IMAGES
of America

NORWELL

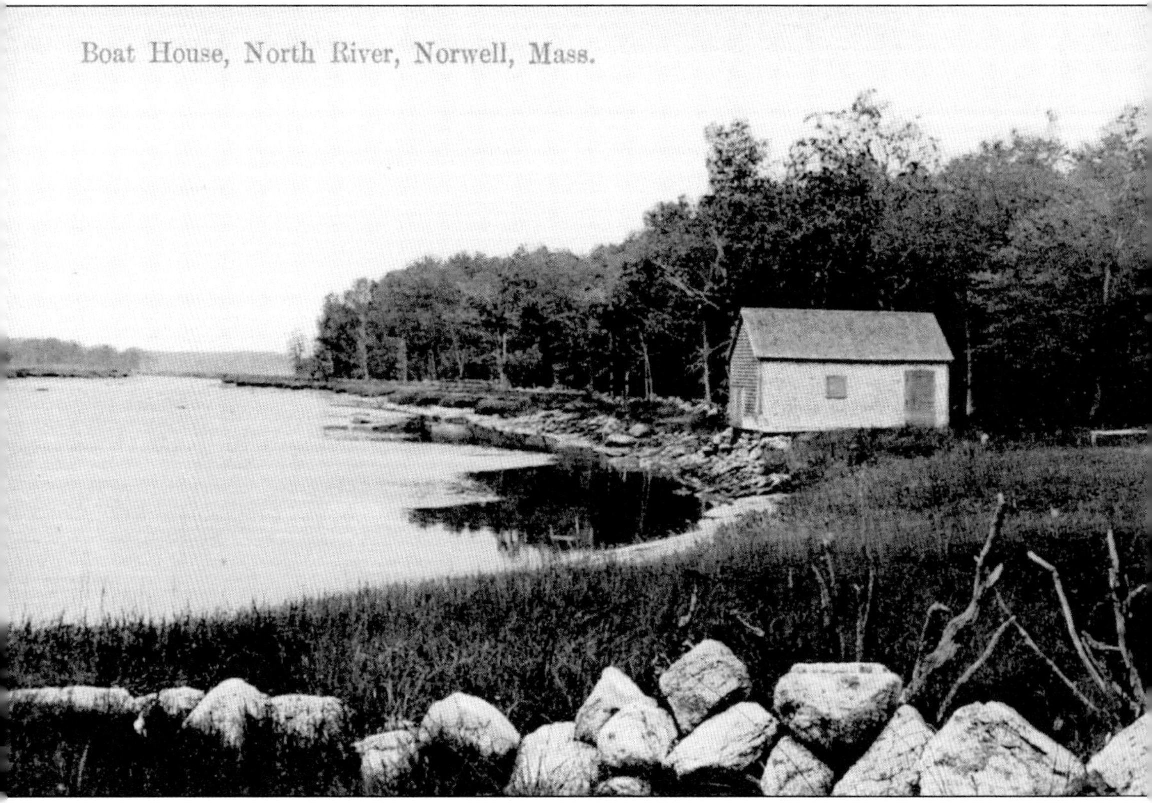

About a half mile down the North River from Union Bridge is the site where many vessels were built at the Block House Yard. Shipbuilders who worked here were William James, David Torrey, and Jotham Tilden. The first ships were built in 1701. The yard was located at the bend of the North River and the blockhouse was used as a garrison to protect the settlers during King Philip's War. King Philip was the son of Massasoit and was determined to get his tribe's land back. He enlisted the help of the Narragansett and Nipmunk tribes. King Philip and his warriors held camp on Mount Blue. From Mount Blue they started their war in Hingham and moved to present-day Norwell near the site of the May Elm Farm. They were stopped by the colonists there but moved on to the North River where they attacked the blockhouse in May 1676, but did not destroy it.

On the cover: Please see page 11. (Courtesy of Jon Bond.)

IMAGES
of America

NORWELL

James Pierotti
Foreword by Jeff Corwin

ARCADIA
PUBLISHING

ISBN 978-0-7385-3841-9

Published by Arcadia Publishing
Charleston, South Carolina

Printed in the United States of America

Library of Congress Catalog Card Number: 2005925269

For all general information contact Arcadia Publishing at:
Telephone 843-853-2070
Fax 843-853-0044
E-mail sales@arcadiapublishing.com
For customer service and orders:
Toll-Free 1-888-313-2665

Visit us on the Internet at www.arcadiapublishing.com

To Jon Bond, Norwell is indebted to you.

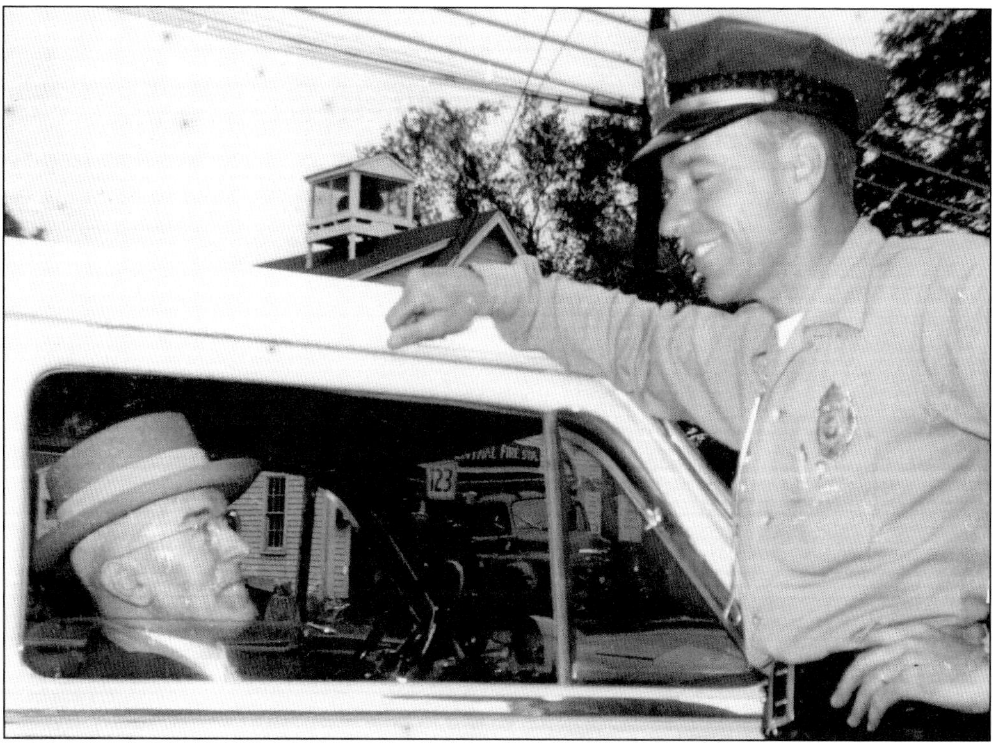

A great conversation is going on in the center of town. In the passenger seat of this car is storekeeper Elmer Josselyn. Josselyn was a merchant who ran a shop in Norwell Center for many years. He is sitting in front of the Norwell Fire Department on Route 123. Chatting with him is Norwell's first full-time chief of police, Kenneth Bradeen.

Contents

FOREWORD

It was the summer of my eighth birthday when my family made the great move from the urban hustle and bustle of Quincy to the more rural retreat of Norwell, Massachusetts. The night prior to our exhausting haul, I sat perched upon my bed, unable to sleep, counting the spackled dots of plaster on the ceiling. The excitement and adventure of the great migration ahead left me restless with anticipation, and the morning to follow just could not come soon enough. My fascination with slimy and scaly critters such as frogs, snakes, and turtles had taken root in early childhood, but, alas, the backdrop of brick and cement, which served as the foundation of Quincy, yielded few opportunities for natural discovery. I was sure, however, that the pristine and diverse ecology of Norwell would provide me with limitless possibilities for wild adventure, discovery, and exploration. The movers had barely begun unloading our things when I quickly made my way past our new home and into the backyard. We had gone from a three-family apartment home on a corner lot of a busy city street to a colonial that boasted a backyard of forest. To an eight-year-old, it seemed to go on forever.

Upon entering the wooded thicket, made up predominantly of pine and oak, I came across a collapsing stone wall. A century of New England seasons had weathered the corridor of rock, and it was settling slowly under the impact of time. I followed the path of fieldstone deeper into the forest, until I stumbled onto an old log cabin, complete with an outhouse, along the perimeter of a small pond. For an inquisitive lad, a find such as this was like honey to a bee. After a further exploration, I came to the conclusion that the cabin had not been occupied for decades. Inside I found a hand-pump faucet and a blackened wood stove. Another curious discovery were the tins of food dating back to the 1950s. The cabin was like a time capsule, complete with old magazines and other literature from an earlier time. What I saw next took my breath away: the stone hearth at the center of the structure had been inlaid with a variety of fossils, including ammonites and trilobites. I felt a profound affinity with the long-gone owner of this cabin and a sudden deep sense of belonging.

The pond and neighboring swamp were home to water snakes, bullfrogs, and a giant snapping turtle. It weighed in at 30 pounds plus, and I would capture and release it year after year, until it was time for me to head off to college. But perhaps the greatest discovery of all was that the cabin had been hand-built by Capt. Bill Vinal, and that the surrounding property served as a sanctuary for him. Of course, to learn more about the life of Captain Vinal and his contribution to the hamlet of Norwell, you must delve into the pages of this captivating book.

In truth, the town of Norwell can be easily missed, accessible by just a couple of exits off the Southeastern expressway. It has no major shopping mall, and a massive center of technology, education, or research will not be found here. Yet this little town possesses its own brand of magic that makes it unique from all other towns on the South Shore. Culture, folklore, and history intertwine here, weaving a rich tapestry of nature. Norwell is a community blessed with pristine resources, which include primordial quaking bogs, meadows, vernal pools, and vast brackish marshes. The meandering waters of the North River, where shad and striped bass abound, once harbored the thriving port for ship construction. Although walking through the hip-high marsh grass along the spongy shores of the North River, you will no longer witness the launch of a clipper ship, you just might discover an ancient arrowhead buried in the tidal muck. With regard to their history, the Norwellians have much to be proud of, and James Pierotti does a superb job at illuminating the town's past and unraveling its secrets. His is a true labor of love.

—Jeff Corwin

Introduction

The rural town of Norwell has had a long-storied history with a few name changes along the way. It began with its northerly neighbor Scituate. The westerly portion of Scituate was the most densely populated part of the large town of Scituate. Most of the town offices were held by residents of the "west end" of town.

The large tax revenue base came mostly from this part of town. There was the shipbuilding industry that prospered for over 200 years on the North River. Many farms also thrived across the west end of Scituate. The westerly residents of the town felt that there was inadequate tax revenues imposed on the seacoast residents.

In 1848, there was a large federal surplus given to the 26 states. Scituate town government changed their minds over what to do with their portion of this newly found bounty. The westerly residents grew frustrated and wanted full control over their finances. They petitioned state legislature to secede from Scituate. They were granted the new state law and Gov. George Briggs signed the law into effect on February 15, 1849. The new town would be known as South Scituate.

Almost 40 years later, a committee of residents approached wealthy summer resident Henry Norwell to ask if he would endow funds for a school to be named after him. The Scottish immigrant, who amassed a fortune in retail dry goods on Winter Street in Boston, declined. Norwell chose instead to contribute $25,000 over a 10-year span for the building and general upkeep of the roads in town. The town residents were so grateful for this gift they voted at a town meeting in 1887 to change the name of South Scituate to Norwell.

Development of Norwell has been carefully planned so as to retain its historic charm, much like its neighbors Hanover, Cohasset, Hingham, and Scituate. Most of the homes that are of historic importance are in the Norwell Village area on Main Street. This part of town served as the seat of government and also as a stagecoach stop for the Boston to Duxbury route.

The Ridge Hill section of Norwell is densely populated and has remnants of a commercial era long since passed. There were shoe factories, mills, and poultry farms on High Street and Washington Street (today's Route 53). Curiously enough, Norwell never had a state highway built through the heart of the town. It was long proposed that the new road would connect Ridge Hill to Scituate Harbor. It never materialized, and as such Norwell's streetscape remains undisturbed with little traffic.

Today, Norwell no longer is a shipbuilding community nor does it rely on agriculture to feed its families. It is an affluent suburb of Boston that is known for its wonderful new homes and excellent school system. The historic character of the town remains because of the efforts of the Norwell Historical Society and the Norwell Historic Commission. In 1982, the Norwell Village area was designated as a National Register Historic District. It is now time to reflect on the proud history of this town as it was once known as Scituate and South Scituate. Today, Norwell remains a rural town with distinct neighborhoods and unique villages. Each has a small-town New England charm of its own. Turn the page to discover how Norwell has evolved.

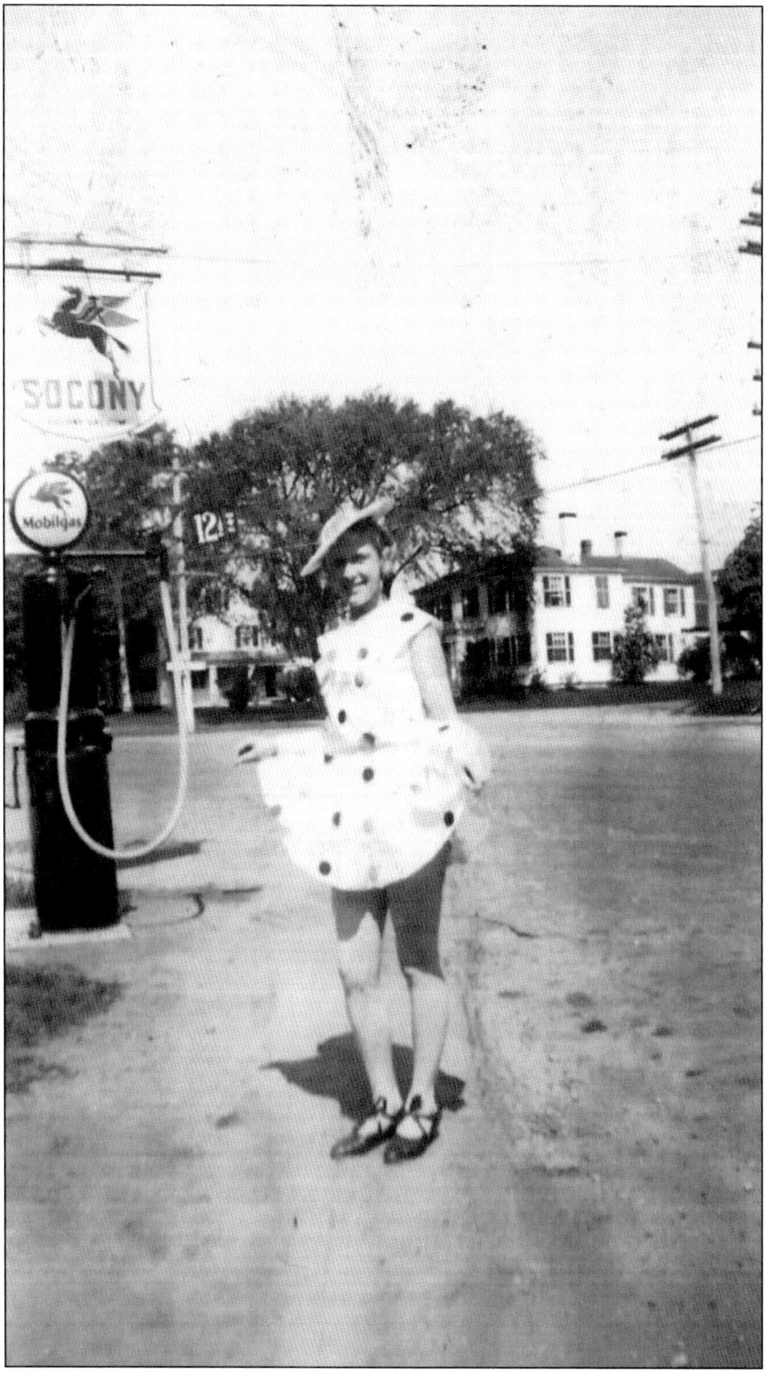

Striking quite a pose in the middle of Main Street is Harry Merritt's older sister Priscilla Merritt Spradlin. Note the sign advertising 12¢ a gallon for gas. Beyond Spradlin is postmaster John Nash's home at the corner of Central and Main Streets. Socony stood for Standard Oil Company of New York. Remember the red, white, and blue sign? Socony stations advertised "Socony gasoline – Pure and Powerful and Uniform." The Socony brand eventually became Mobil in 1966. This photograph was submitted by Spradlin's son Don.

One

Main Street

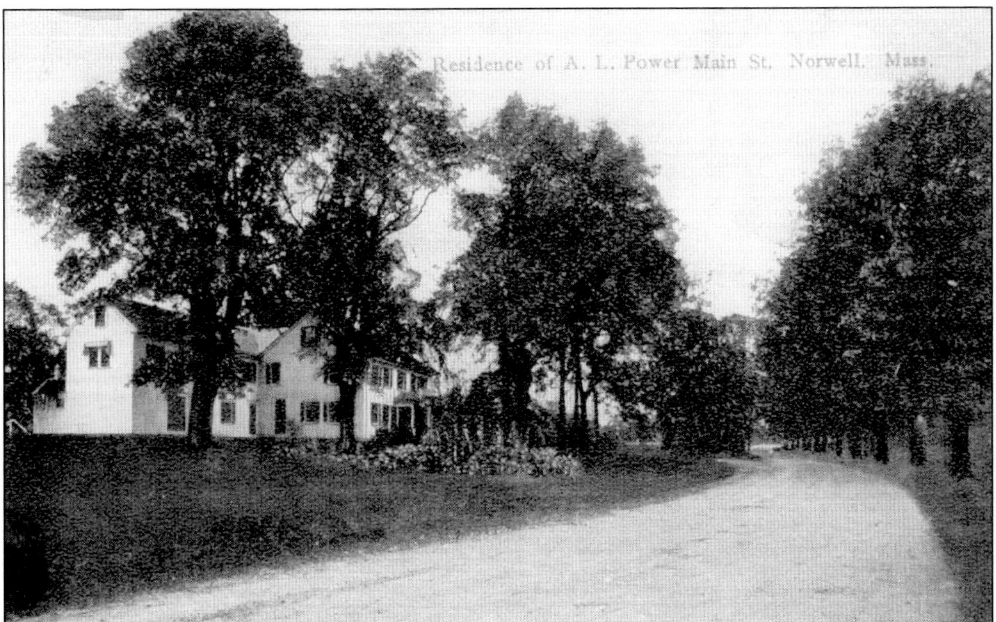

Arthur L. Power lived at 841 Main Street in the early 1900s. This home, built in 1786 by Elijah Curtis, was originally called the May Elms Farm. After his death, Curtis's widow rented the property to Rev. Samuel May, pastor of the Second Parish of Scituate. Among the notable guests at the home was his niece Louisa May Alcott, author of *Little Women*.

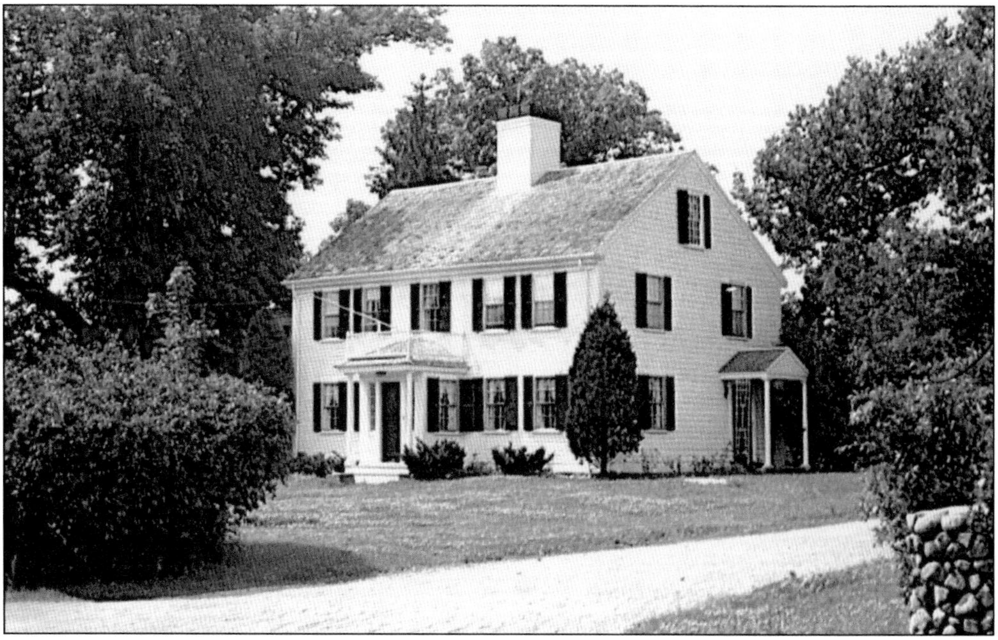

Louisa May Alcott moved to Concord with her family in 1840. Her father's friend, Ralph Waldo Emerson helped them settle in the area. Alcott befriended another poet, Henry David Thoreau, and she was well on her way to being influenced by prolific writers. She visited her uncle's home from 1837 to 1842. It was through her childhood experiences that she based her book, published in 1868, called *Little Women*.

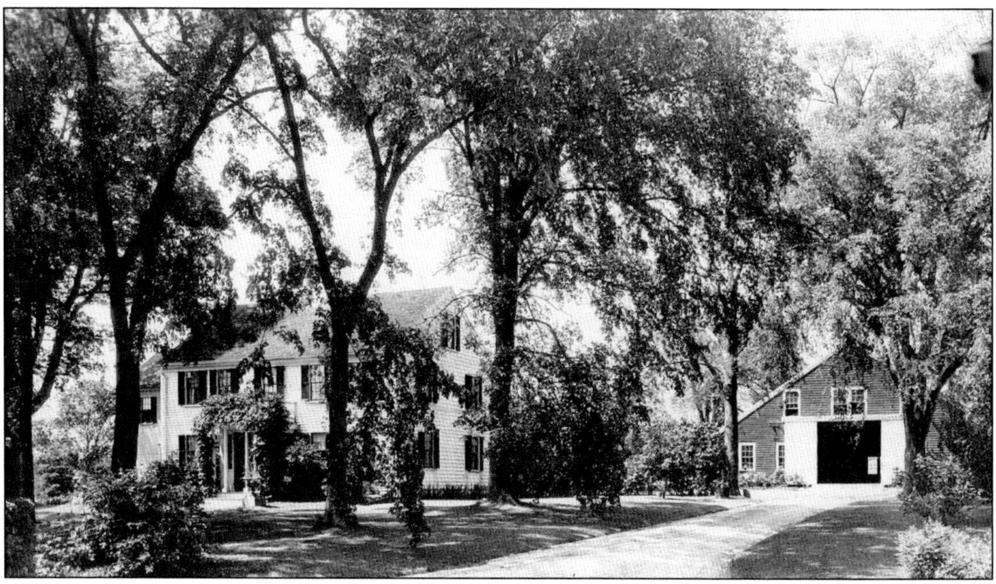

The name May Elm was derived from the elm trees that Reverend May had planted there. In 1935, Arthur L. Power and his wife held the first organizational meeting of the Norwell Historical Society. The estate encompassed over 65 acres, a windmill, a barn, and an outbuilding. After discharge from the navy in 1944, Com. John Chipman purchased the May Elms property for $19,000. His daughter, Ruth Chipman Bailey, is currently a library volunteer at the historic James Library in Norwell Center.

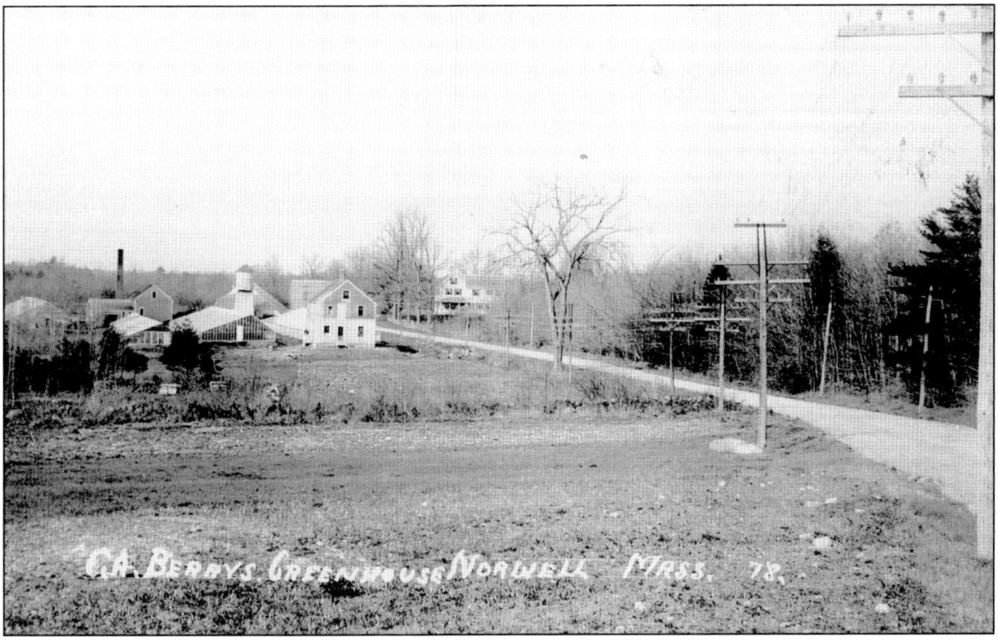

For over 300 years, most every resident of South Scituate used farming as a means to support his family. Most of the farming that was identified with Norwell's rural character was greatly diminished by the early 1930s. This greenhouse was operated by Charles A. Berry and was located on Main Street, west of the United Church of Christ. By the late 1920s, the greenhouse business folded and the land was rented out to various tenants.

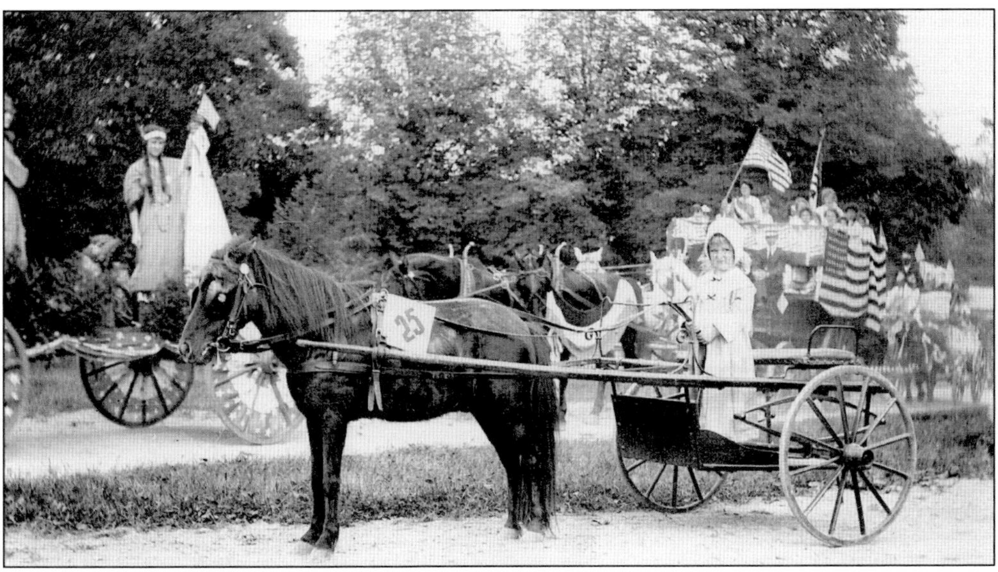

Four-year-old Lillian Foster has her photograph taken in a carriage during the Flag Day exercises in Norwell. She is posing for the photographer on September 4, 1915. This image was captured on a real photo postcard. The festivities of Flag Day were held on the town common.

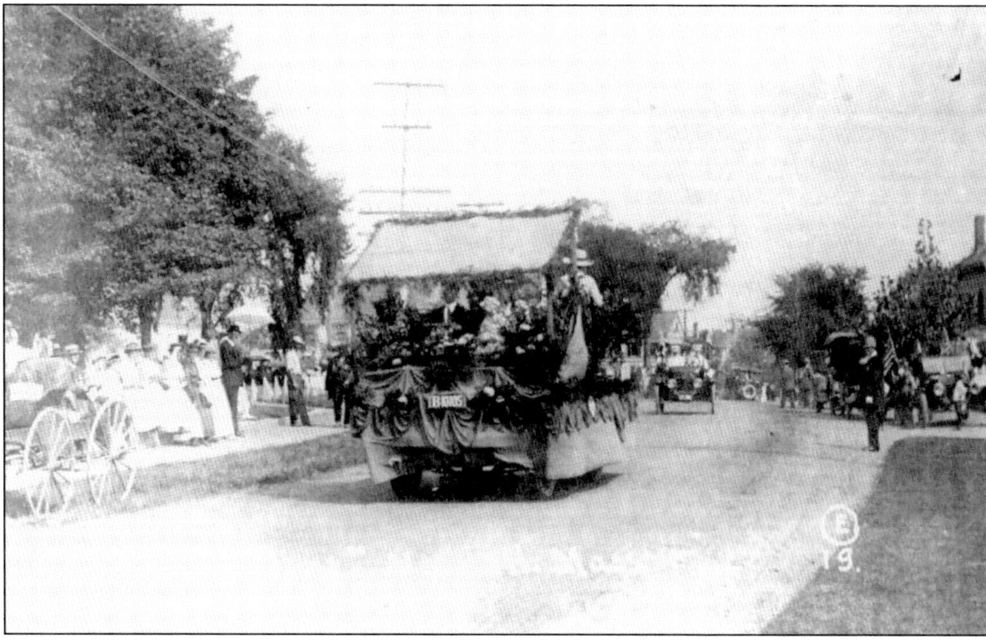

Members of the Norwell Improvement Association organized the event because of the looming world war. Patriotic fervor was indeed on the minds of many. Among the organizers were Horace T. Fogg, Arthur L. Power, Ernest H. Sparrell, and John F. Wilder.

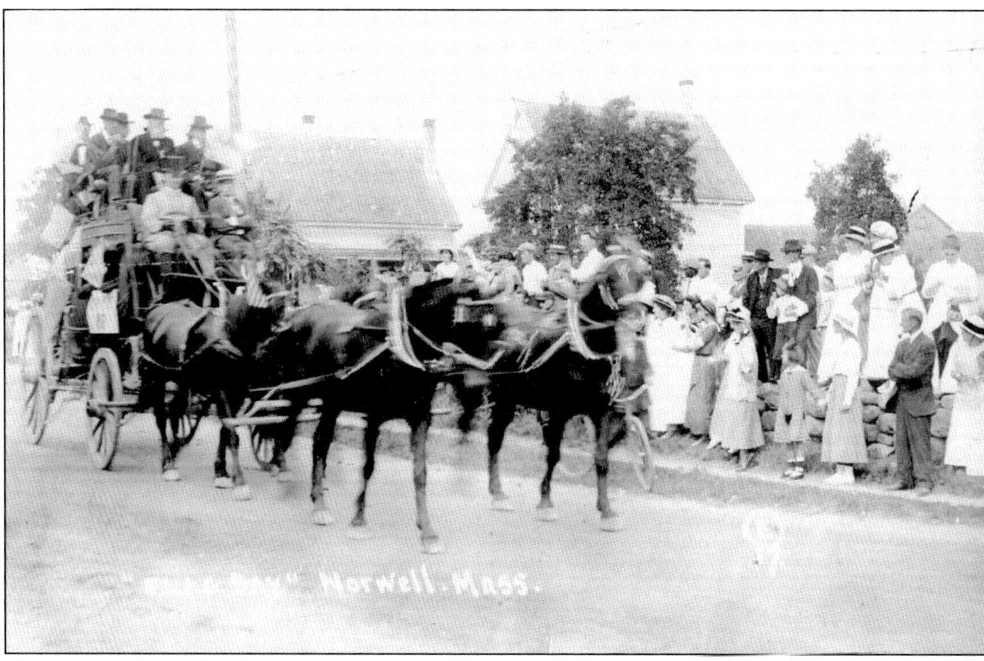

On the agenda for the day was a parade at 1:00 p.m., a dedication ceremony of the newly installed flagpole, and the raising of the American flag. The distinguished guest of the proceedings was U.S. Senator Henry Cabot Lodge who addressed Norwell's largest gathering of townsfolk ever.

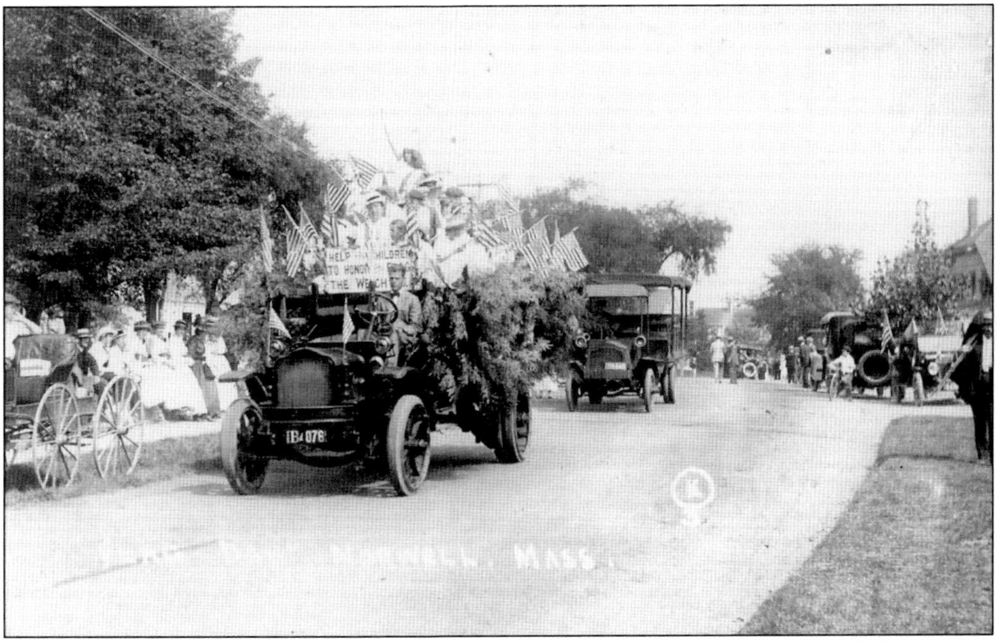

Henry A. Turner did the official unfurling of the flag after Horace Fogg welcomed the citizens. At 3:30 p.m., a baseball game was played out between Kingston and Norwell at Cushing's Field. At the conclusion of the day's festivities was a band concert. The crowd on hand was encouraged to sing along with tunes such as "America" and the "Star Spangled Banner."

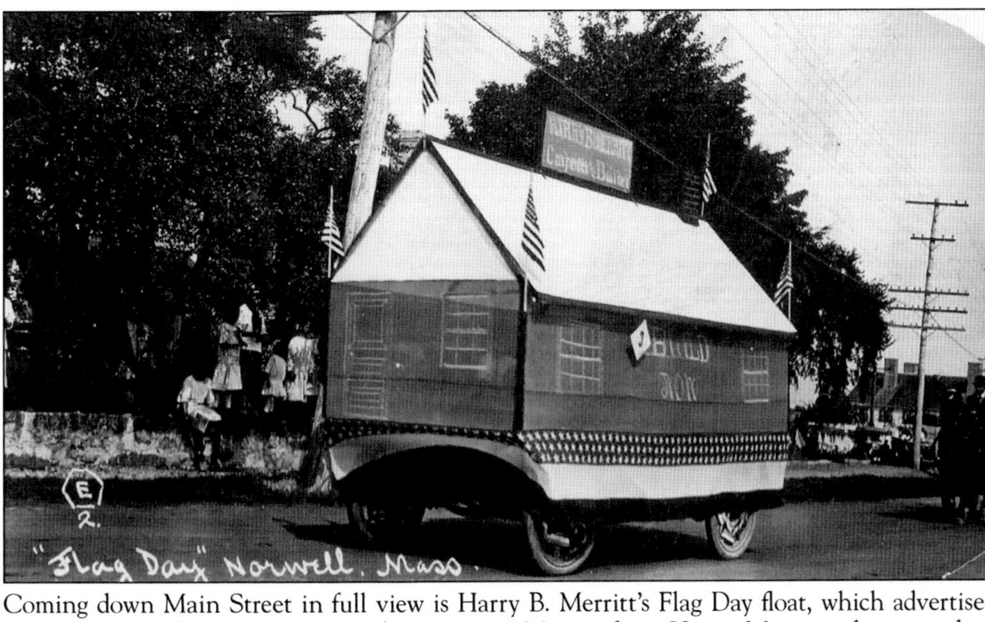

Coming down Main Street in full view is Harry B. Merritt's Flag Day float, which advertises his building trade. Harry was a 10th-generation Merritt from Henry Merritt, who arrived in America in 1626. Harry Merritt was a carpenter and builder who had a big business in town. His children are Priscilla Merritt Spradlin and Harry A. Merritt. Notice the parade goers sitting on the stone wall in the shade.

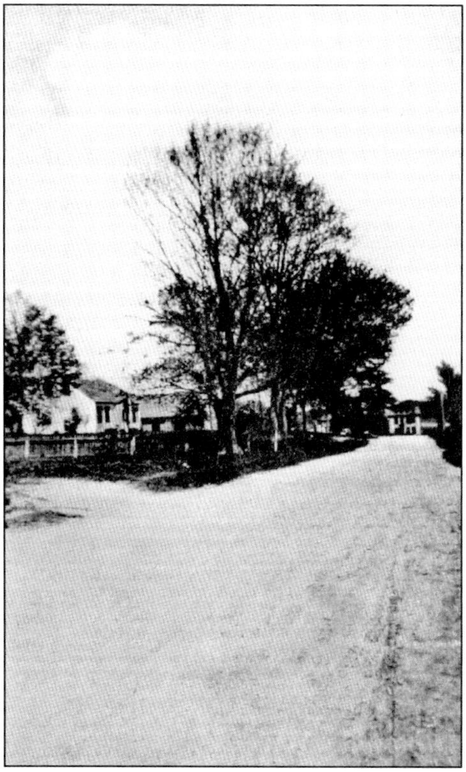

Heading towards Scituate, one would be riding his horse and buggy down Main Street in this direction. The greeting on the back of this postcard was indicative of many correspondences. Most writers were on vacation in the country in Norwell. Francis Dana writes to Olive Morris on September 6, 1911, "I didn't see you before I left on vacation. Did William get the bottle? I am staying here for a while longer." What was in the bottle for William?

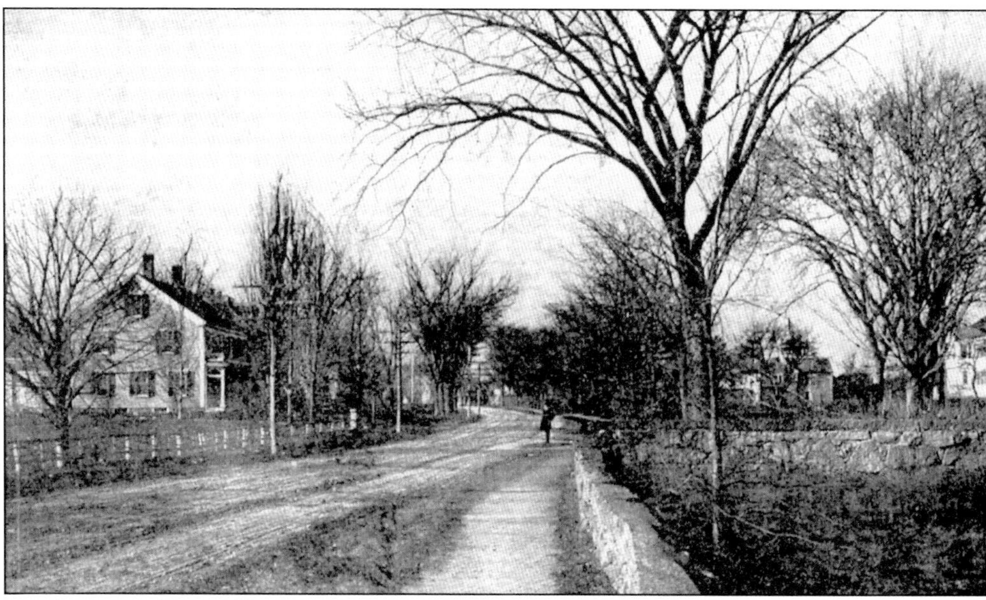

Heading out of Norwell Center toward Assinippi and Hanover, this would be the view on Main Street. The stone wall on the right can be prominently seen. A stone wall in New England is a part of its celebrated heritage. During the winter, the earth would freeze and then thaw. The stones would then rise to the surface of the fields. Farmers would unearth these large stones to be able to cultivate a field. The farmers would then put the large rocks into large piles around their property.

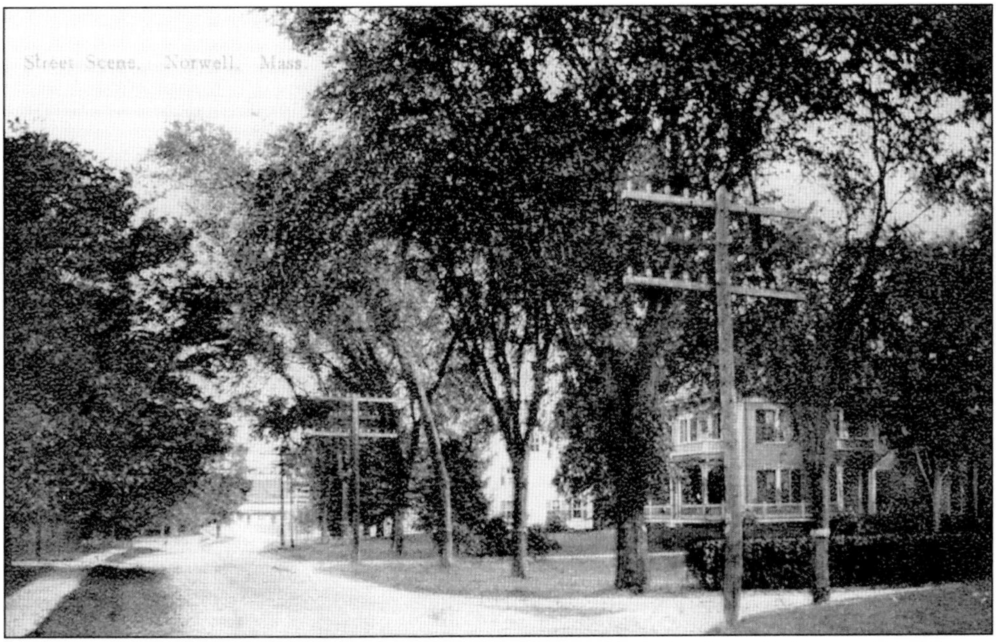

This is a postcard scene of Main Street looking east towards Norwell Center. The South Scituate Savings Bank can be seen off in the distance. The summertime was always filled with out-of-town visitors from Boston who were entertained by the rustic features of Norwell. Seeing cows and various farm animals was a delight to the youngsters who came to see their brethren.

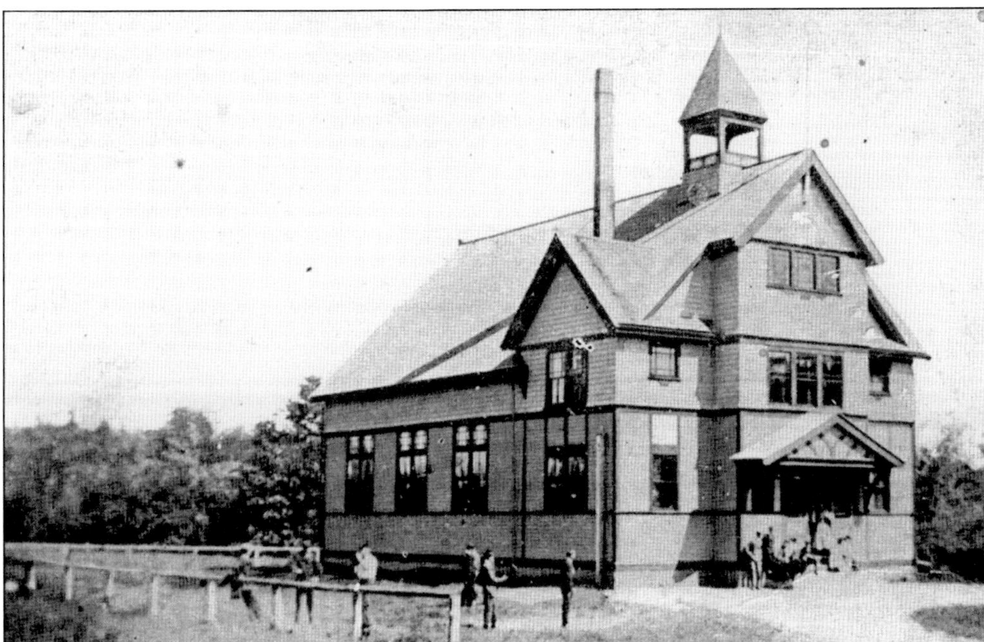

The second town hall of South Scituate was built at 345 Main Street in 1885. However, it was not easy to get the building approved by town meeting. It took well over 10 years to get enough people to agree that a new town meeting place was so sorely needed. On April 3, 1876, a town meeting voted to build a new town hall large enough to accommodate the high school.

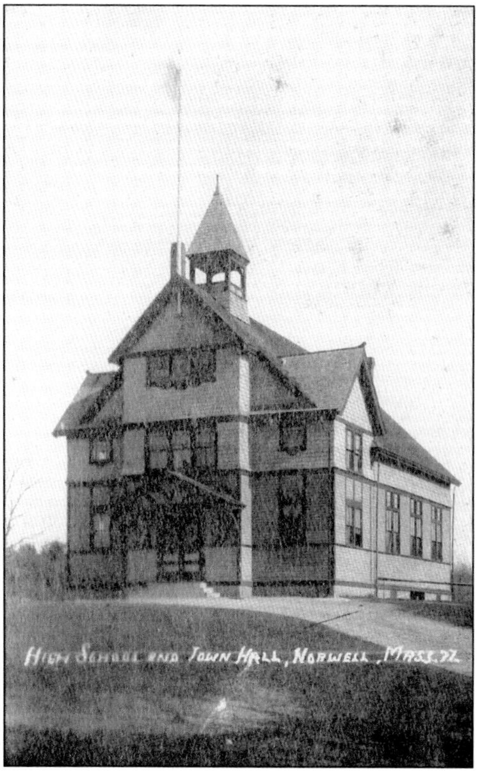

The town meeting stalled over the amount of the cost to build the new town hall/high school. The sum was $6,500, and it was deemed to be exorbitantly expensive, so the matter was bickered over for nine more years. It was not until the town hall burned to the ground in 1884 that the town voted to put their differences aside and build the town hall, and, incidentally, the costs went up since the original estimate.

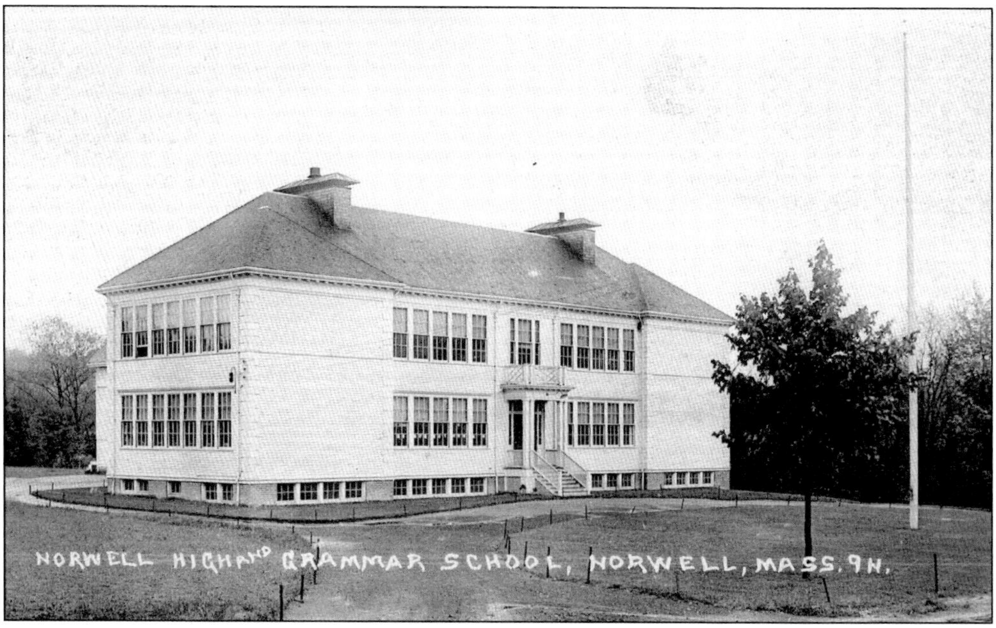

The new town hall was erected, and in 1896, the high school moved into the building. Because of a burgeoning population growth, in 1922, a new combination grammar and high school was built (shown in this postcard) and attached to the town hall at a cost of $40,000. The building was gutted by fire on December 20, 1935, and the students were relocated to the Sylvester School in Hanover.

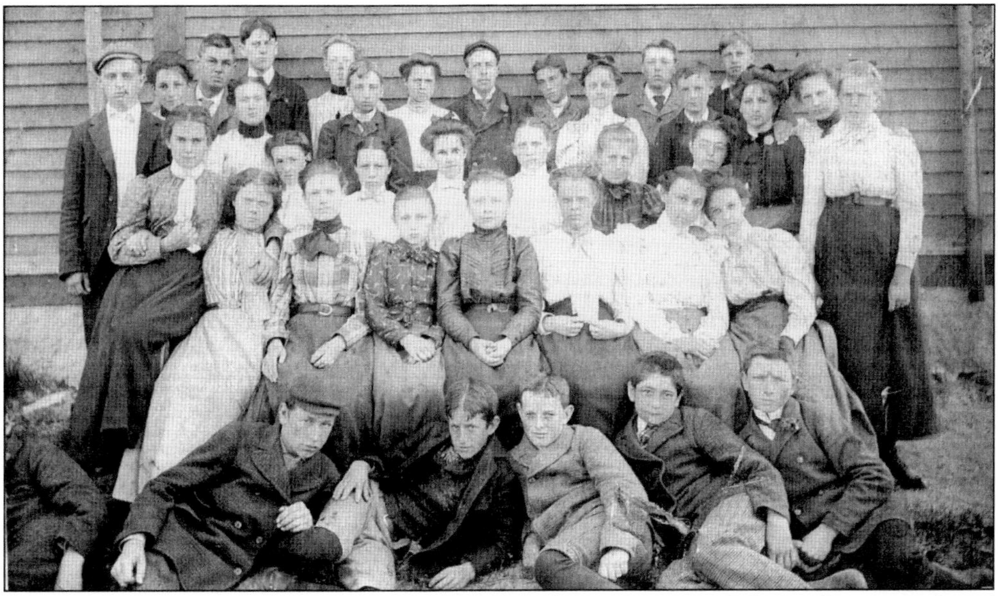

After the fire, the town rented space from Hanover for two years, and the students were forced to take classes in the afternoon. The town meeting was moved to the First Parish Church. The town fathers, however, did not deem it wholly appropriate to conduct elections in the church, so an alternative location had to be decided upon. Less than a month later, the town broke ground on a new town hall due to the generosity of the Cushing family. Pictured here are several Norwell High School students.

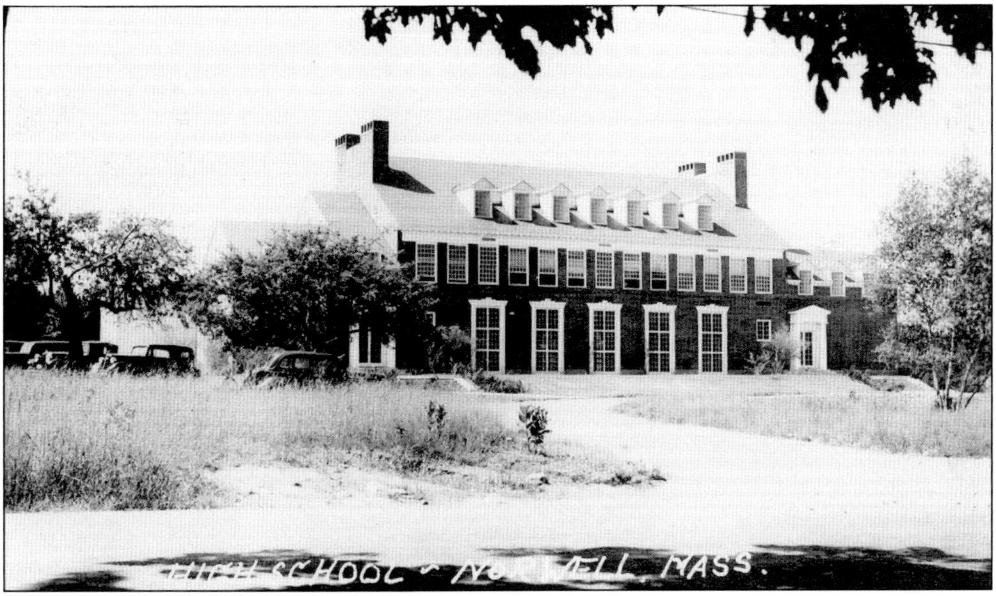

After the fire razed the Norwell Grammar and High School, the town set forth to build a new improved building to educate the growing population of Norwell youngsters. In 1937, the new school was opened on the former Brooks Farm, just down the street at 322 Main Street. In 1956, a new wing was added, and it was named the Sparrell Wing. The town built a new high school next door in 1961, and the original building was named the Sparrell Elementary School 10 years later. Today, it is the site for the Norwell School Administration.

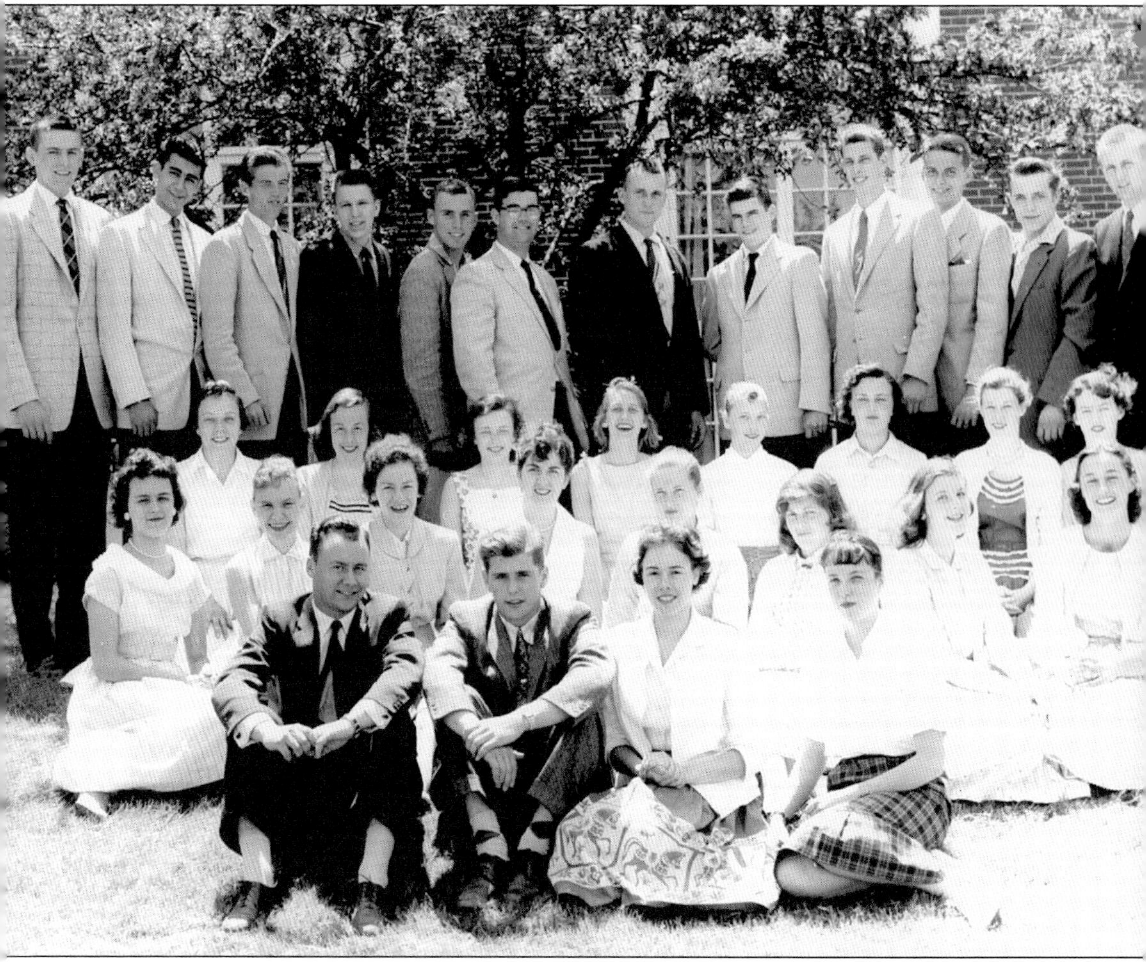

Graduation day has arrived for the class of 1957 at Norwell High School. Among the classmates pictured here are, from left to right, (first row) David Oman, Paul Knight, Gayle Falconer, and Judith Mederos; (second row) Norma Swain, Janine Anderson, Jean Jackman, Arlene Stokes, Nancy Chase, Dorothy Panico, Natalie Carruthers, and Laura Cunningham; (third row) Jane Merritt, Sandra Hakanson, Margery Joseph, Kathryn Leslie, Betty Long, Barbara Spinney, Arlene Brown, and Jean Wheeler; (fourth row) Robert Kroeger, Joseph Pompeo, George Laing, John Slupsky, Peter Gilbert, Peter Smellie, George Cavanagh, Edward Walsh, Hobart Wright, Leslie Titcomb, Sidney Goss, and Richard Maxwell.

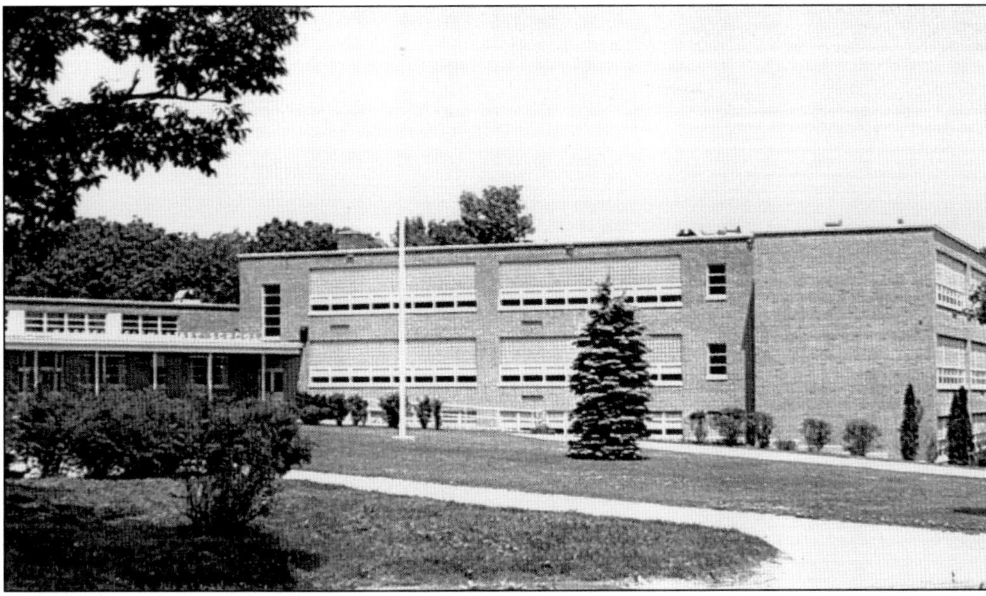

Jon Bond was a valuable member of the Norwell School Committee prior to his death in 1968. He was instrumental in helping to build the Center Elementary School on the grounds of the former town hall at 345 Main Street. A young Jonathan Bond remembers seeing all the building plans for the new school built in 1950. His father, John, was a member of the school building committee. It was renamed the Ella F. Osborn Elementary School in 1956. Today, it is the site of the Norwell Town Offices.

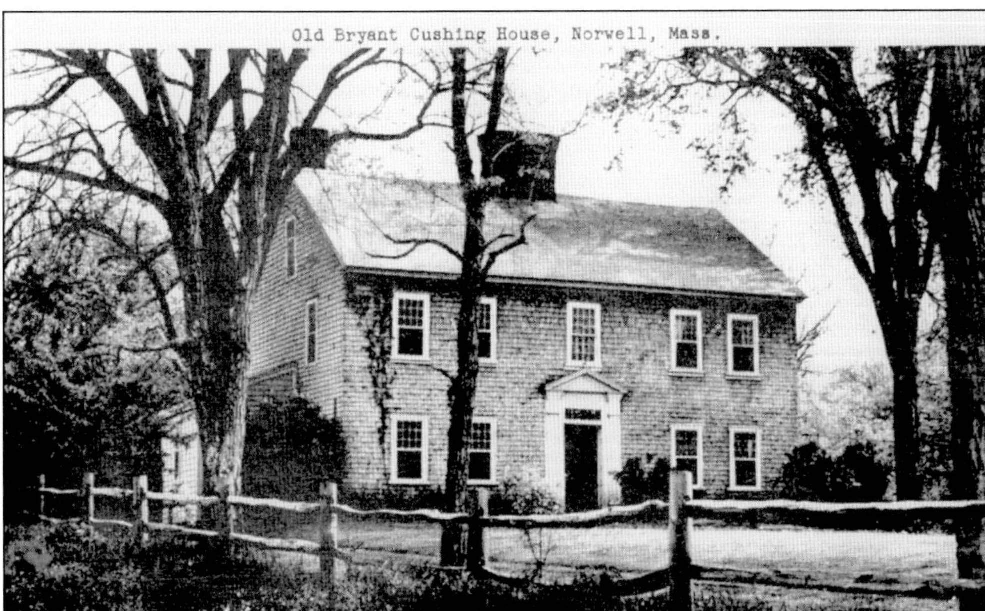

Located on lower Main Street is the colonial Bryant-Cushing home. This home is listed on the National Register of Historic Places and was built in 1698. Deacon Thomas Bryant was the first occupant of the home until 1769, when Hawkes Cushing purchased the property. Cushing installed a mill site, and a year later, he and his brother established a saw mill on Second Herring Brook.

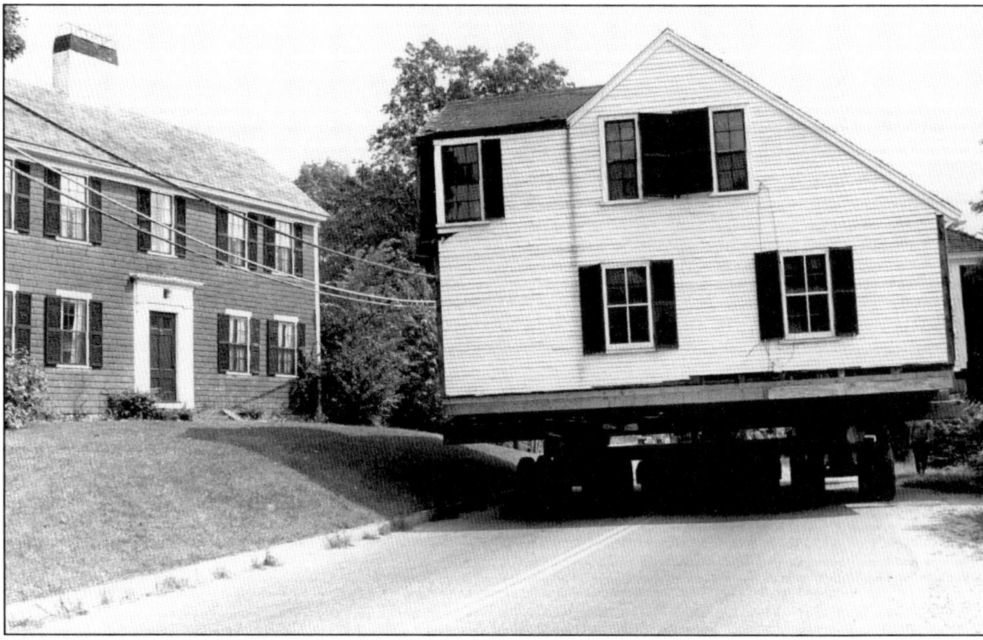

When driving down the street, perhaps anywhere in America, you may be driving behind a prefabricated house en route to a plot of land. Prefabrication homes have grown in popularity and thus it is not uncommon to see a home being driven down the street. It was a sight to behold when, back it the late 1950s, Nellie Sparrell's home was moved a mile down Main Street past Joseph's Pontiac. The move was made to accommodate the building of a commercial property. This area now is home to Mug Shots, Mount Blue restaurant, and Day Lily.

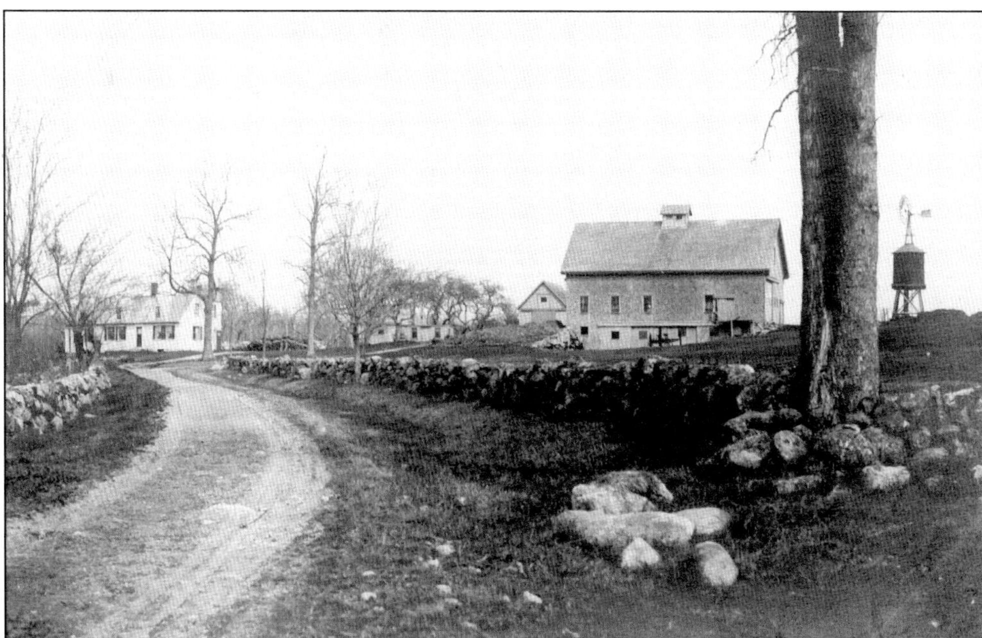

Today, 1035 Main Street is called Stoney Brook Farm. Norwell residents remember it as the Henry Ford Farm and recall when Mrs. Ford ran a printing business from this location.

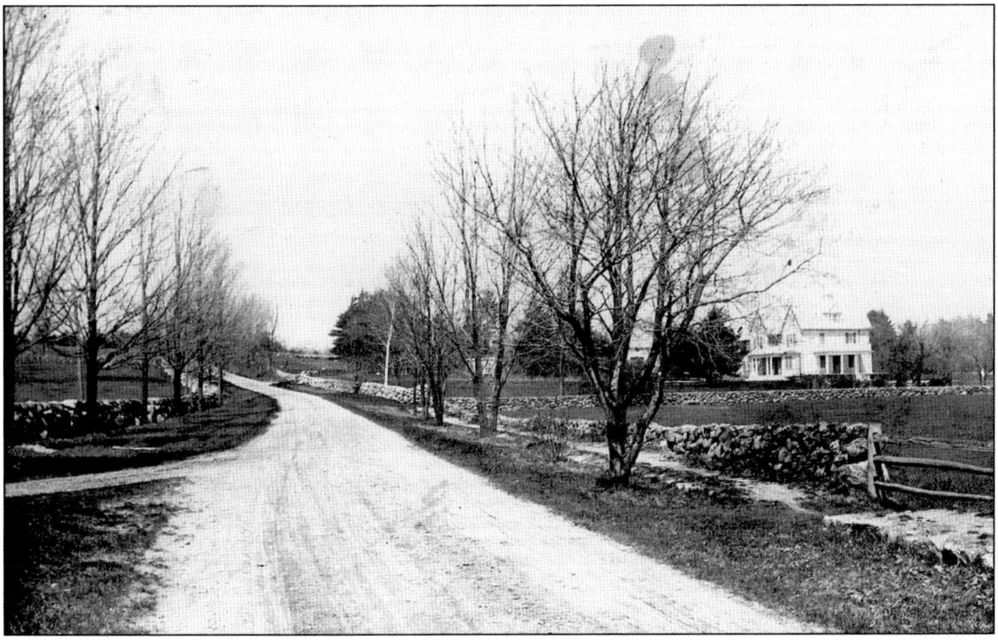

This house on Lincoln Street near the corner of Main Street was for many years the home of the Whiting family. Today, it is the home of Bruce and Marcia Humphrey. Many Norwell organizations benefited from the generosity of the Wearguard Company on Longwater Drive during Bruce's time as president.

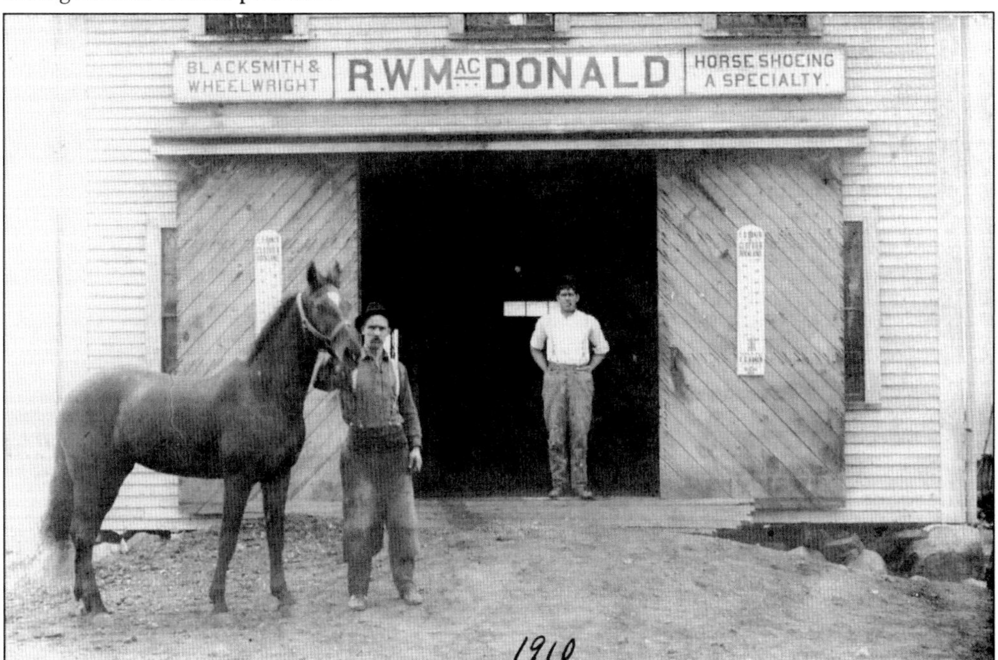

The R.W. MacDonald blacksmith shop was moved again in 1923 to the south side of Main Street, numbered 808, at the foot of Winter Street, where it is now a private home. MacDonald was an avid clock collector, and his heirs donated a grandfather clock from his large collection to the town in 1931. This clock can be viewed in the Osborn Room in the town hall today.

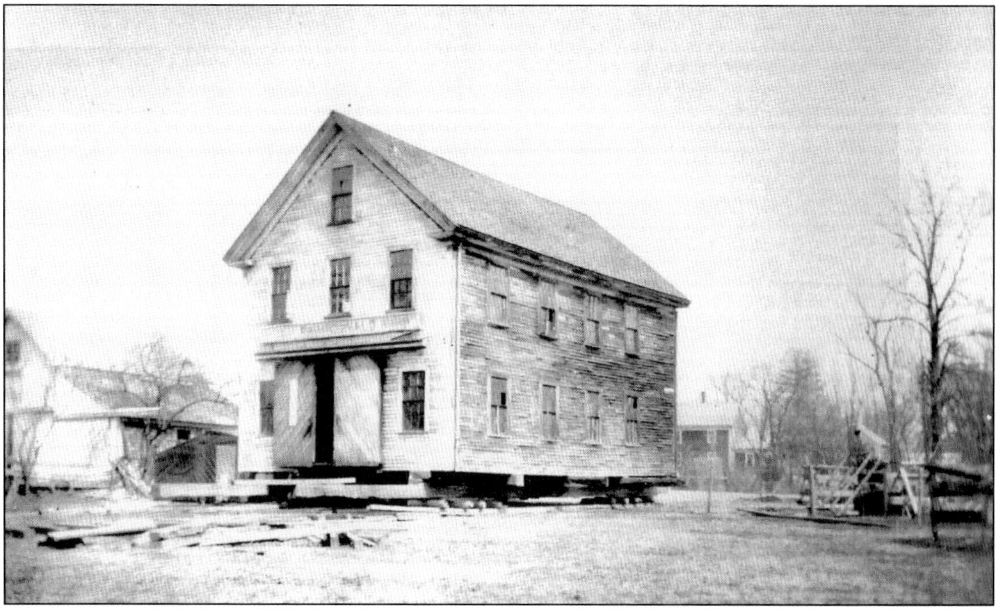

R.W. MacDonald ran a blacksmith shop in Norwell Center. This business also did horseshoe work and was a carriage smith and a wheelwright. This building was originally Charlie Young's shoe factory on Washington Street. It was moved to the junction of Bridge and Main Streets in 1905 by J. Franklin Turner and MacDonald. It is shown here in the process of being relocated on braces and log skids by oxen for the five-mile trip. MacDonald actually kept his fire going throughout the move.

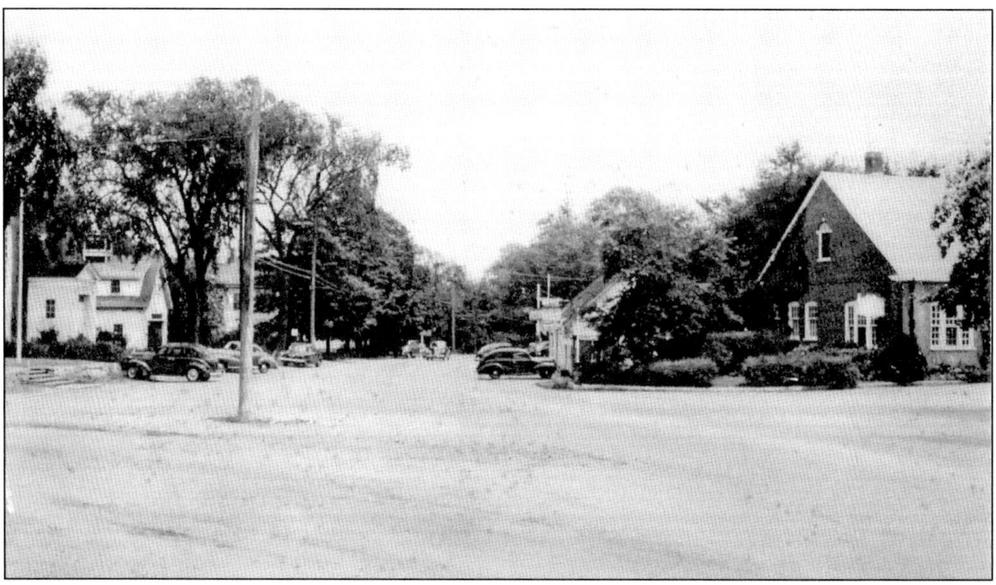

It is a busy day downtown with a few cars in Norwell Center. This picture was taken around 1940, and it shows the Central Fire Station on the left and the South Scituate Savings Bank on the right. The telephone pole in the foreground is no longer there, as it does seem odd that it is located in the middle of the intersection.

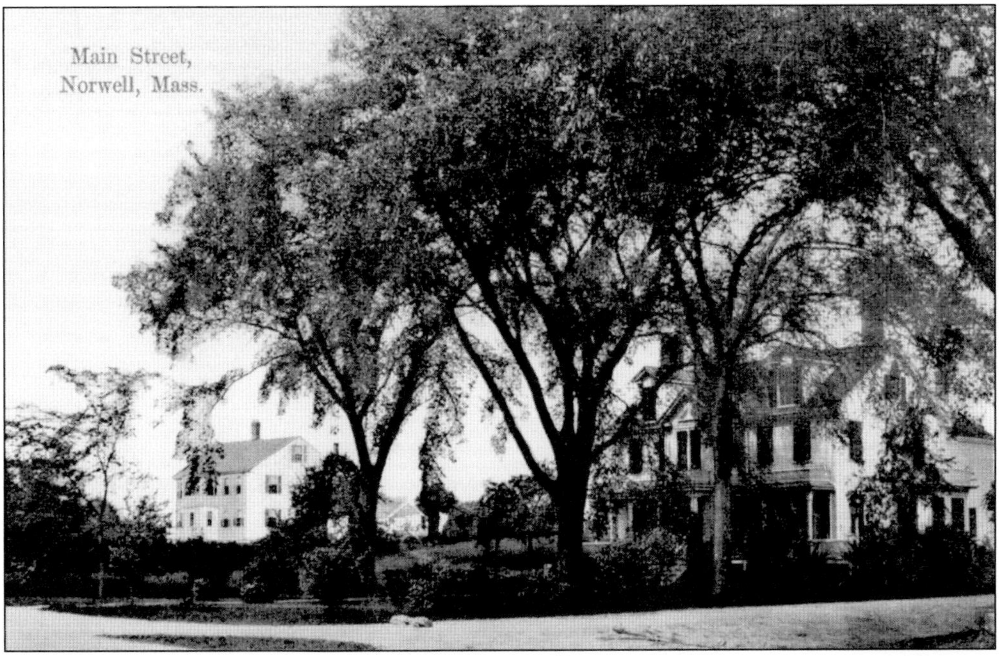

This is a photograph postcard of a home near Norwell Center. It was sent to Minnie McLernon of Lynnhurst by her friend Lizzie. Lizzie wrote in 1915, "You will no doubt be surprised to know I am down here. It came as a surprise to me. I was asked to come and cook for sixteen so you see I am very busy. I came by auto and it was a lovely ride."

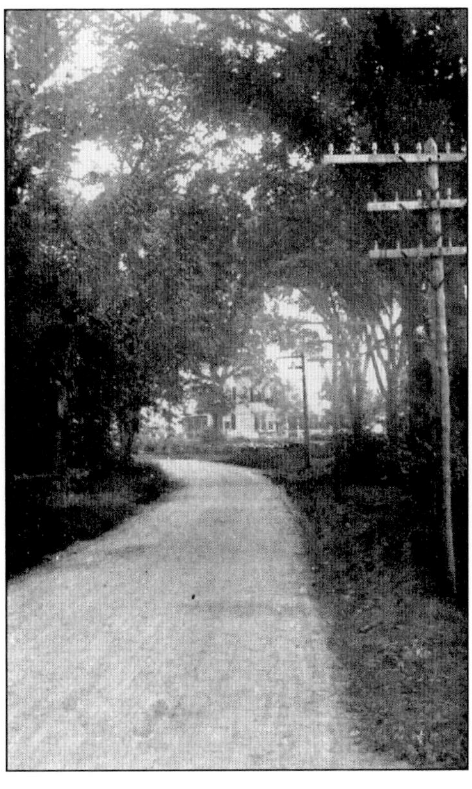

At lower Main Street is the intersection of Parker and Main Streets. Number 975 Main Street can be seen in the foreground. Across from Parker Street is Kings Landing Marina, which rents out kayaks for use on the nearby North River.

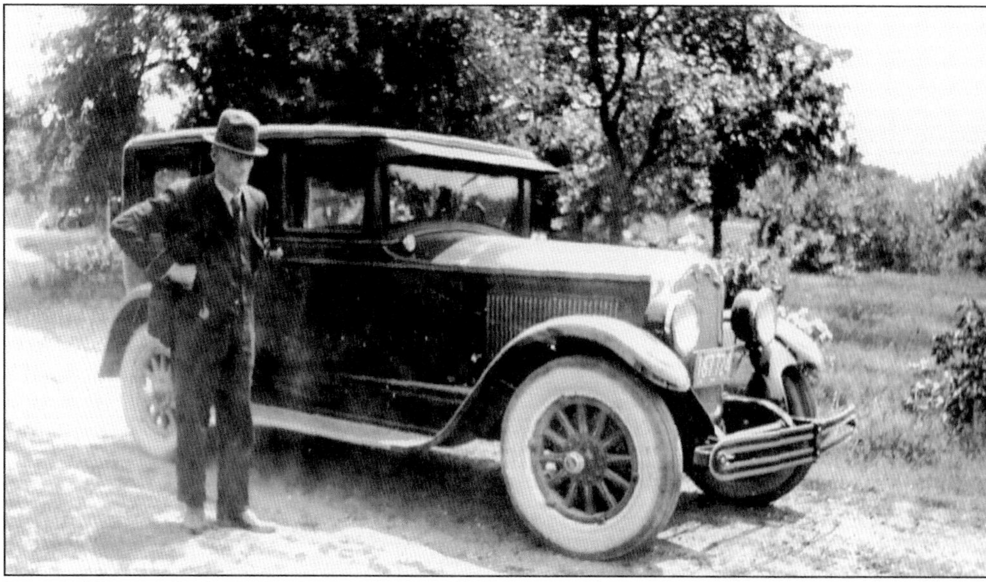

Pictured here is Dick Tedeschi's great-grandfather Samuel Turner. He was also the father of the town switchboard operator, Caroline Turner. He is posing for a photograph along a country road with his new 1929 Ford sedan. One of this popular Ford model's unique features was the auxiliary awnings that pulled down over the windows. Samuel most likely paid $525 for this new car in 1929. In 2006, $5,600 would be the equivalent.

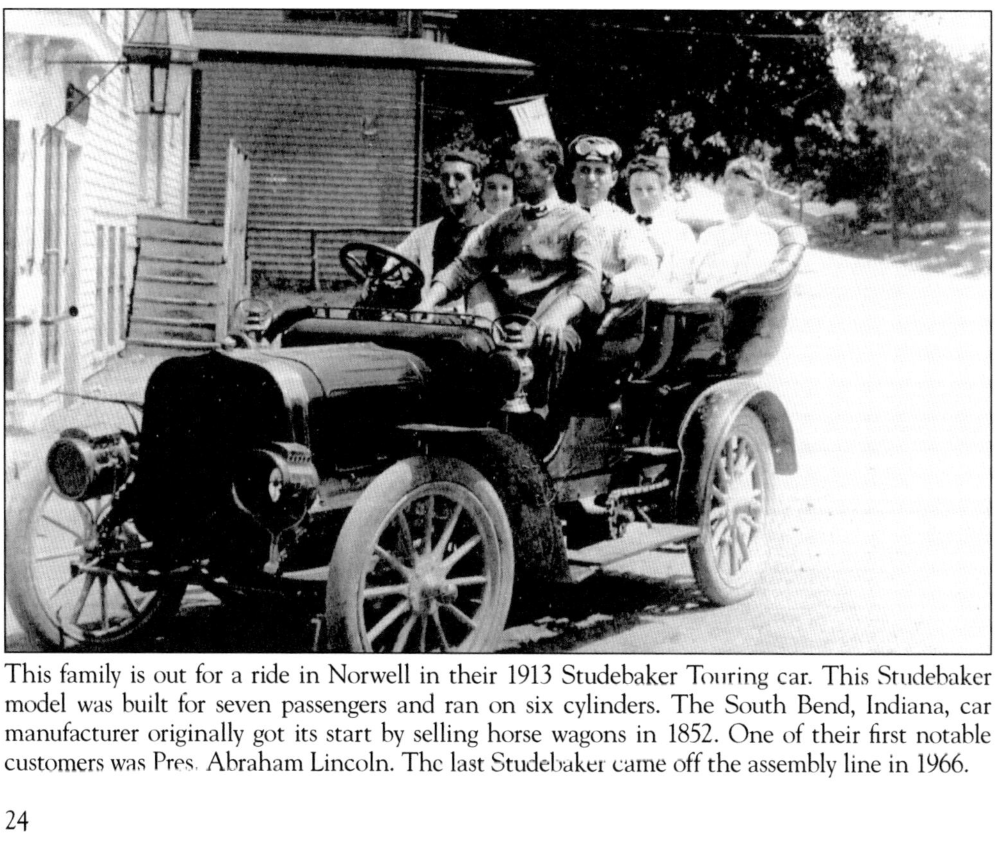

This family is out for a ride in Norwell in their 1913 Studebaker Touring car. This Studebaker model was built for seven passengers and ran on six cylinders. The South Bend, Indiana, car manufacturer originally got its start by selling horse wagons in 1852. One of their first notable customers was Pres. Abraham Lincoln. The last Studebaker came off the assembly line in 1966.

Two

NORWELL VILLAGE

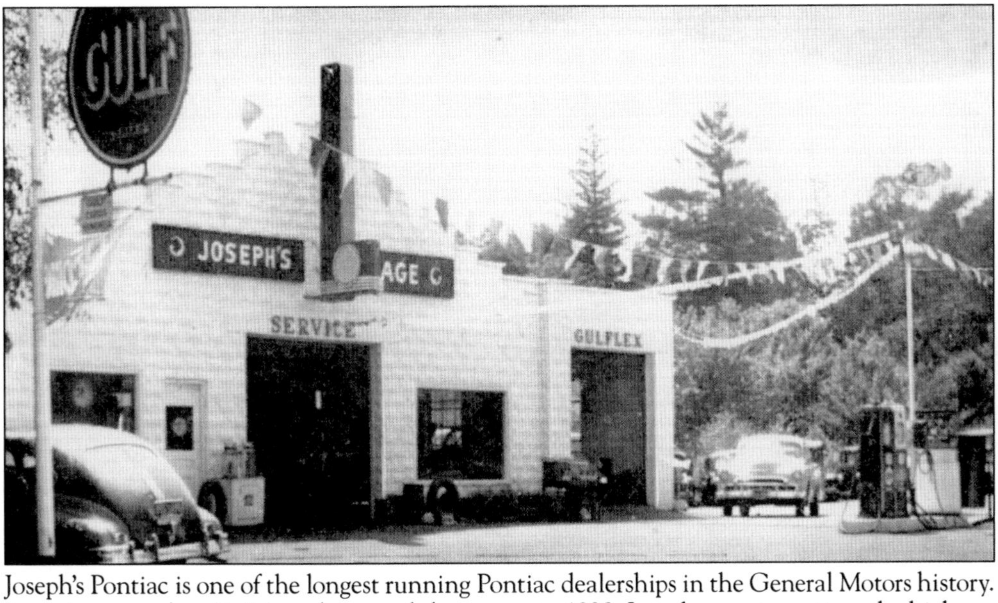

Joseph's Pontiac is one of the longest running Pontiac dealerships in the General Motors history. It got its start when E. P. Joseph opened the garage in 1928. Joseph was at one time the highway surveyor for the town of Norwell. Today, John and Art Joseph Jr., two Babson College graduates and sons of Art, run the auto business. This third-generation family enterprise has been able to withstand the test of time and ably provides old-fashioned customer service in Norwell Center.

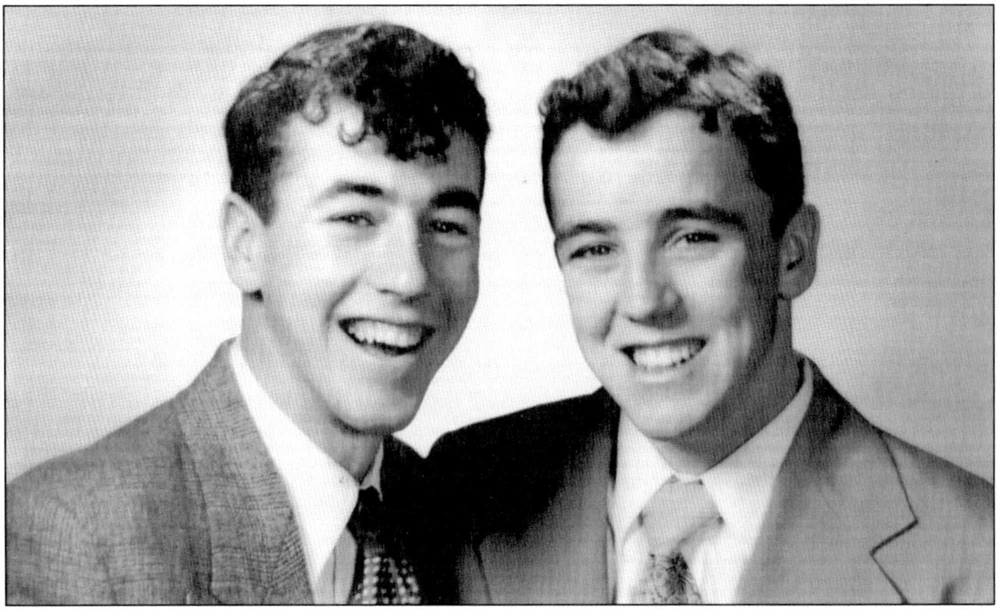

Here is the graduation photograph of Arthur (left) and his brother Phil "Philly" Joseph. They are part of the proud Norwell High class of 1951. Both Art and Philly served in the Korean War. When they returned home, they helped their father, Herbert, run their Pontiac dealership. The auto business began as a filling station and repair shop in 1928. It became a Pontiac dealership in 1940.

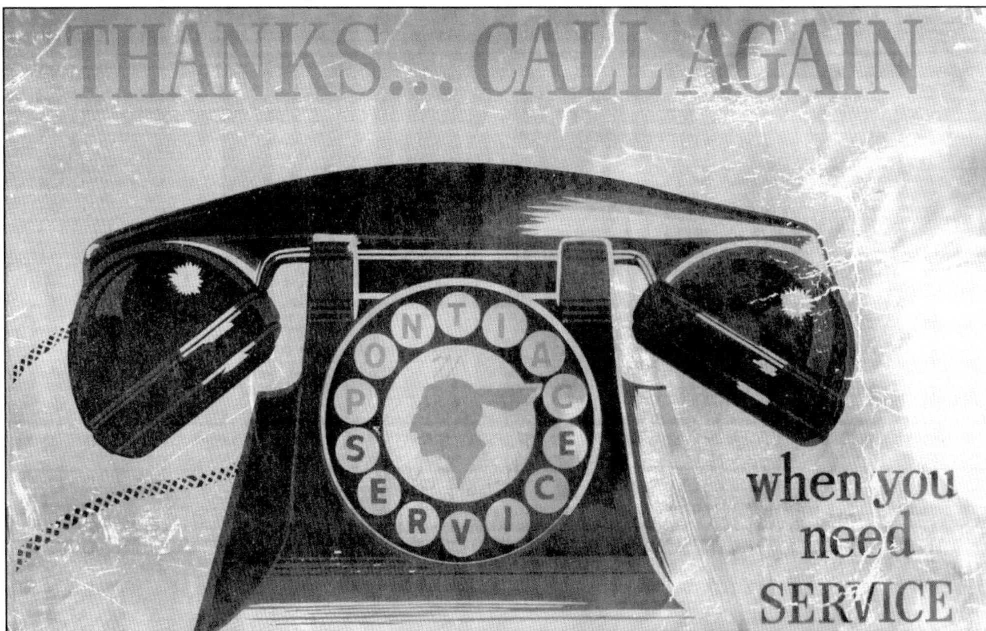

This is an original sign from the early 1940s at Joseph's Pontiac. The telephone exchange of 71, for Norwell Center, is handwritten inside the logo of the rotary dial. The Pontiac brand was first established by General Motors (GM) in 1926. The Indian logo seen here is no longer used by GM, as it was replaced by a red-colored arrowhead. Pontiac was the chief of the Ottawa tribe and fought along other American Indian tribes at the Siege of Detroit in 1760.

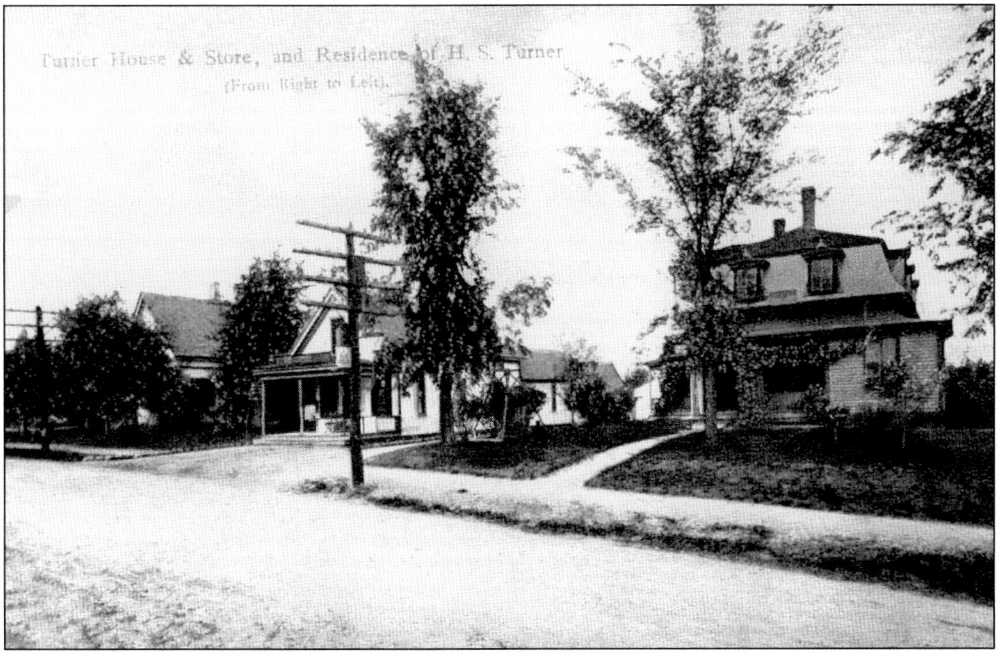

The Turner House was located on Main Street in Norwell Center. E. A. Tuner ran it as a hotel for summer guests from Boston. Among the visitors were actors and entertainers who performed on the second floor of the South Scituate Savings Bank, which was known as Fogg's Hall. Today, the well-known Joseph's Hardware operates on the former site of the venerable Turner House.

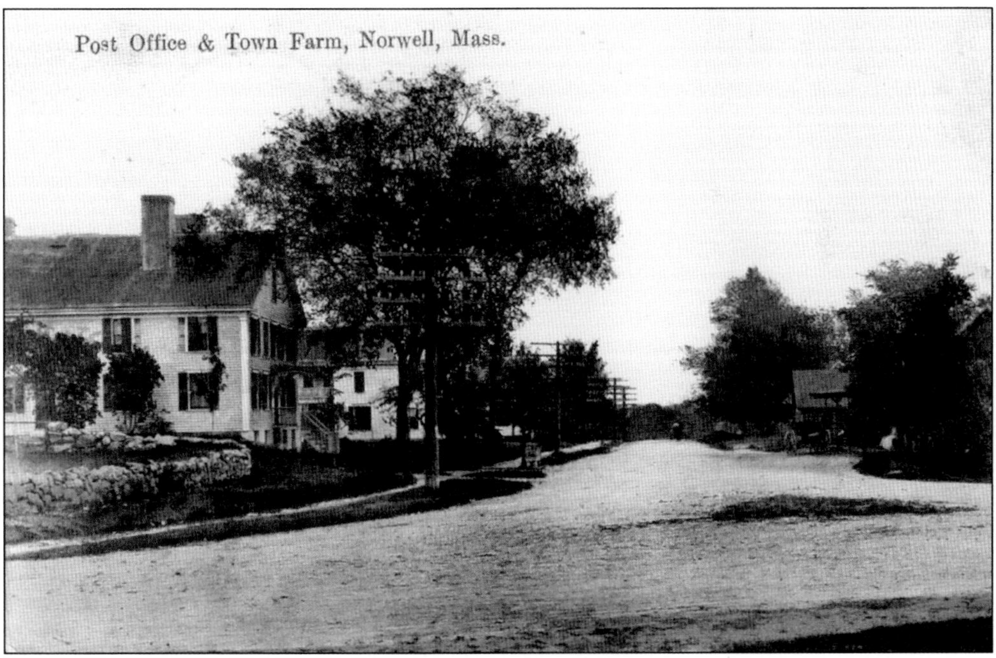

A pretty scene is shown here in Norwell Center. On the left is the Norwell old almshouse on Main Street. It was also called the town farm, which was another term for the home for the town's indigent. Across Main Street is the post office and M. E. Curtis General Store.

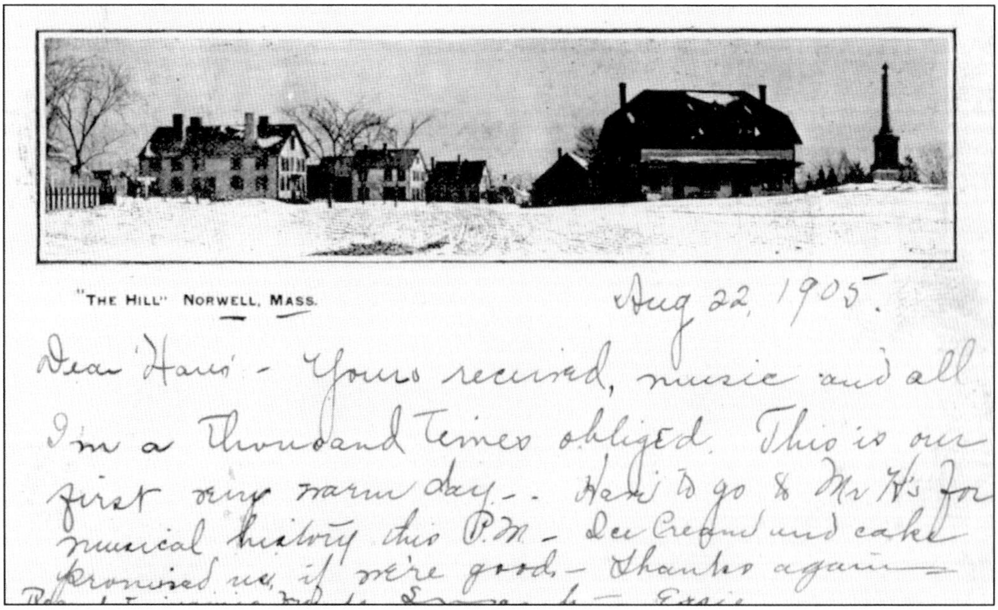

This is a picturesque scene of Norwell Center after a snowstorm. Prominently featured are the South Scituate Savings Bank and the Town Farm across Main Street. This area was also known as Norwell Hill. Today, Norwell Center merchants and several supporters are undergoing a planning initiative to beautify the streetscape.

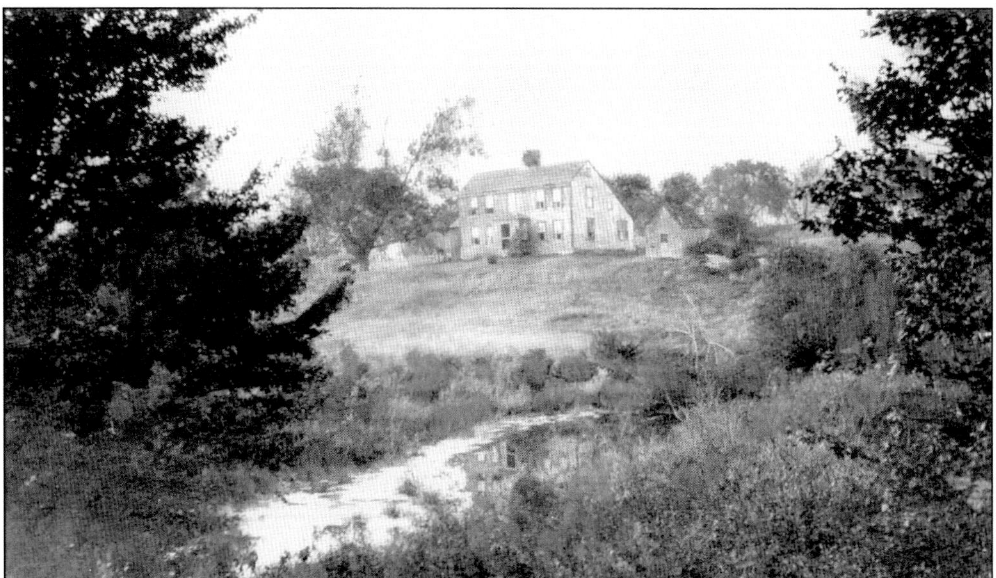

Perched high on a hill is a home built on Upper Ferry Lane by Jonathan Turner. This saltbox colonial was erected in 1645 near the center of Norwell Village. This home is in the area that was once called Up River Way, which crossed the Bryant Mill and the Bryant-Cushing home.

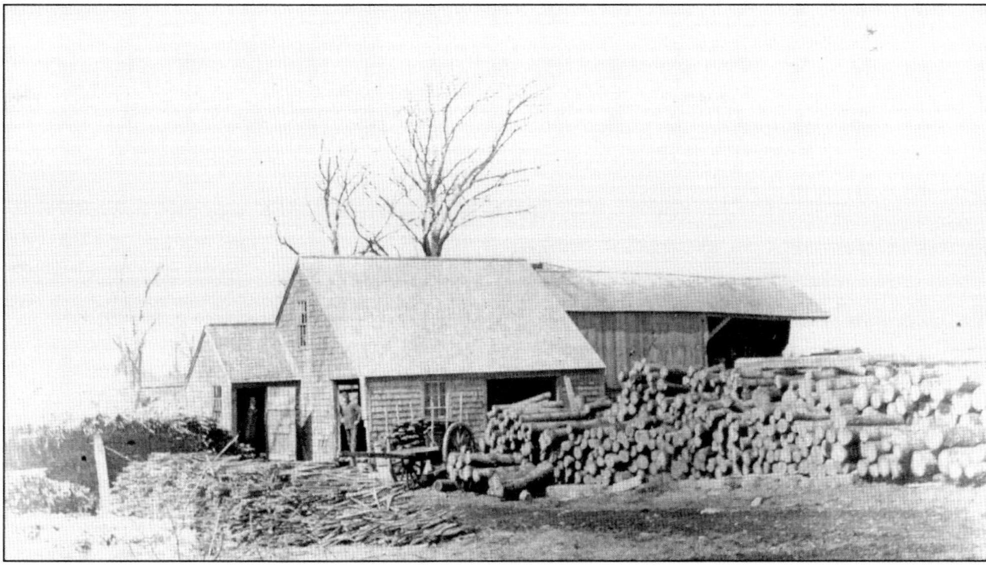

Here are loads of lumber being readied for processing at a saw mill named the Bryant Mill. This structure was originated by John Bryant in 1690 as only a gristmill. It was located downstream from the Second Herring Brook, not far from Norwell Village. It expanded to a saw mill in about 1770 by Hawkes Cushing. It was a vital business to the residents of Norwell Center for generations. It eventually closed in early 1927.

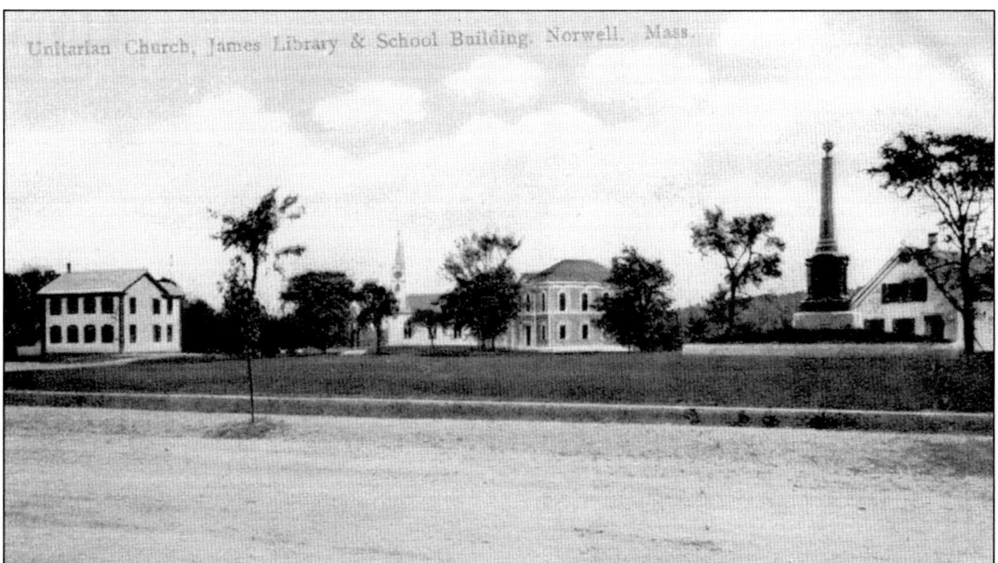

This postcard image of Norwell Common was taken around 1906 and shows prominent Norwell landmarks. From left to right are the Norwell School District No. 5 Building, the First Parish Unitarian Church, the James Library, the Civil War Monument, and No. 18 West Street. Norwell Common is part of the Norwell Village Area National Register Historic District, which was awarded to the town in 1982 by the U.S. National Park Service.

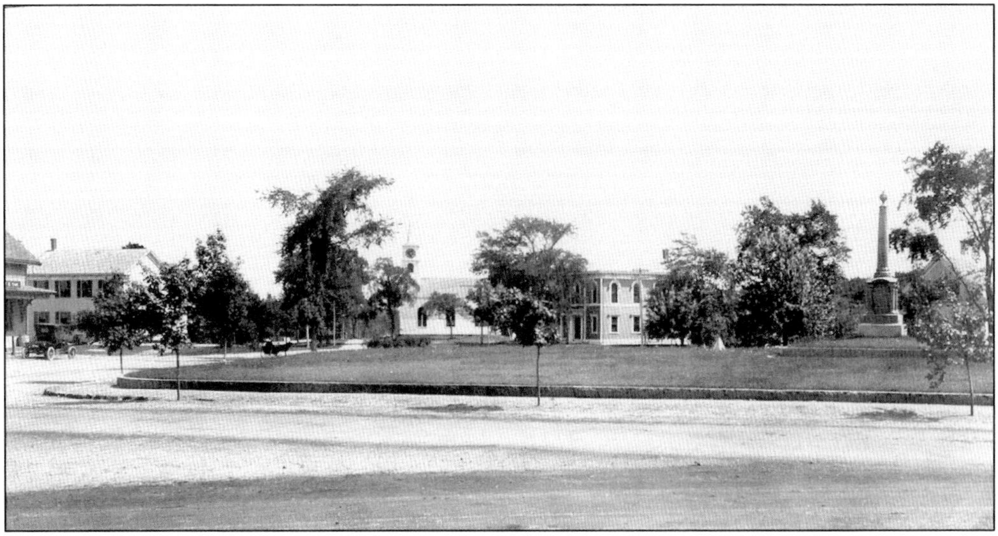

Pictured here on the far left, the South Scituate Savings Bank and the Norwell Schoolhouse District Number Five can be seen. Jon Bond remembers his older brothers going to school here before the Center Elementary School was built. School No. Five was returned to the Unitarian Church, and later this building was the home to the Pfc. Samuel B. Turner Jr. American Legion Post 192. The building was eventually sold to the South Scituate Savings Bank, which in turn razed it to make room for a parking lot.

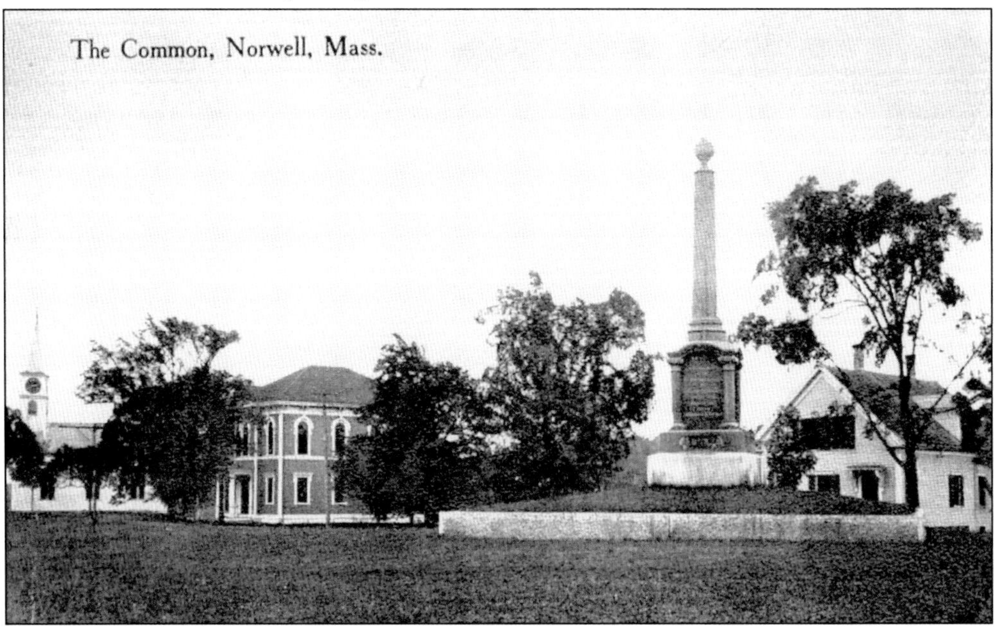

Pictured here on the town common is the Civil War monument which was dedicated on Memorial Day 1878, by a large group of South Scituate veterans. On the inscription of the monument it stated "Erected in Honor of the Soldiers and Sailors of South Scituate Who Fell in The War of 1861 for The Preservation of The Union." There are 24 names inscribed on two sides of the monument. This tribute to the servicemen has a powerful statement inscribed on the side by the James Library. It says "Liberty and Union Established By Our Fathers Preserved Unimpaired By The Patriotism of Their Sons."

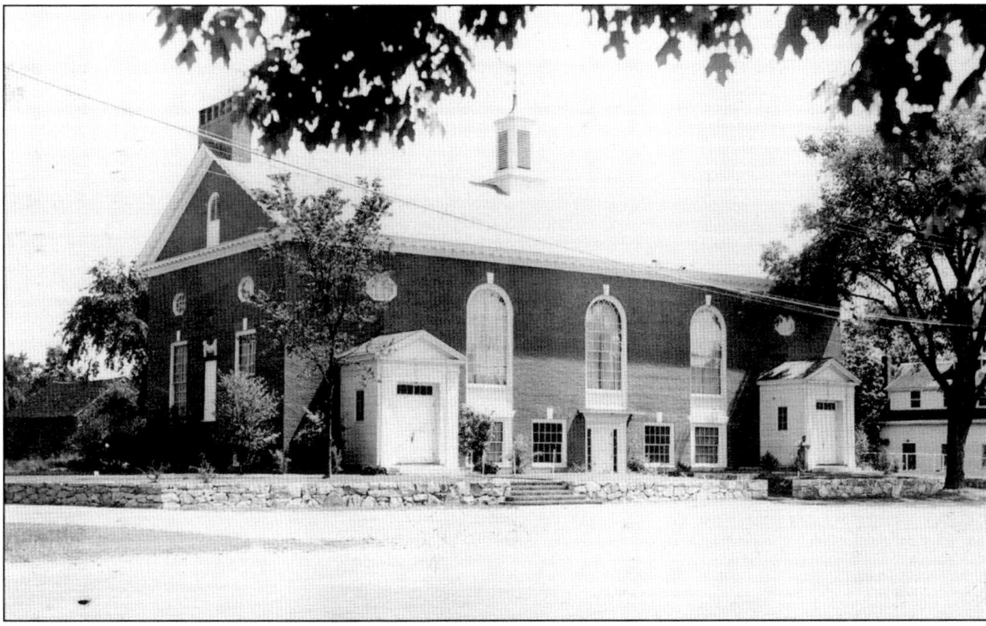

Florence M. Cushing left in her will funds for the town of Norwell to build a large hall that would house town meetings, lectures, and shows. Florence wanted the hall to be built in memory of her father, Nathan Cushing, and her uncle Hayward Pierce Cushing, two prominent men who helped shape Scituate, South Scituate, and finally Norwell. The hall was built on the site of the former infirmary and dedicated on November 2, 1936.

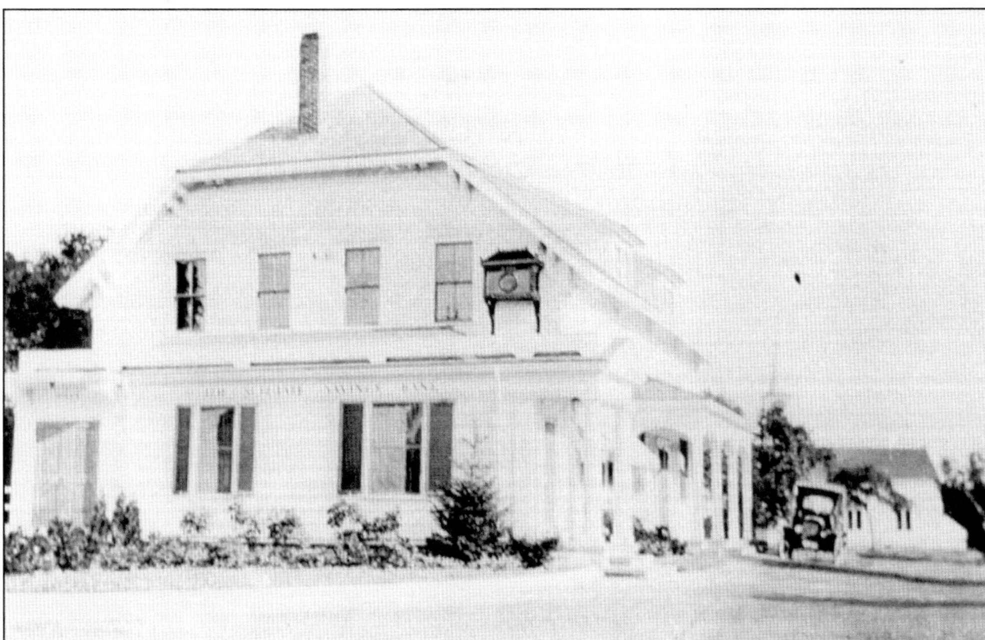

The South Scituate Savings Bank got its roots by a special act of legislature in 1834. It was named the Scituate Institution for Savings. Ebenezer T. Fogg, Samuel Turner, and Anson Robbins started the bank as partners. When the town divided in 1849, the bank shareholders changed the name to the South Scituate Savings Bank.

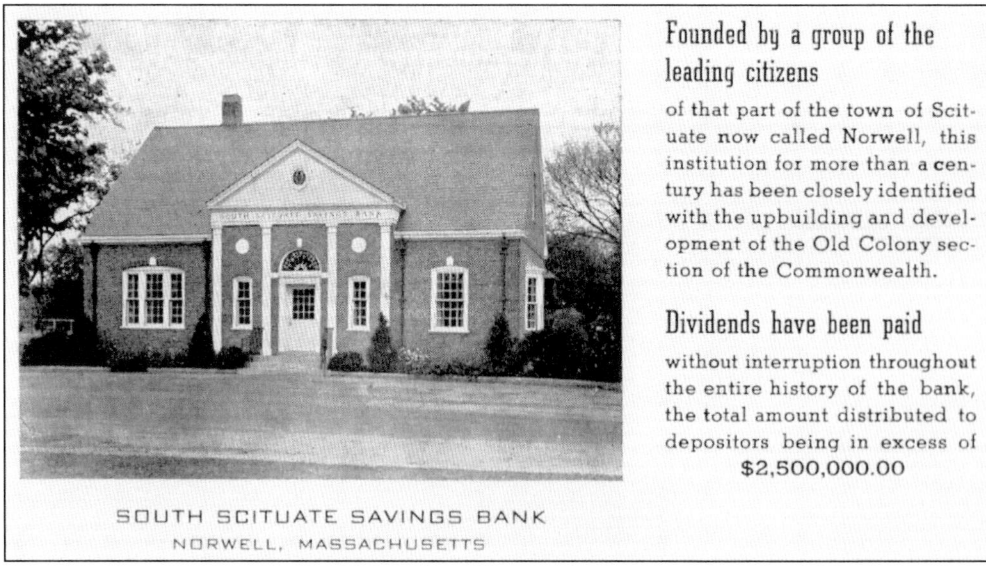

The bank had humble beginnings inside the home of Fogg. It later grew to its present site in Norwell Village in 1885. From 1885 to 1921, the second floor of the bank was used for vaudeville type shows in the venue known as Fogg's Hall. The present bank is located at 1 River Street, and in 1936, it was completely remodeled into a brick structure, replacing its wooden exterior.

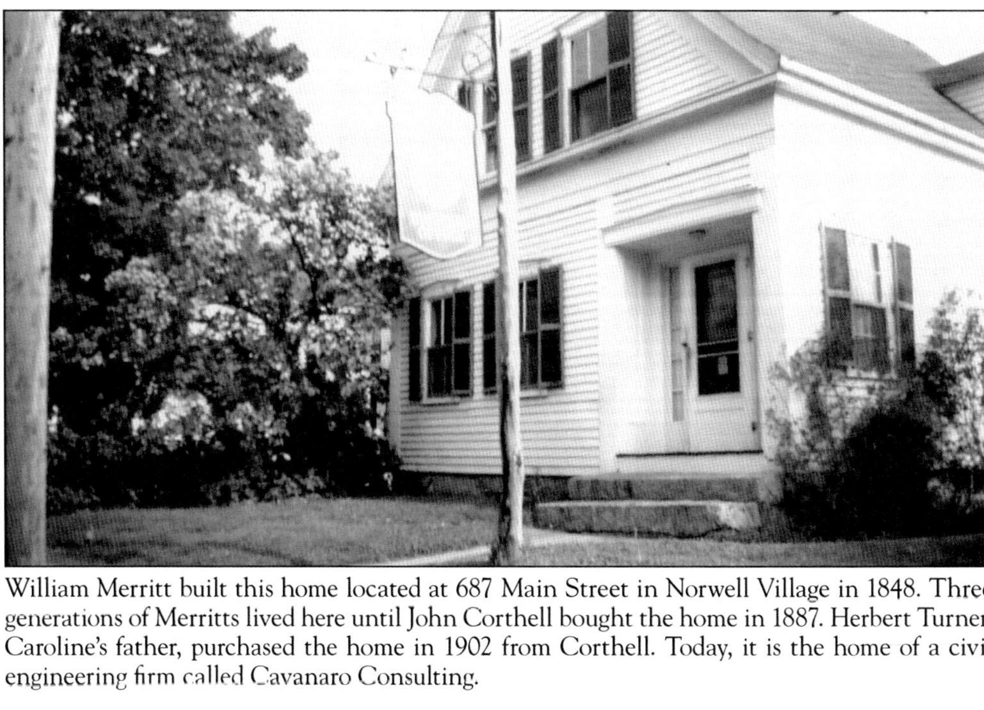

William Merritt built this home located at 687 Main Street in Norwell Village in 1848. Three generations of Merritts lived here until John Corthell bought the home in 1887. Herbert Turner, Caroline's father, purchased the home in 1902 from Corthell. Today, it is the home of a civil engineering firm called Cavanaro Consulting.

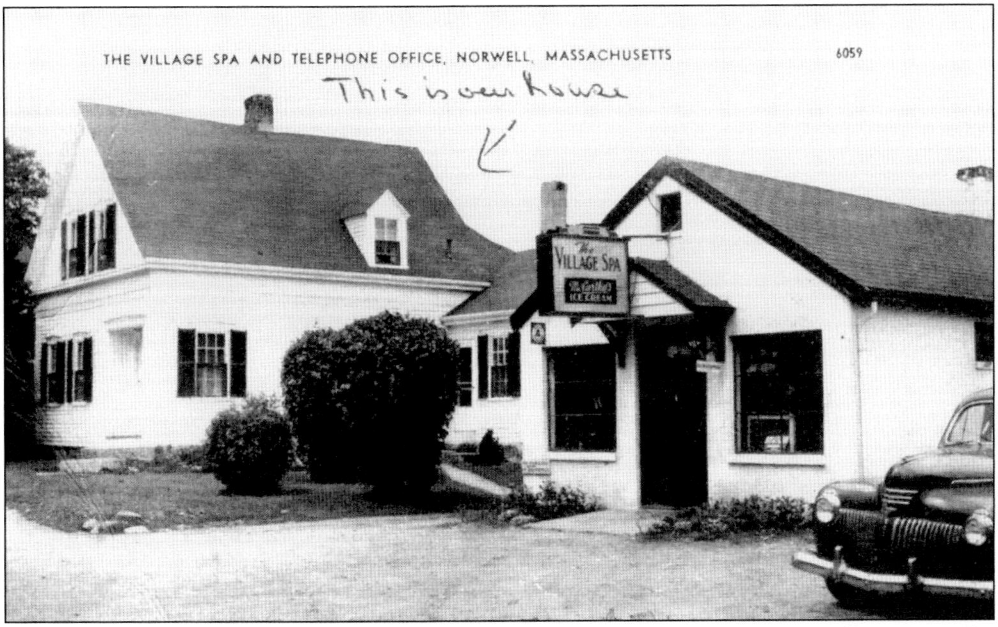

Here is the New England Telephone and Telegraph exchange office and the Village Spa. The Village Spa is now Aveni Cleaners. Caroline Turner wrote on the face of this postcard "This is our house," to her aunt Olive Sanford Damon of St. Petersburg, Florida, postmarked on October 29, 1951. She wrote, "Elizabeth is home from the hospital and gaining slowly. Sam is very, very, poorly." She also lamented, "We missed seeing you this summer."

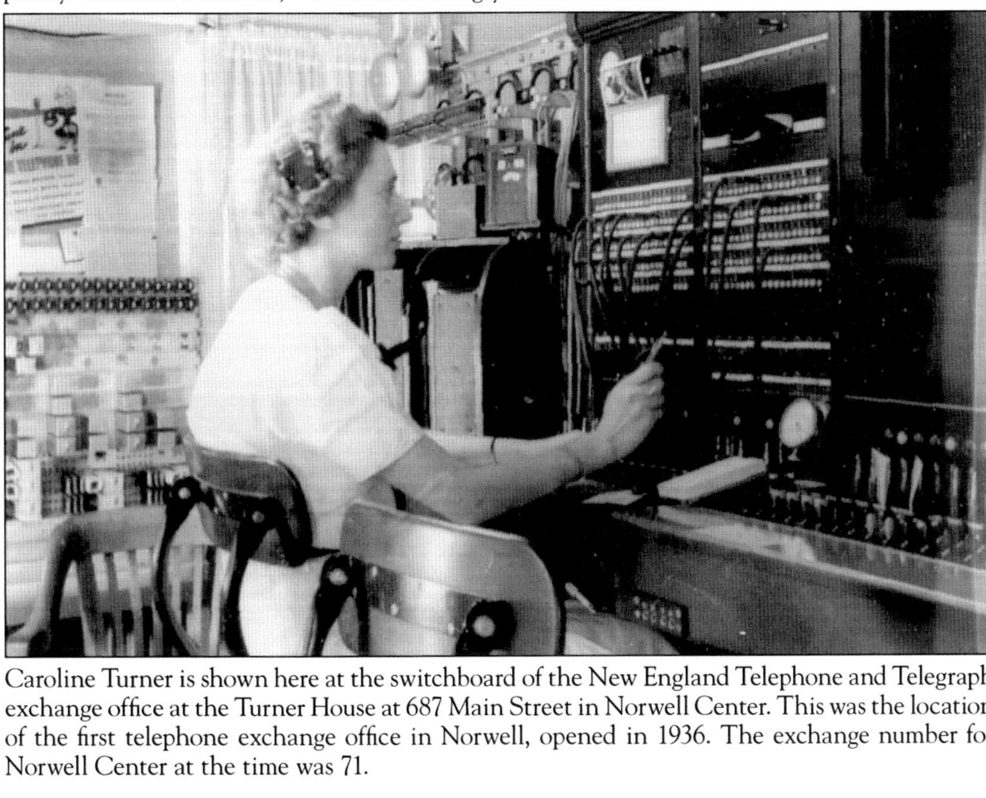

Caroline Turner is shown here at the switchboard of the New England Telephone and Telegraph exchange office at the Turner House at 687 Main Street in Norwell Center. This was the location of the first telephone exchange office in Norwell, opened in 1936. The exchange number for Norwell Center at the time was 71.

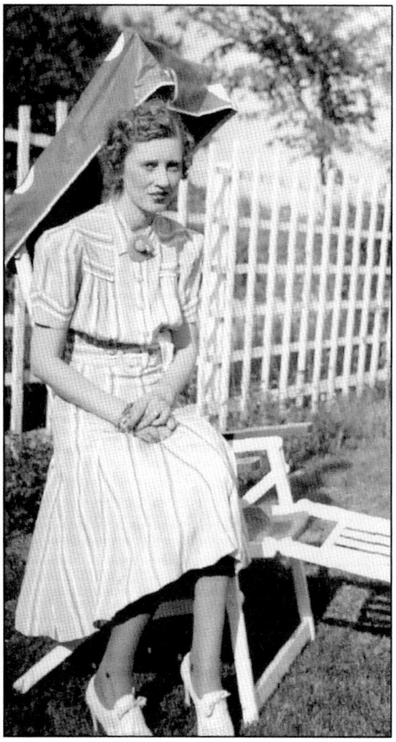

Caroline Turner's photograph was taken outside at her family home, the Turner House. Caroline Turner was the sister of Elizabeth Turner and the great-aunt of Dick Tedeschi. Caroline was a graduate of the Norwell High Class of 1912. She was one of four graduates that spring of 1912. Dick Tedeschi remembers his aunt telling him that for their class trip that year the seniors took a trip to Washington, D.C.

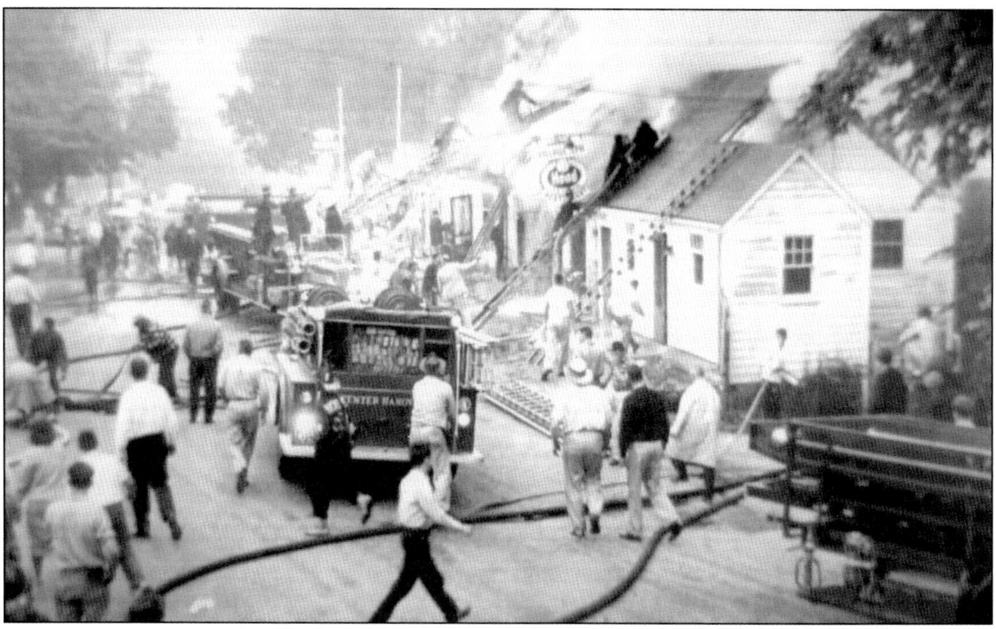

In the fall of 1957, a terrible fire raged through the center of Norwell's business district. Geoff Gordon, the owner of Andrew Gordon Insurance Agency, remembers hearing a story that while the blaze was erupting, firefighters rushed into his father Andrew's office to save their copies of insurance policies! Norwell Fire Company One was the first to respond, as it was situated right in front of the blaze. The town had two other fire stations in addition to Norwell Center, which were Company Three in Church Hill and Company Two in Ridge Hill at 209 Washington Street.

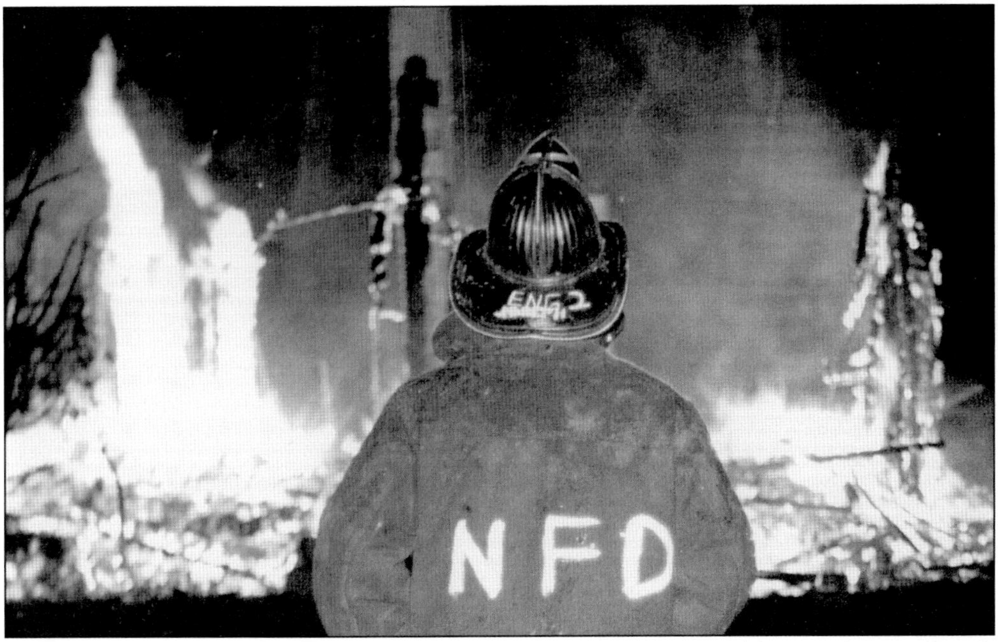

Extensive damage was done to the historic center of town. Depicted here is fireman Joseph watching as a structure succumbs to the overwhelming heat. The Hanover Four Corners, Scituate, and Rockland fire departments assisted the Norwell Fire Department in this five-alarm blaze. Most businesses had to be rebuilt; however, the Cushing Memorial Hall was spared the fire's wrath.

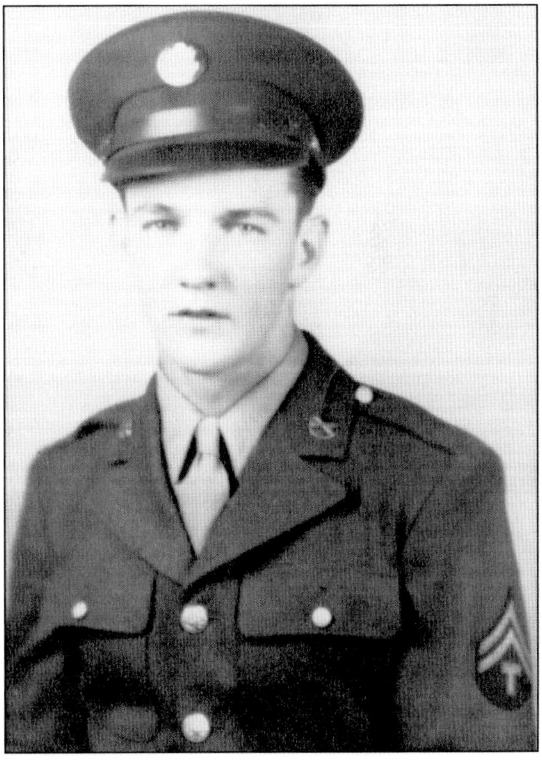

Samuel B. Turner Jr. was the first GI from Norwell killed in World War II. Turner, or "Bart" as he was also known, was the uncle of Dick Tedeschi, and he lost his life fighting in France shortly after the Invasion of Normandy on July 16, 1944. He was in the U.S. Army's 120th Infantry, 30th Infantry Division, and he valiantly fought against the Germans as a machine gunner. The American Legion Post 192, located at the former School No. Five, was named for Pfc. Samuel B. Turner Jr.

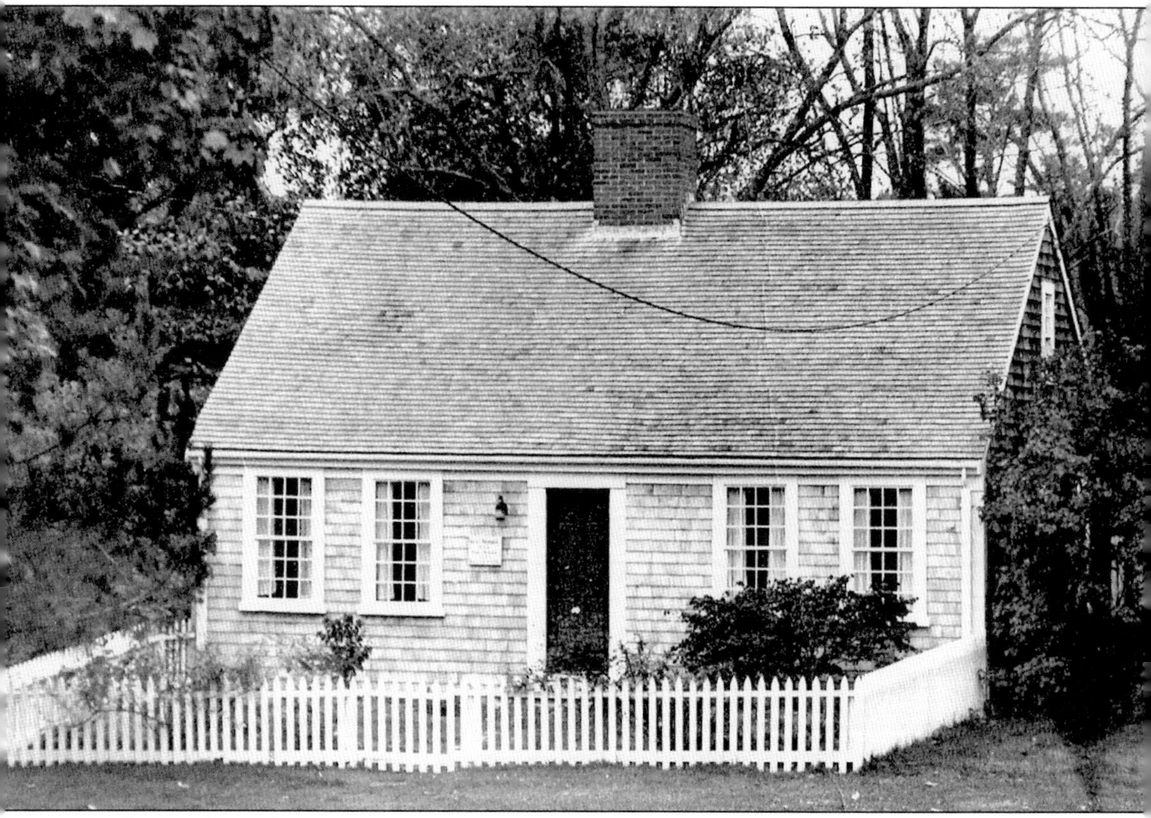

This residence located in Norwell Center has had a long history. This Cape-style residence was built in 1680 by James Bowker from Scituate. Capt. William Vinal was born in this home in 1881. The house is located on River Street between the First Parish Church and the James Library. When Vinal was 91 years old, he wrote about the history of the property on the back of this postcard that he addressed to Cape Cod Community College Chemistry Professor B. Carson French of Osterville, Massachusetts, on December 20, 1972. Vinal wrote, "This house was given to First Parish in 1930 moved to Norwell Center. Barn went to Cudworth house, historical center Scituate. Its now cared for by Norwell Garden Club. Am retired. Greetings Cap'n Bill"

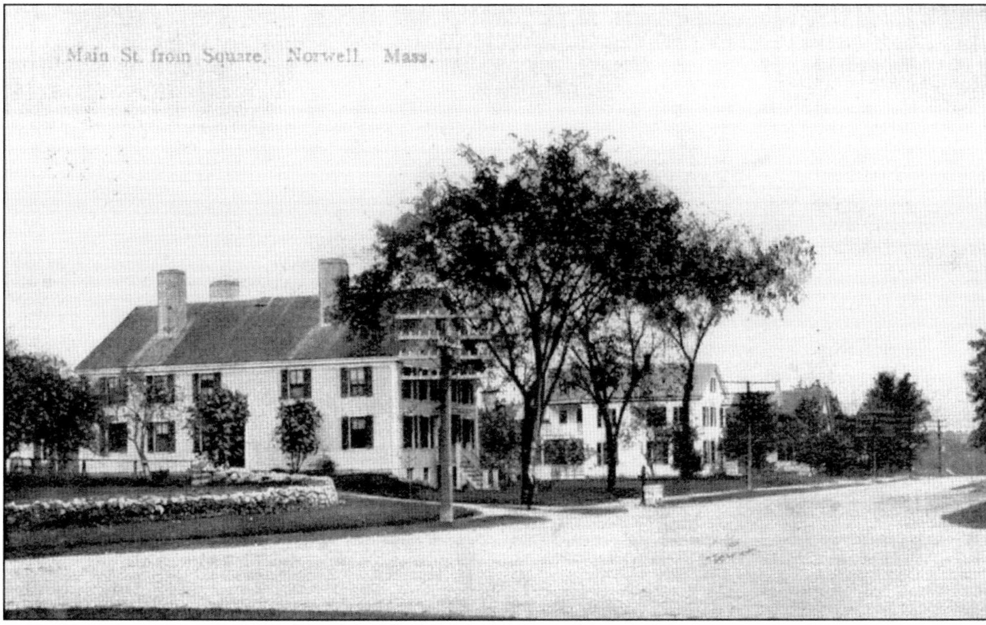

The old almshouse was built in 1821, replacing the original almshouse which was a victim of arson by John Woodward. Woodward was quite upset that his wife was placed there, so he torched the almshouse and he was promptly put to jail where he later died. The town of Scituate rebuilt the almshouse with four large chimneys and a fireplace in every room. Soon thereafter, it continued to serve the indigent and needy residents of Scituate and later South Scituate.

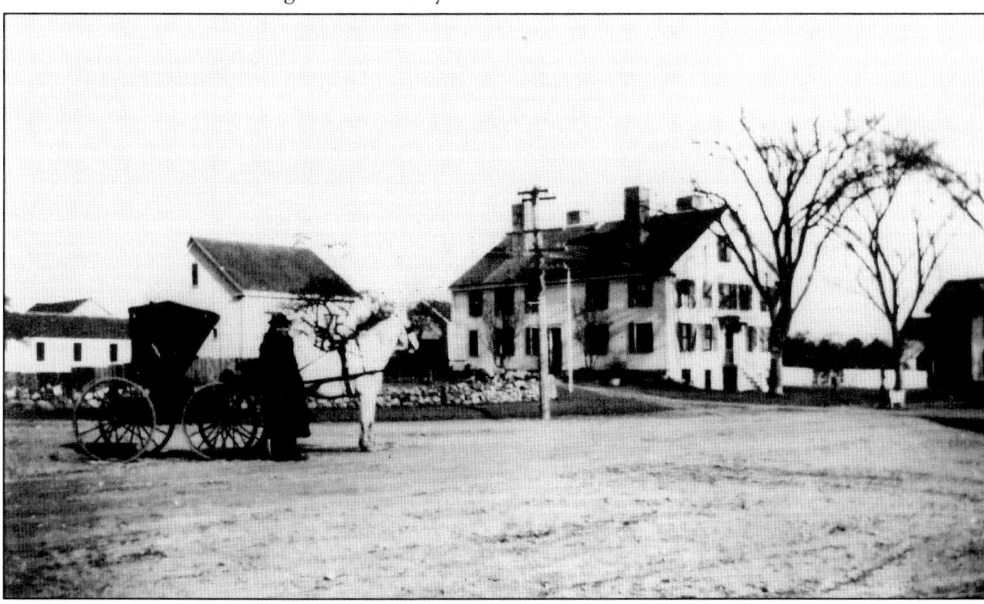

After the secession of South Scituate in 1849, the town of Scituate agreed to let the newly incorporated town take over the almshouse. The almshouse was very busy, particularly after the Civil War, when employment was difficult to find. Drifters in search of work utilized many almshouses across the region for lodging. Their required payment was to cut wood or complete chores on the property. Behind the almshouse was a prison house that held local perpetrators, prostitutes, and the mentally ill.

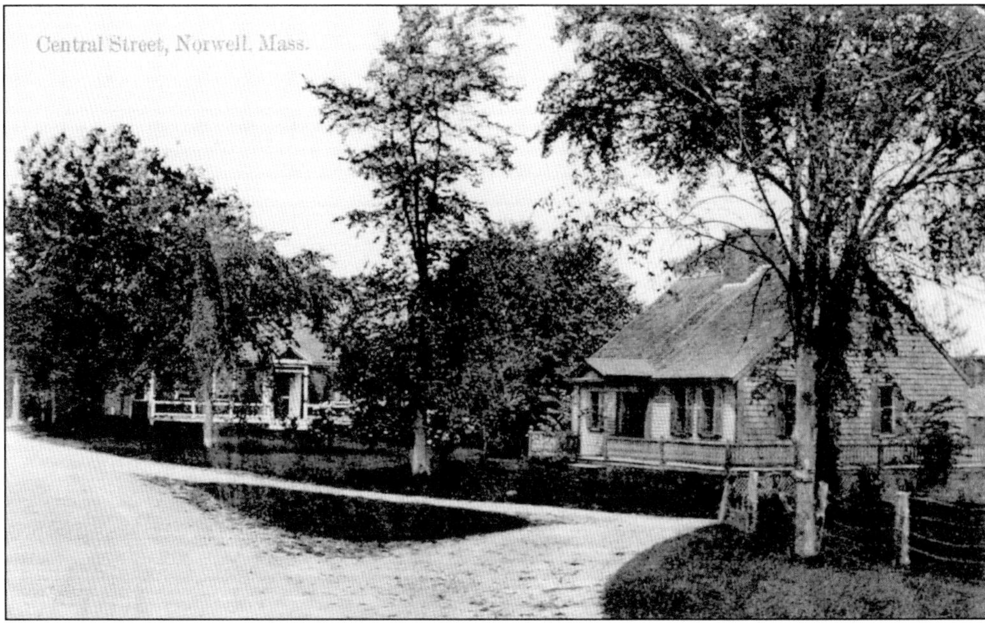

In the heart of historic Norwell Center stands a home with wonderful period features. Robert W. Turner Sr. is an inspiration and a reminder of years gone by in Norwell. He has been farming on his land for generations, and is one of the true Norwell lifelong residents.

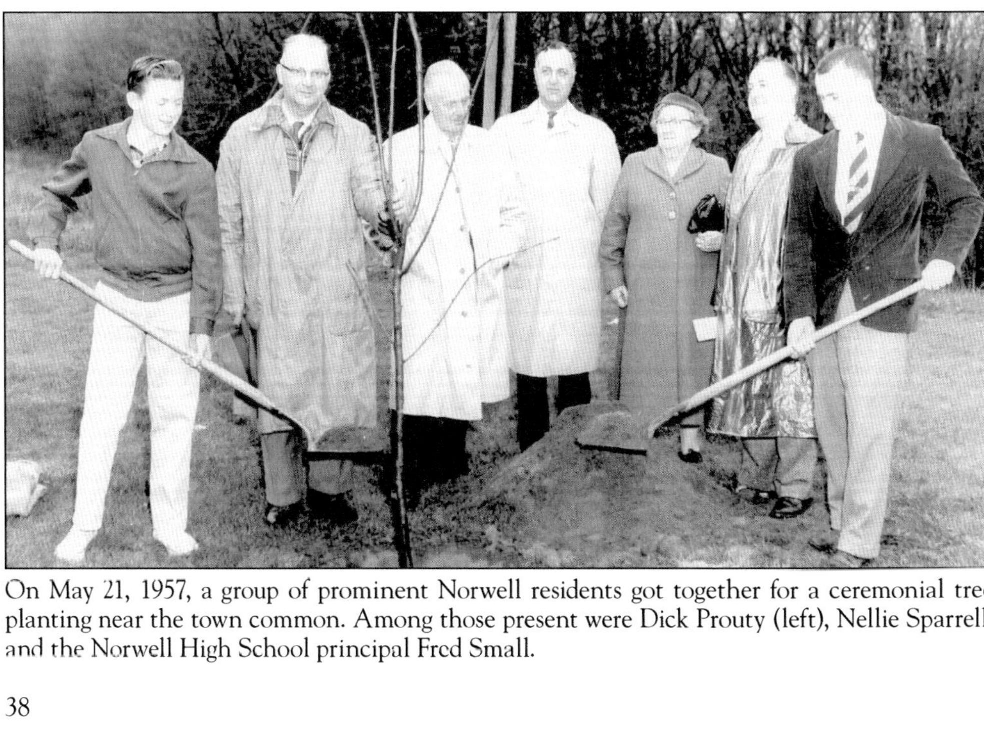

On May 21, 1957, a group of prominent Norwell residents got together for a ceremonial tree planting near the town common. Among those present were Dick Prouty (left), Nellie Sparrell, and the Norwell High School principal Fred Small.

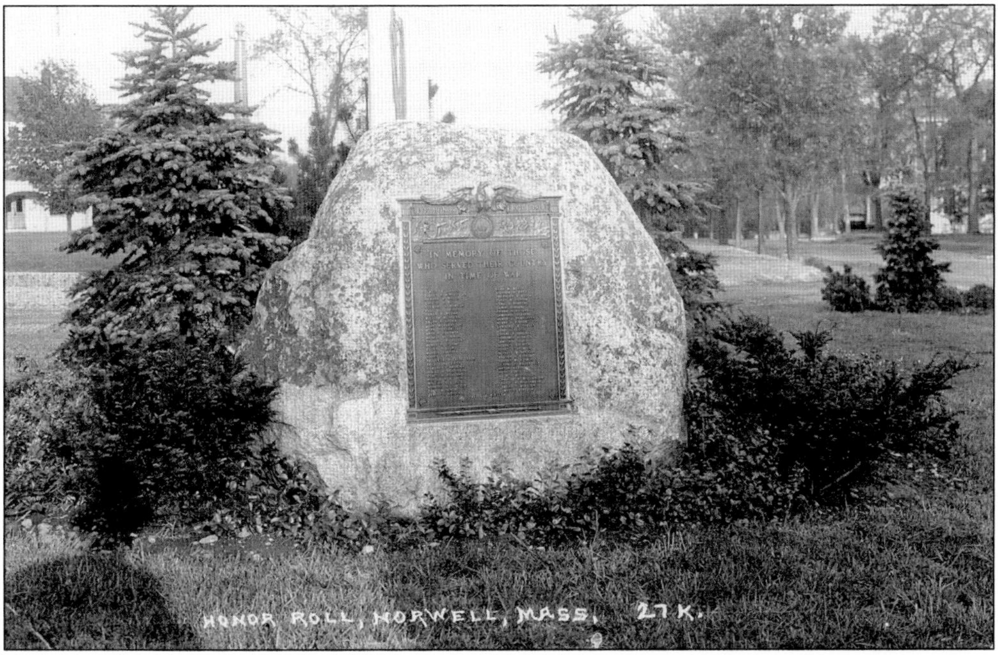

Here is a memorial tablet on a granite stone honoring the servicemen from Norwell that served their country during World War I, which was then known as the Great War. The tablet is located on the town common in Norwell Center. It is estimated that over 10 million people across the globe lost their lives during the war.

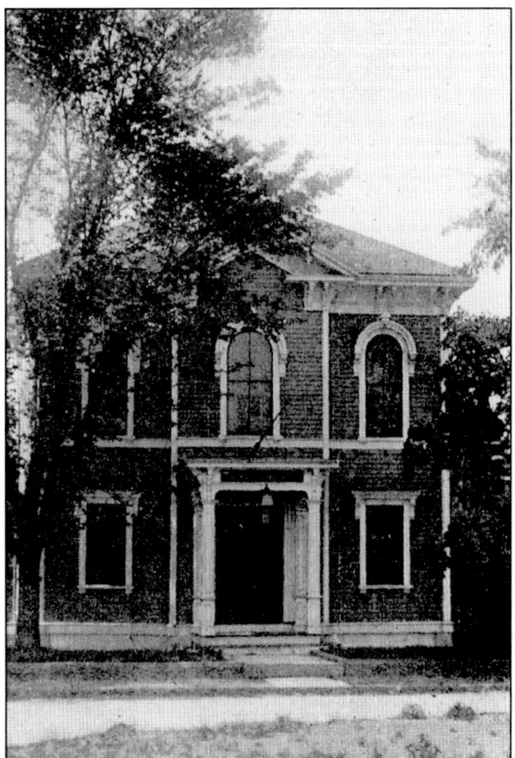

After the Civil War, talk came up that South Scituate was in dire need of a library for its residents. First Parish of South Scituate minister Rev. William Fish had written to his friend Josiah James to see if he had any interest in helping out his old hometown. James was a successful businessman who at the time lived in Chicago. He agreed to help establish a library if members of the parish would also contribute. The library was officially dedicated on May 1, 1874, and Reverend Fish became its first librarian.

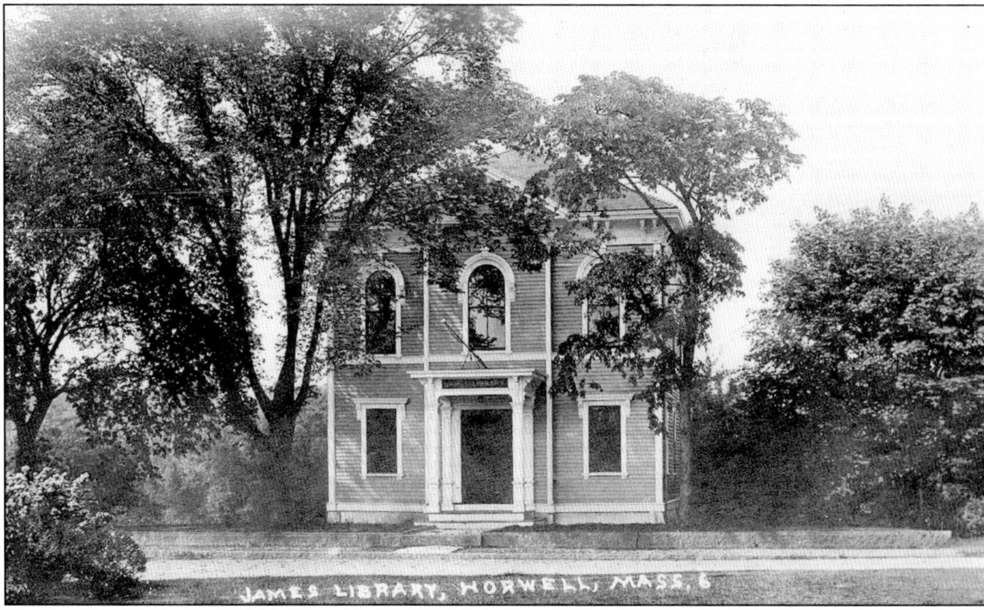

The James library was owned and controlled by the First Parish of South Scituate for over 75 years. It became a free library, which meant that it was available to all of the townspeople, in 1902. Today, the James Library has experienced a renaissance of sorts. The Victorian-era structure underwent a renovation project in the 1990s and has hosted many performing arts events in its upstairs hall. There is also an art gallery in the basement featuring local artists' works.

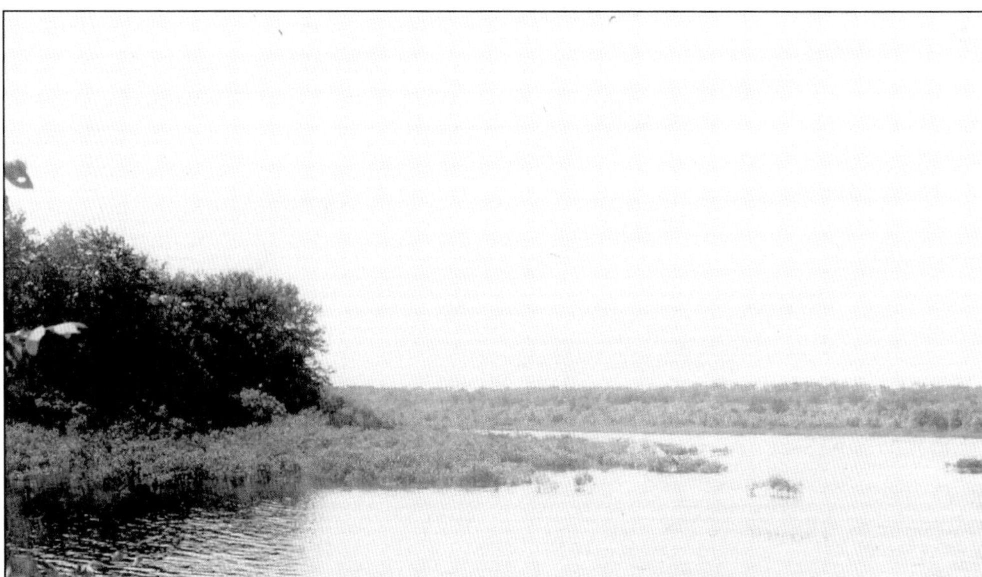

Located off Mill Lane near Norwell Center is Torrey's Pond. The pond was named for the Torrey brothers who operated a saw mill at a site of an old beaver dam. Everett, Willard, and David Torrey operated the mill for decades. The dam was originally built around 1800 by Lemuel Turner.

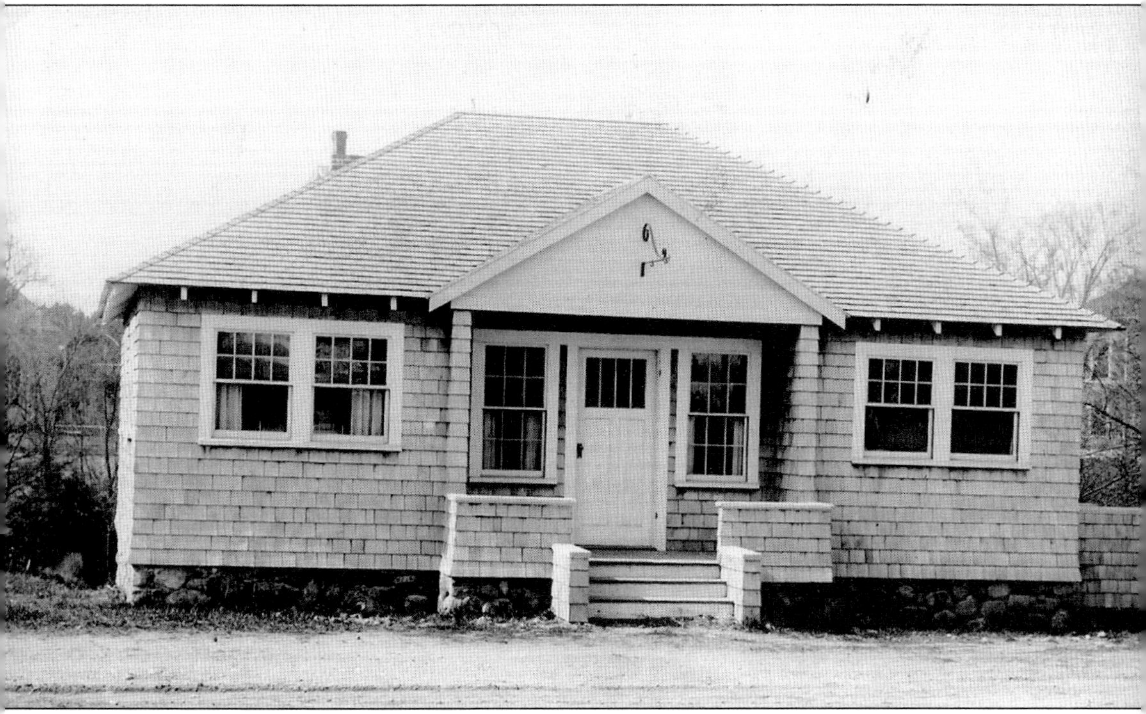

Located at 688 Main Street in the heart of Norwell Village stands the Arts and Crafts Building. In 1907, a group of ladies formed the Norwell Arts and Crafts Society. The society was organized to be primarily a social club. There were works of art available at the annual Christmas sale. The building was also used for the Red Cross, a post office, a dentist office, a state police station, and an American Legion auxiliary. The society disbanded in 1927, and its membership sold the building to John Sparrell. Today, it is Jardins Antiques. In 1919, the Massachusetts State Police were deployed to Norwell because of a serious poultry theft problem. They had five troopers working out of the Arts and Craft Building. D Troop Station 1 is now located in a barracks built on West Street by the state in the early 1930s.

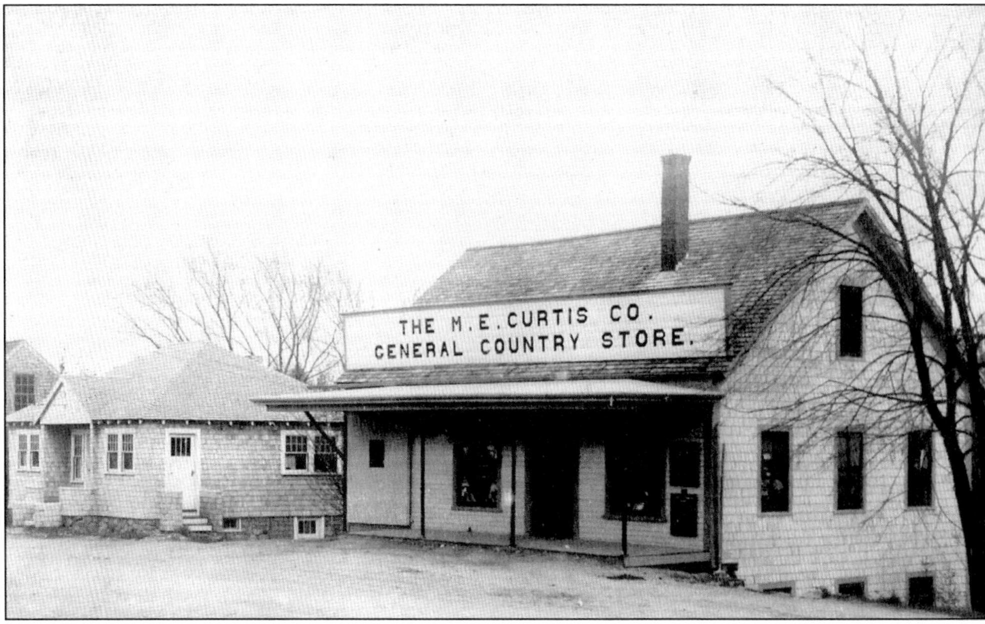

Pictured here on Main Street in Norwell Center is the M. E. Curtis general store. To the left of it, the Arts and Crafts building can be seen. Years later, it was known as Josselyn Market, owned by amicable shopkeeper Elmer Josselyn. In 1957, when fire broke out at the Village Spa in Norwell Center, this structure suffered serious damage. It was rebuilt, and today it is known as the popular Drums Emporium.

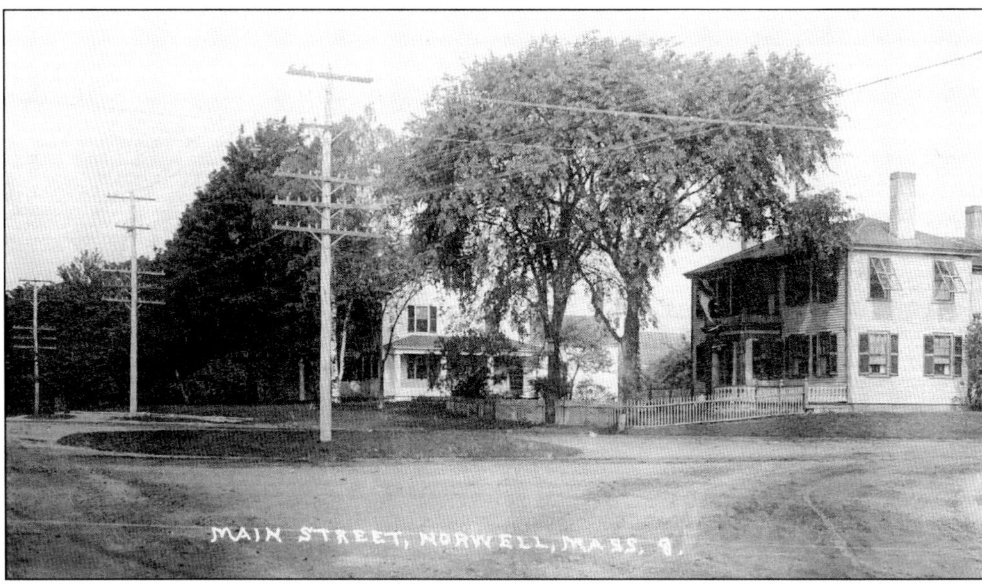

In 1788, John Nash opened a successful grocery store at the corner of Central and Main Streets, specializing in West Indies wares. Six years later, Nash built a home next to his store. His homestead overlooked Norwell Common in the village of Norwell Center. In time, Nash's home would serve as the village club room, library, and later, the post office. The Duxbury-bound stagecoach would make regular stops here as well. Years later, Daniel Webster would travel this route and stop at the Nash home.

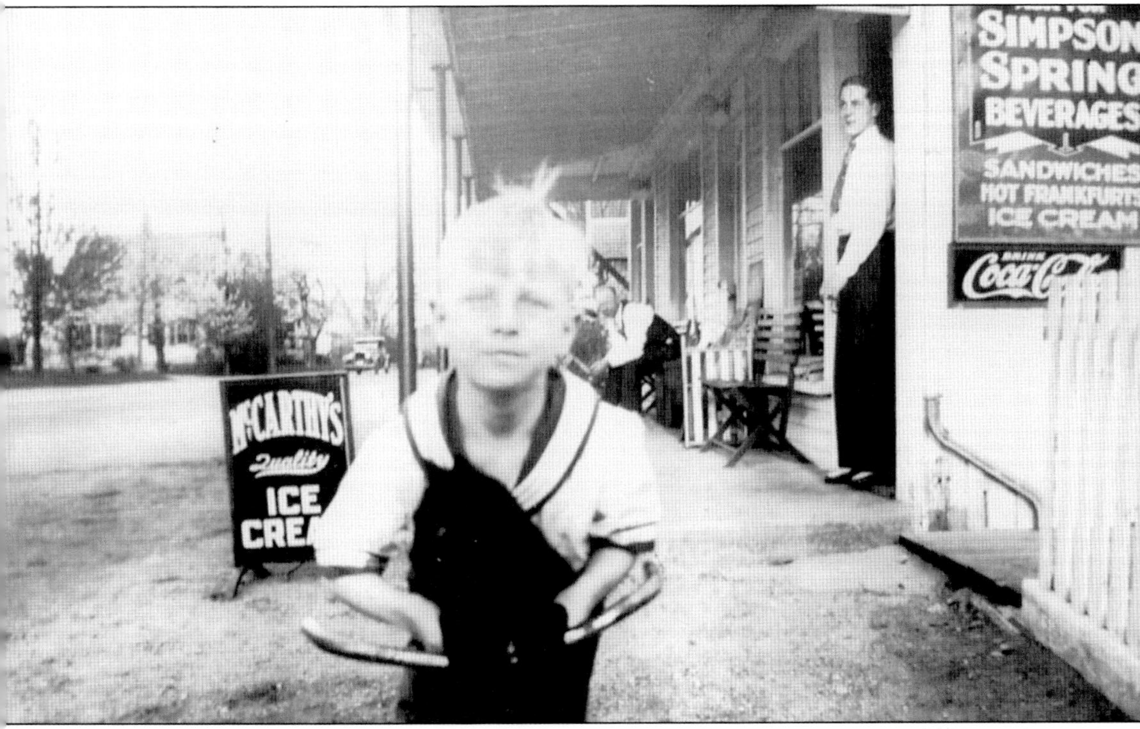

Posing on Main Street in Norwell Center with his cat on his bike is young, 13-year-old Harry A. Merritt. This photograph was submitted by his nephew Don Spradlin and it was taken in 1939. Merritt is sitting on his bike in front of the general store that is known as Drums Emporium today. Simpson Springs is an old fashioned soda company from Easton and is still available today. The McCarthy's Ice Cream sign is very nostalgic indeed as this company is no longer in business. Merritt worked for years as the maintenance department head for the Norwell Public Schools. He lives happily in retirement after serving on many town boards through the years.

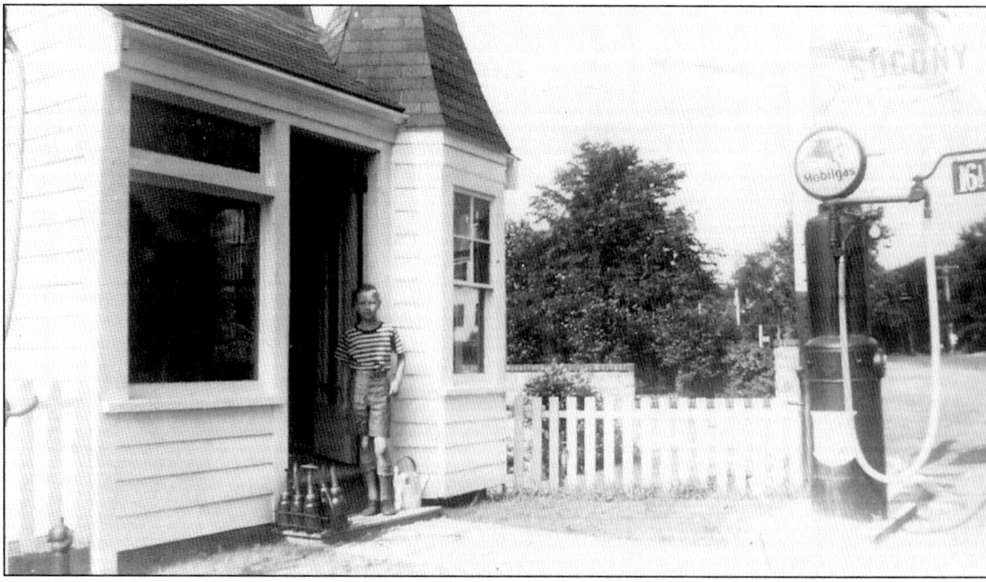

The gas prices seem to have soared to 16½¢ to the gallon. That is a price everyone would all like to see today. Young Harry Merritt has his photograph taken in front of the Socony gas station on Main Street in Norwell Center. This location today is the well-known Andrew Gordon Insurance Agency. In the doorway, there are quite a few oil cans ready to go for Merritt to service the customer's automobiles. That was truly full service back then!

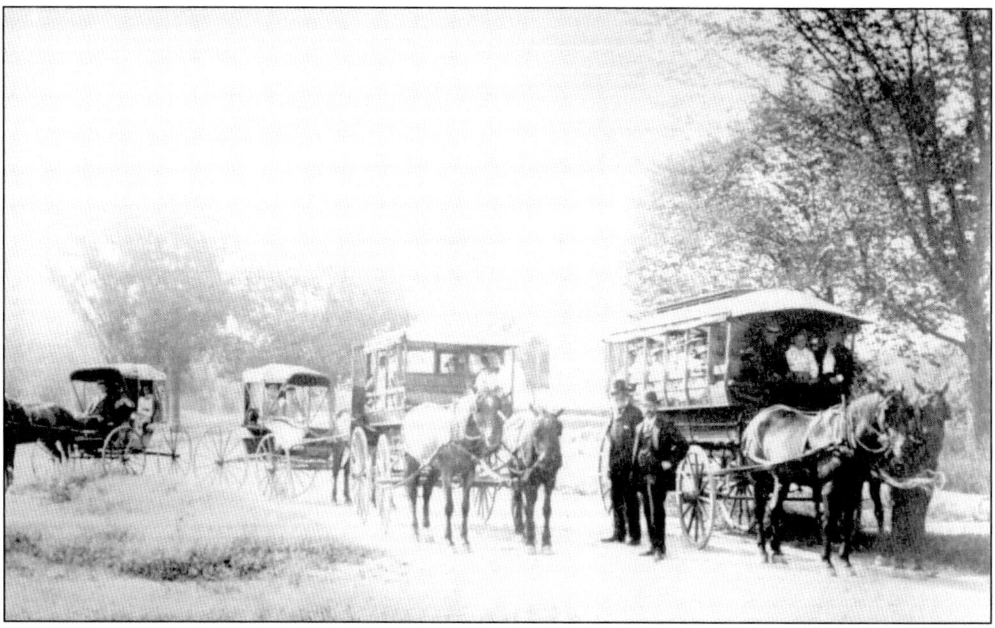

This looks like a major traffic jam for Norwell in 1900. The school barges can be seen on the right-hand side. Beginning around 1903, Henry Ford invented a four cylinder fuel combustion engine and devised a way to mass produce his motor car. This landmark innovation would spell the end of the horse-and-carriage, and thus change the landscape of Norwell and America forever. By 1917, Norwell was utilizing three new motorized school barges, putting the horse drawn barge out of business.

Three

NORTH RIVER

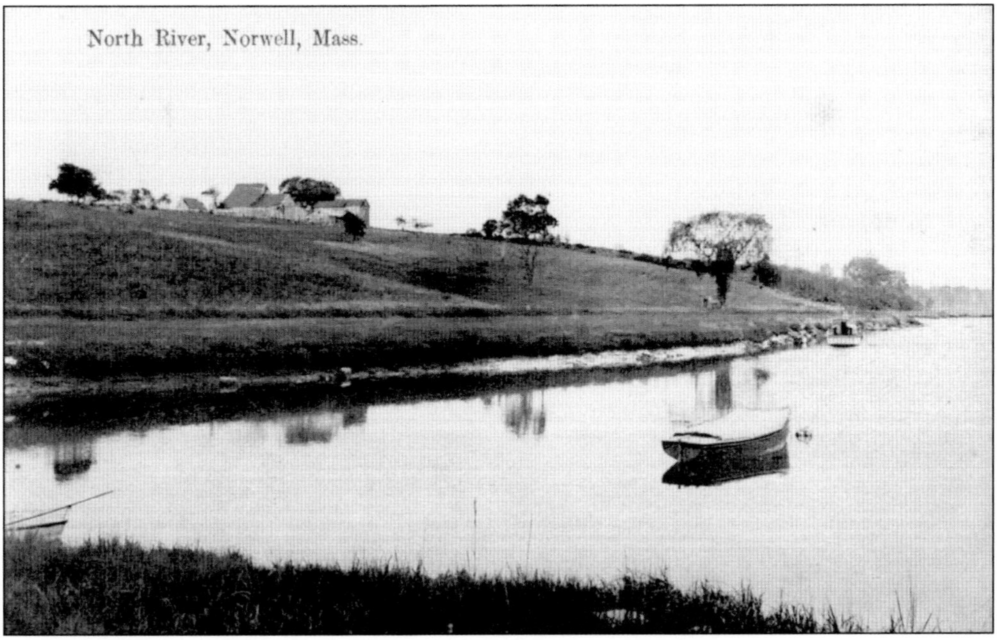

At the beginning of the 19th century, the North River was indeed one of the world's busiest shipbuilding areas. The shipbuilding area encompassed Scituate, Marshfield, Pembroke, and Hanover. Vessels were not known to be built in one of those towns but rather just "North River." On average, over two dozen ships were churned out each year in the early 1800s. By an unofficial count, the North River produced over 1,025 ships. Ironically, many of the ships used by the British Navy during the Revolutionary War were built along the banks of the North River.

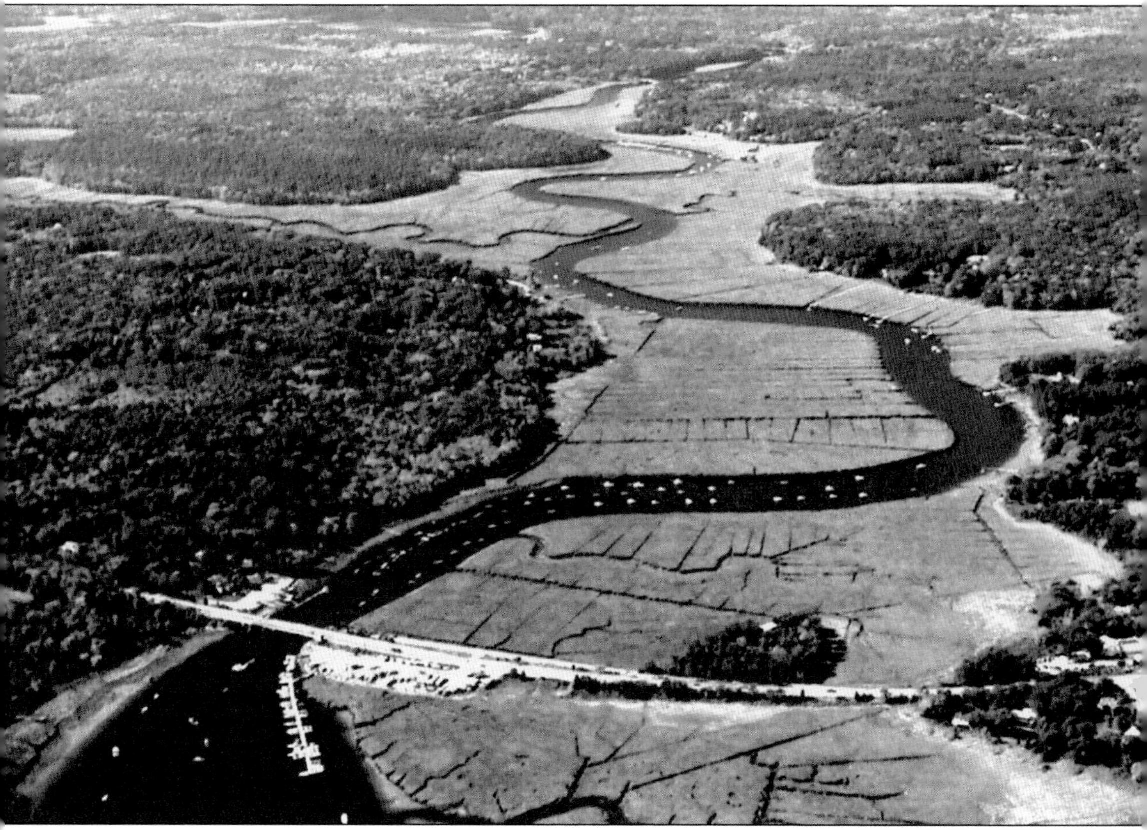

This is a beautiful aerial shot of the winding features of the North River. The Barkers were the first settlers to navigate this historic river, around 1628. The sources for the river are the Indian Head and the Namassakeesett Rivers. Many shipyards, such as the Wanton and the Chittenden Yards, thrived on the North River for over 100 years. Other prominent shipbuilders of the North River in South Scituate were the Cudworths, Southers, Clapps, and Fosters. The *Essex* was a ship built on the North River in 1796. It was the sinking of *Essex* and its horrible aftermath for the captain and crew that became the inspiration for the famous novel *Moby Dick*, written by Herman Melville. Another prominent vessel built on the North River by James Briggs was the *Columbia*. It was the first ship to carry the Stars and Stripes around the world. The last vessel built and launched from the North River was the *Helen M. Foster*. It was only a 65-ton schooner, and quite small compared to the Delano-built *Mount Vernon*, which weighed in at 464 tons and was the largest vessel ever built at a North River shipyard.

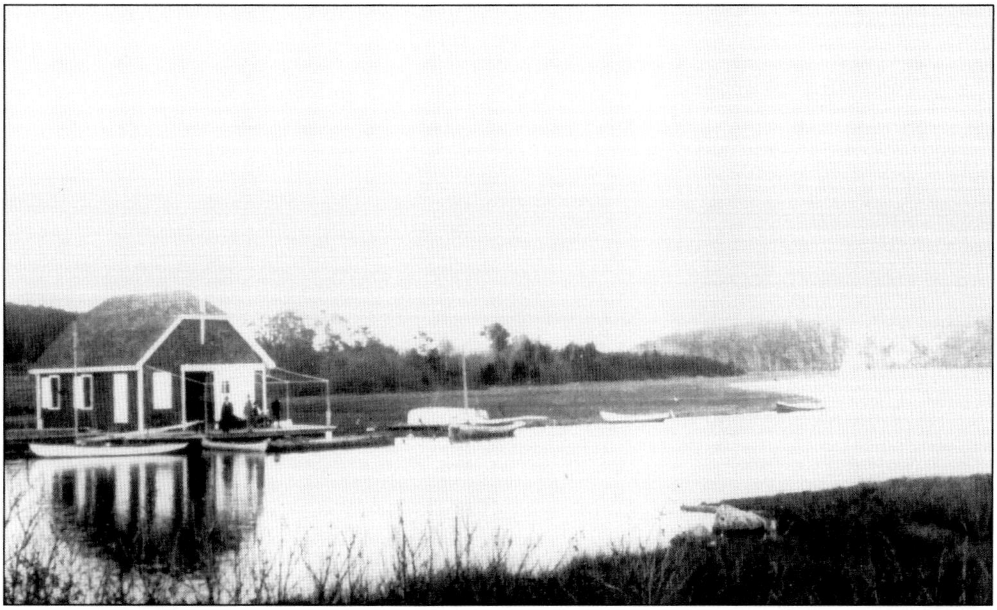

Henry Norwell, Horace T. Fogg, Charles E. Lincoln, Arthur L. Power, and Henry J. Corthell organized the North river Boat Club on September 4, 1893. The club's founders were the town of Norwell's power brokers of its day, which also included George Cushing, Joseph Merritt, and Samuel Turner. The club members enjoyed minstrel shows, dances, and races. After a terrible storm on the day after Thanksgiving in 1898, the boathouse floor became continuously flooded. The club voted to dissolve the organization the next fall, and the boathouse was sold and moved to 33 Winter Street.

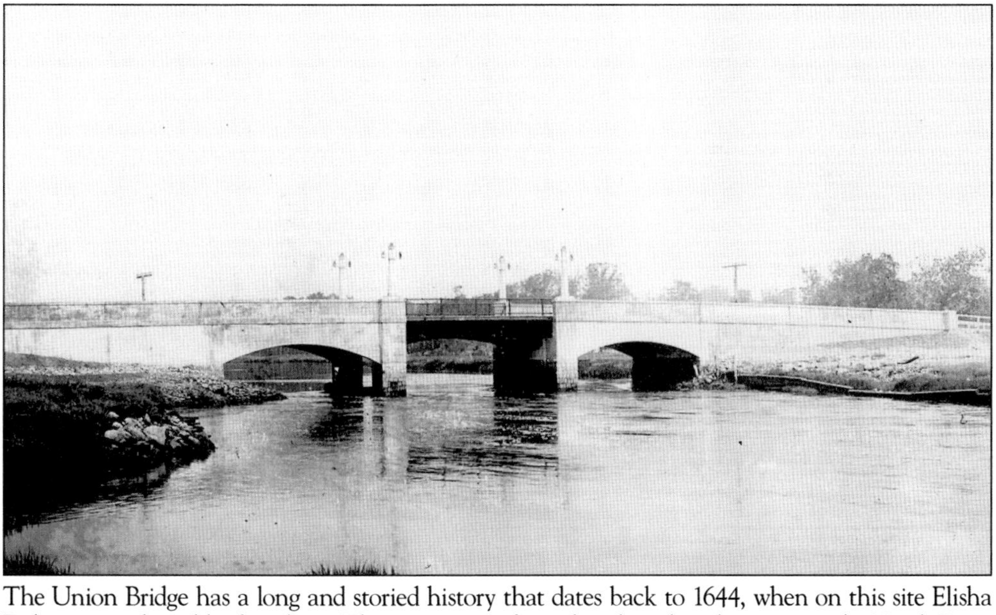

The Union Bridge has a long and storied history that dates back to 1644, when on this site Elisha Bisby operated a public ferry boat. This service was for early colonial settlers to cross the North River from Scituate to Marshfield. Bisby's home stood near this bridge next to his son Elisha's tavern. The ferry was known as the Upper Ferry, and the colonists also used a town landing there.

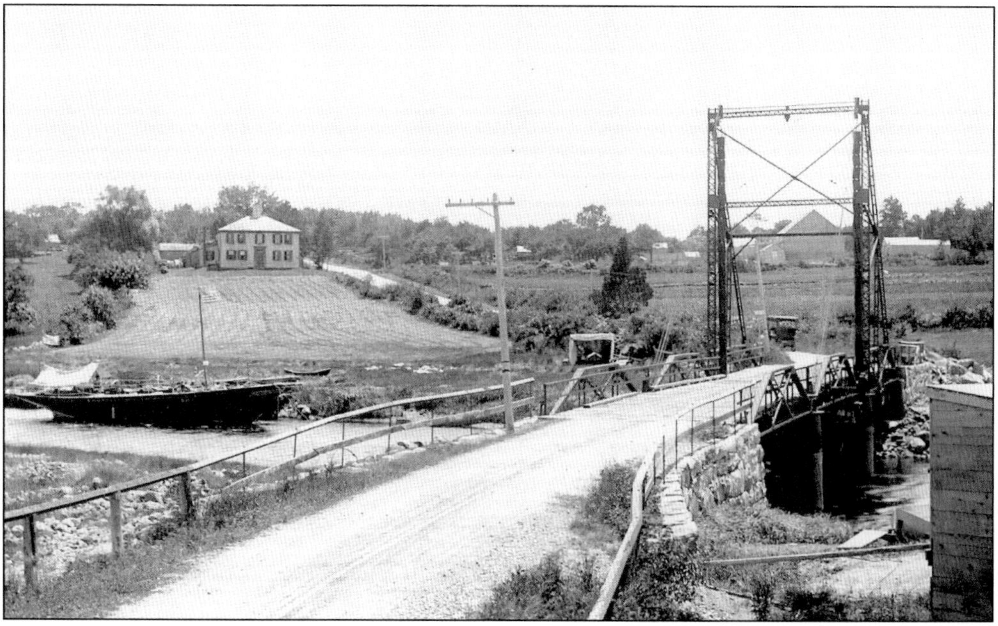

The Upper Ferry was run by the Oakmans of Marshfield until 1760, when John Tolman took over the ferry. Tolman would be the very last ferryman to work at this site because in 1799, the towns of Scituate and Marshfield agreed to build a bridge over Oakmans Ferry. Initially, $370 was raised, but the venture ultimately failed when Marshfield did not contribute its share.

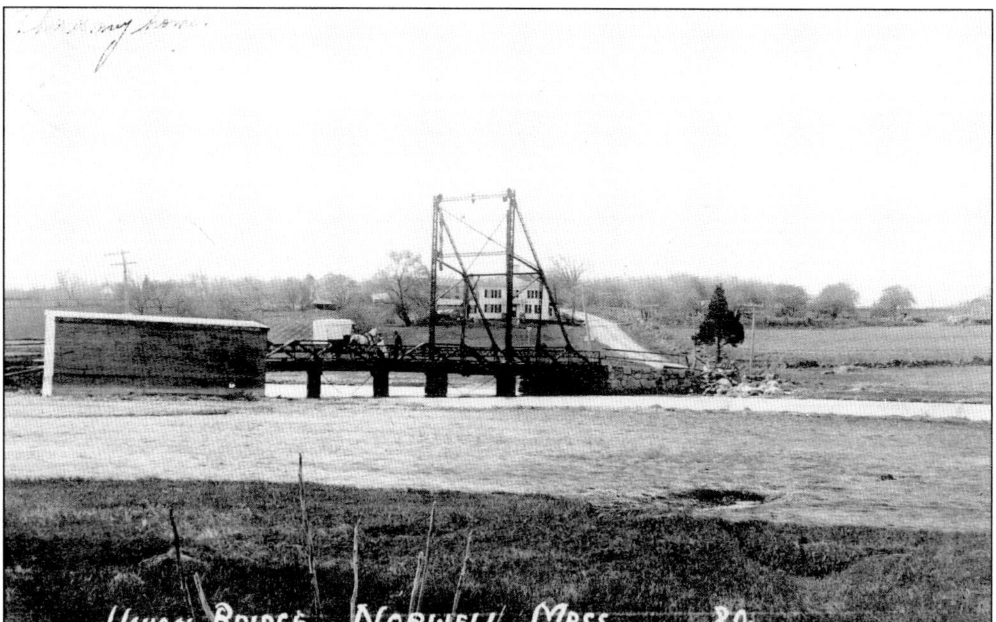

In 1801, a corporation was formed to build a drawbridge that would charge a toll. It would be a bridge big enough to span the North River, which was eight rods wide at ordinary tide. A rod is defined as a being a linear measure of 16 ½ feet. Very soon thereafter, Union Bridge would be built.

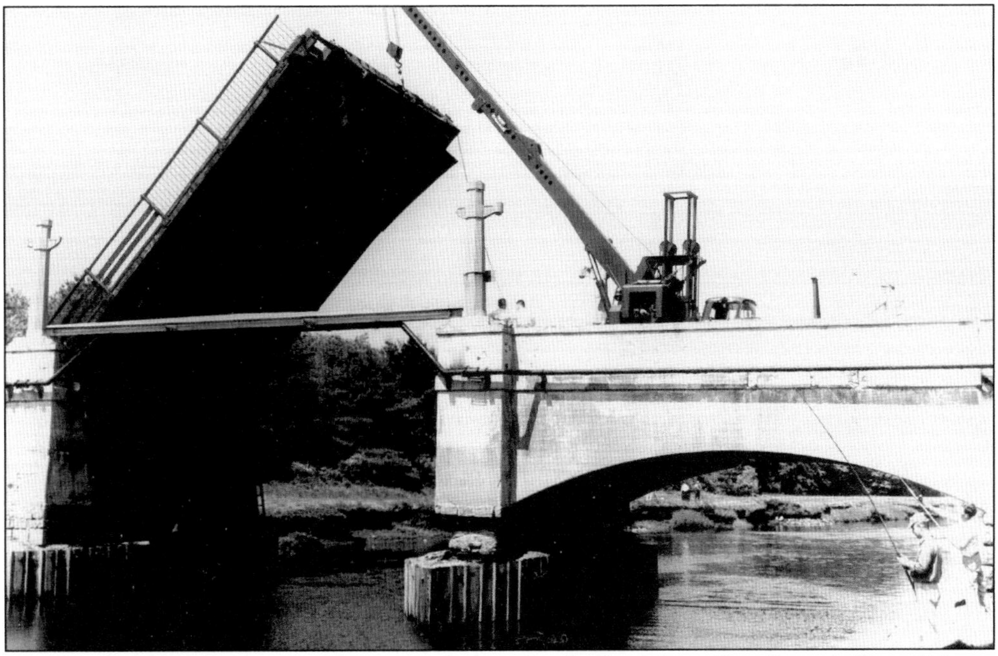

In 1850, the Union Bridge would be turned into a free bridge. The tolls collected allowed Union Bridge to be able to stay in good repair, and the unused funds were invested at seven percent interest. Hatch Tilden, the brother of prominent shipbuilders Jotham and Luther Tilden, was the toll collector for over 40 years.

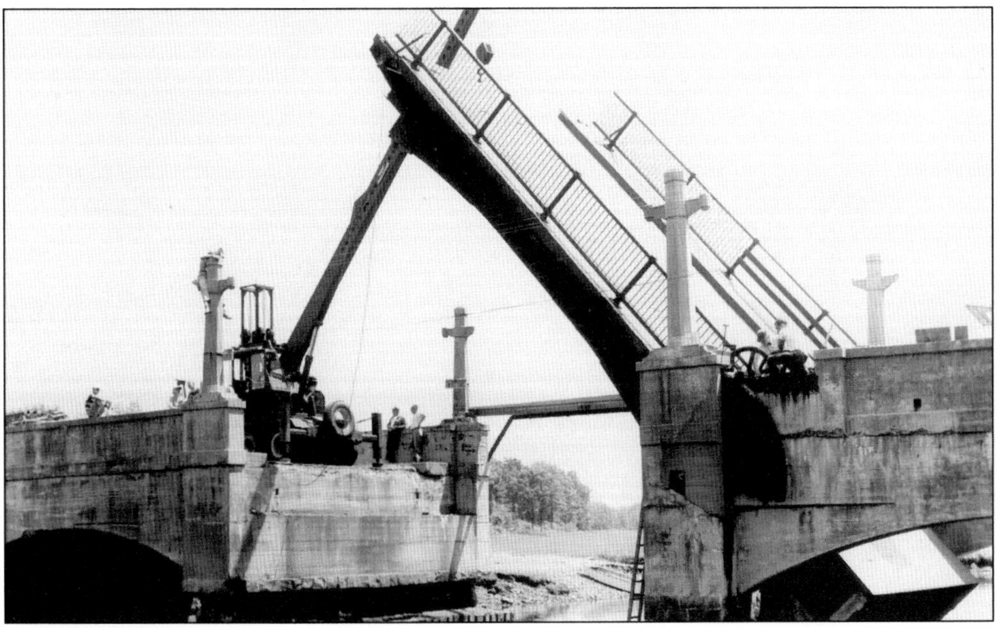

Over the course of more than 200 years, the Union Bridge has been constructed four times, consisting of wood twice and then steel and its present form of concrete with a steel draw. The wooden bridges lasted almost a hundred years, from 1802 until 1899. In 1899, the Town of Norwell contracted with the Pittsburg Bridge Company for a steel bridge. It was later replaced in 1917 with Marshfield, Norwell, and Plymouth County sharing the costs.

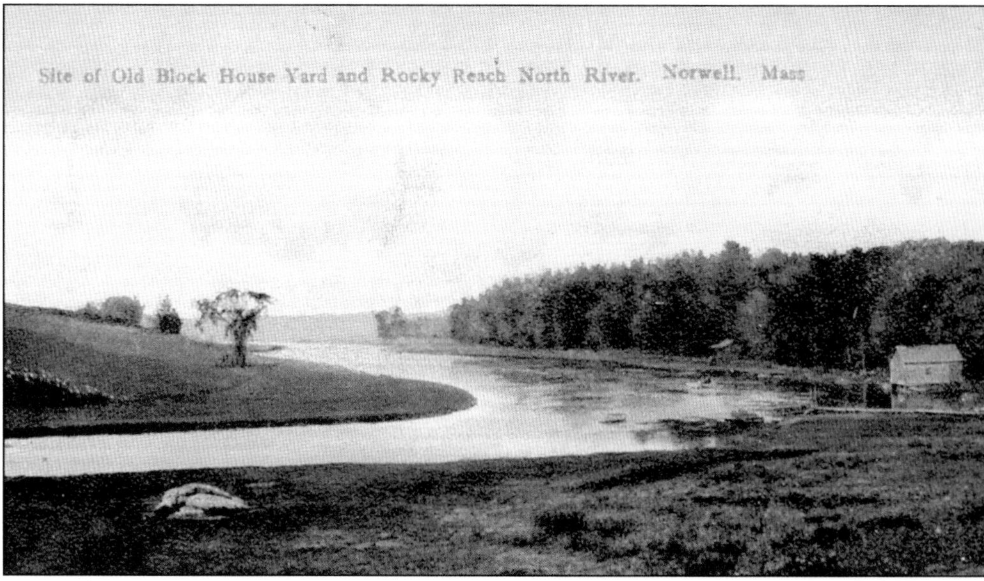

Situated on the North River where the well-known Block House shipyard once thrived is the Norris Reservation. Eleanor Norris generously donated land for generations of Norwell residents to enjoy. This is one of the most frequently visited spots in Norwell. The property is under the care of the Trustees of Reservations. This non-profit organization also administers World's End and Weir River Farm in Hingham. The property has been enlarged by donations from the McMullan and the Gordon families.

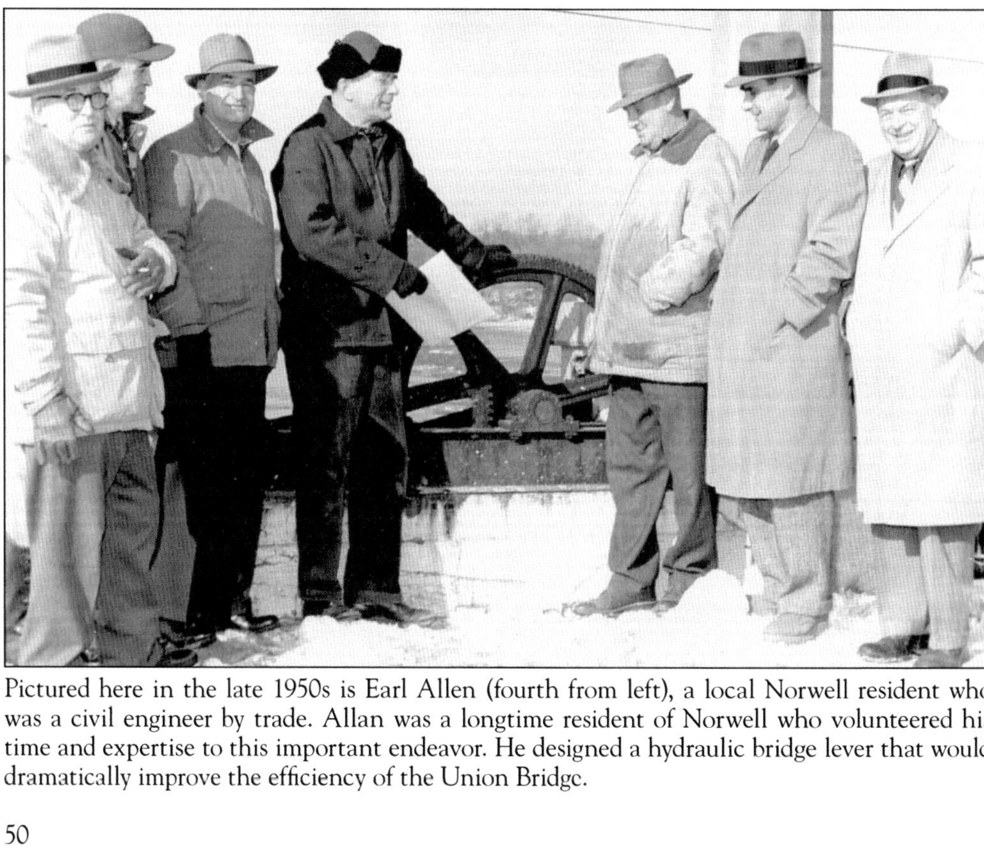

Pictured here in the late 1950s is Earl Allen (fourth from left), a local Norwell resident who was a civil engineer by trade. Allan was a longtime resident of Norwell who volunteered his time and expertise to this important endeavor. He designed a hydraulic bridge lever that would dramatically improve the efficiency of the Union Bridge.

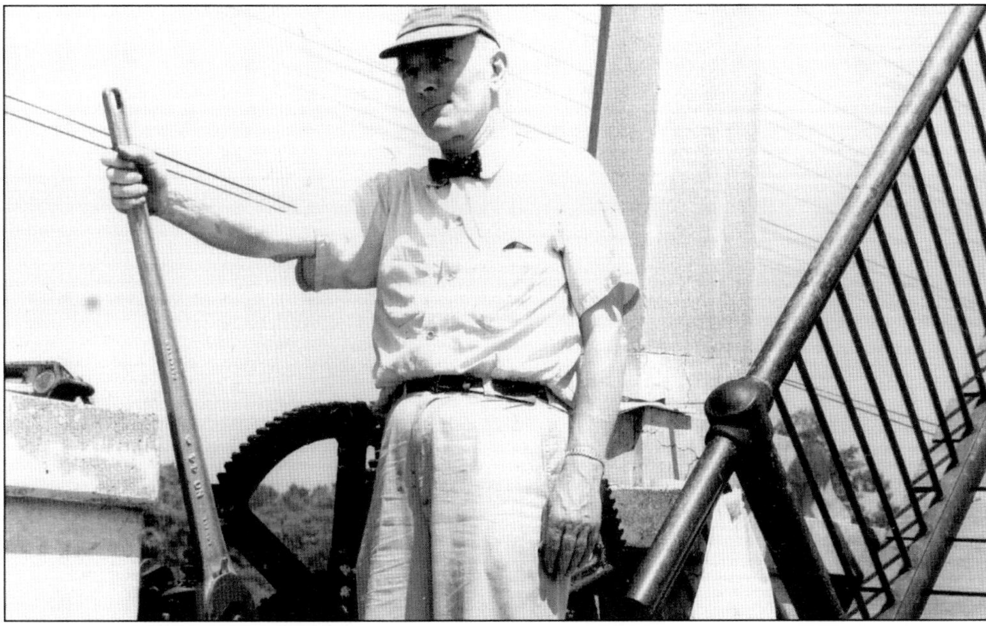

The Union Bridge was not a heavily traveled road, but the North River was used by a considerable amount of boats. Bridge traffic would have minimal disruption due to the bridge being raised. Boats would flow under Union Bridge on the North River while the new hydraulic lever would quickly raise the bridge.

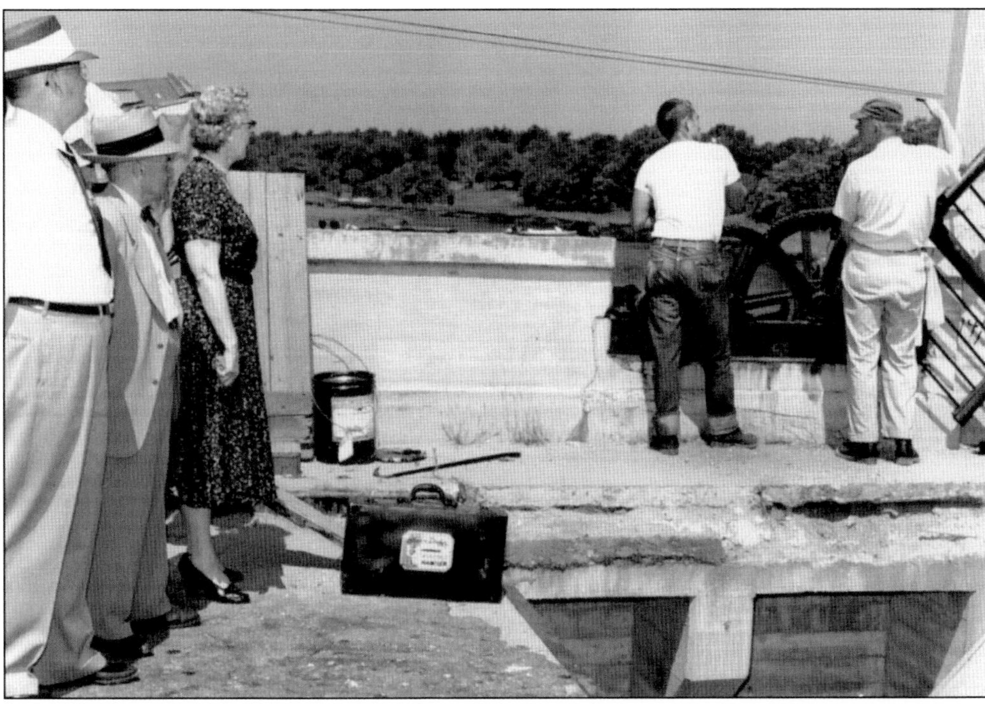

Alas, the new lever would not survive long. On the first day of the official raising of the new bridge, a truck hit the hydraulic lever. As a result, the initiative had a short life span. Discouraged, Earl Allan decided not to repair the hydraulic lever.

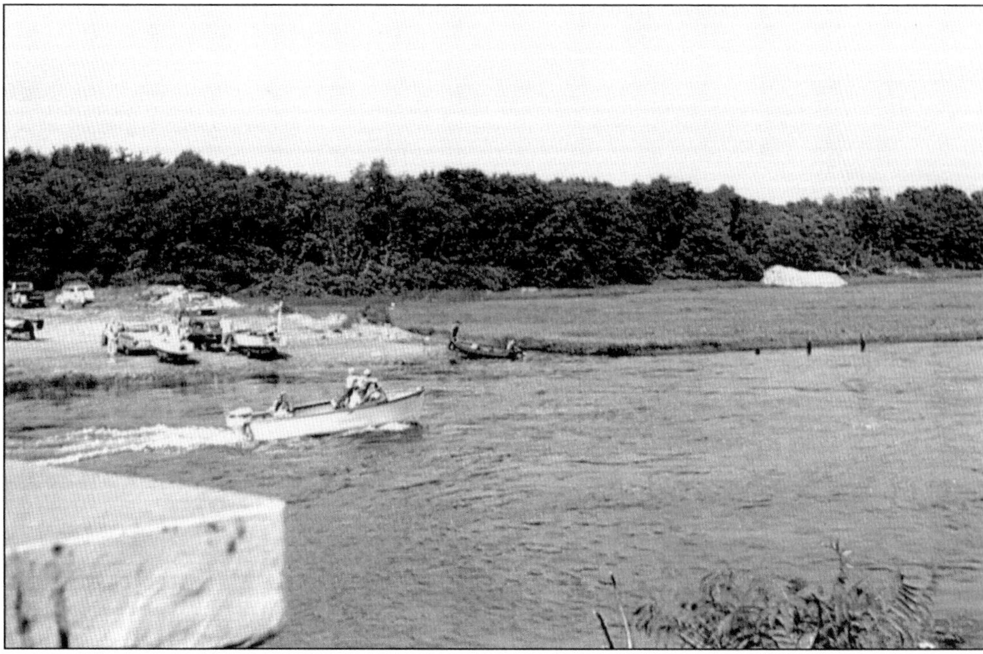

The North River has proven to be an ample space for recreation through the centuries. This is a shot taken of the Norwell town landing while a motorboat zooms down the North River in the early 1960s. Many homes off of Bridge Street have docks allowing the residents unbridled access to the river and the Atlantic Ocean in Scituate.

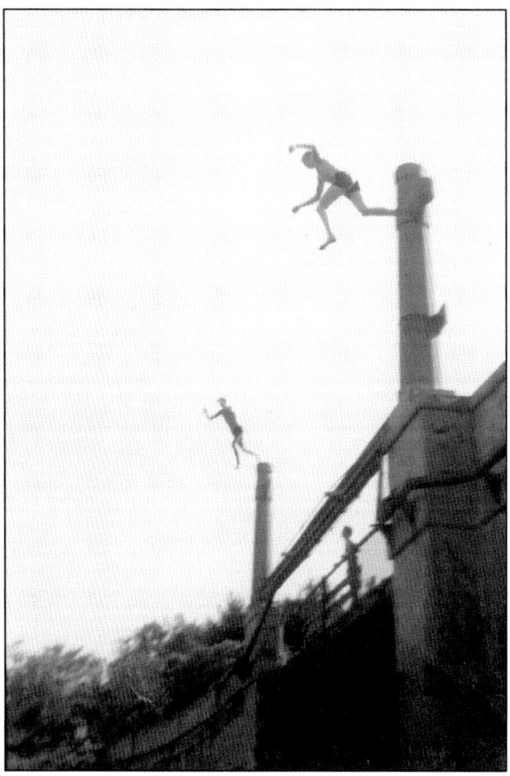

Boys will be boys! Two youngsters and one waiting in the wings are seen jumping from the Union Bridge in the mid-1950s. They are jumping off the ornamental stanchions that have now been removed. This must have been a great deal of fun on a hot summer day, but most likely is frowned upon today.

Four

River Street

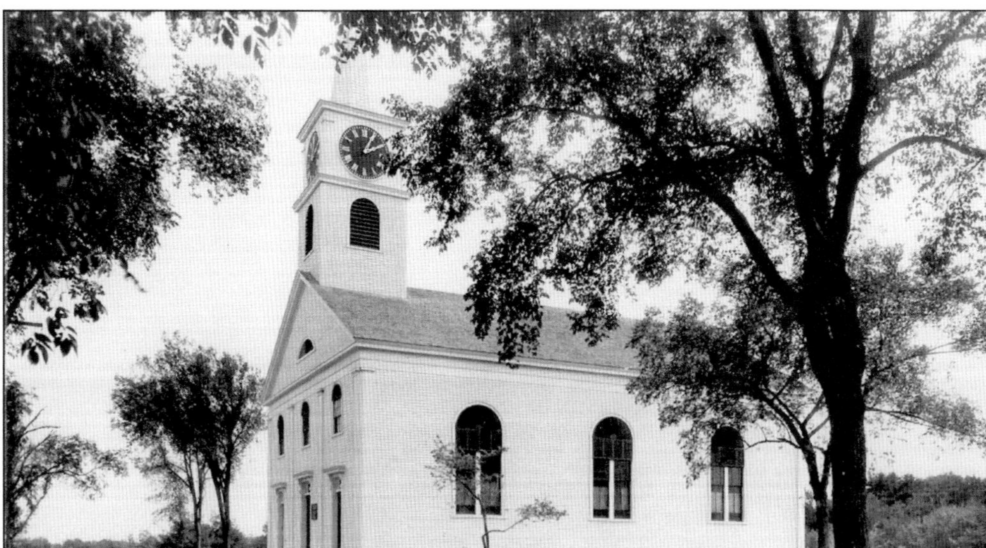

Located on the town common in Norwell Center at 24 River Street is the Unitarian church, also known as the First Parish Church, whose origins date back to February 2, 1642. In South Scituate, the parish was established as the South Parish, also known as the Second Parish. The church was organized as a result over the difference of opinion on how baptism should be conducted. When a minority disagreed over the baptism proceedings, they left the First Parish of Scituate and formed their own church.

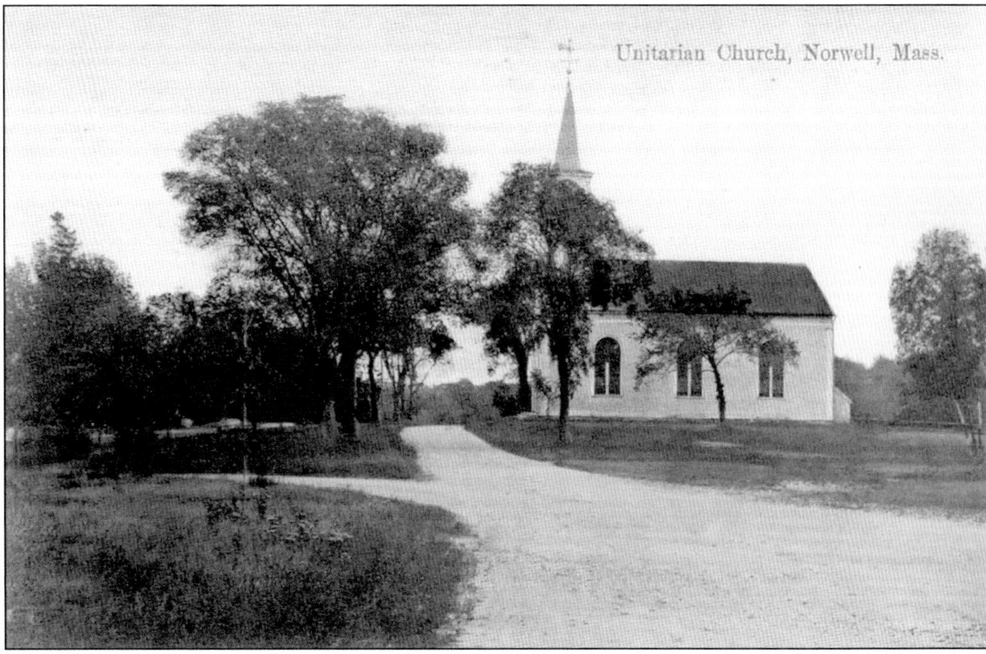

The first building that housed the new congregation was located on Main Street near the top of Wilson Hill. In 1680, a new meetinghouse was built on Main Street not far from Joseph's Pontiac. The Second Church flourished soon thereafter under the ministry of the Reverend Dr. Barnes and thus expanded its meetinghouse three times over the course of 50 years.

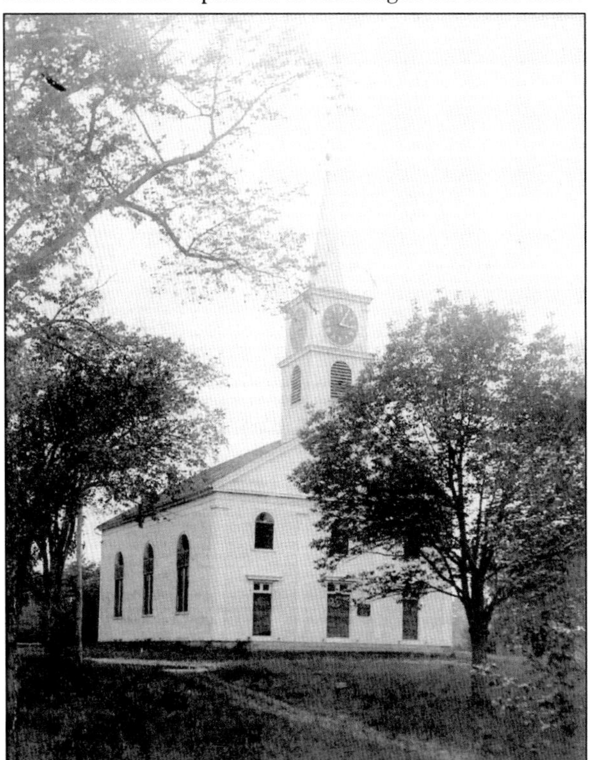

The present Unitarian Church was erected in 1830 and was officially dedicated on October 13. The architect of the church was William Sparrell. The pews were sold at auction and the congregation bid heavily for the right to sit in a good spot in the new meetinghouse. Among the bidders were Ebenezer and Betsy Fogg, Elijah Turner, Samuel Foster, and John Nash. In 1849, when South Scituate voted to secede from Scituate, the Second Parish of Scituate changed its name to the First Parish of South Scituate.

The Methodist church is located on River Street just south of Church Hill. The church building was erected in 1852 and had its humble beginnings in the home of Samuel Stetson on Stetson Road in 1844. Samuel's wife, Mary Kimball Stetson, organized the Methodist class meetings in their home and then later at the schoolhouse on the town common.

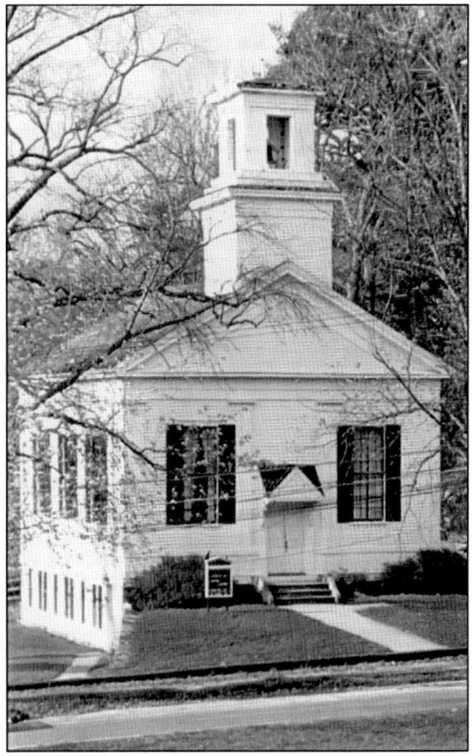

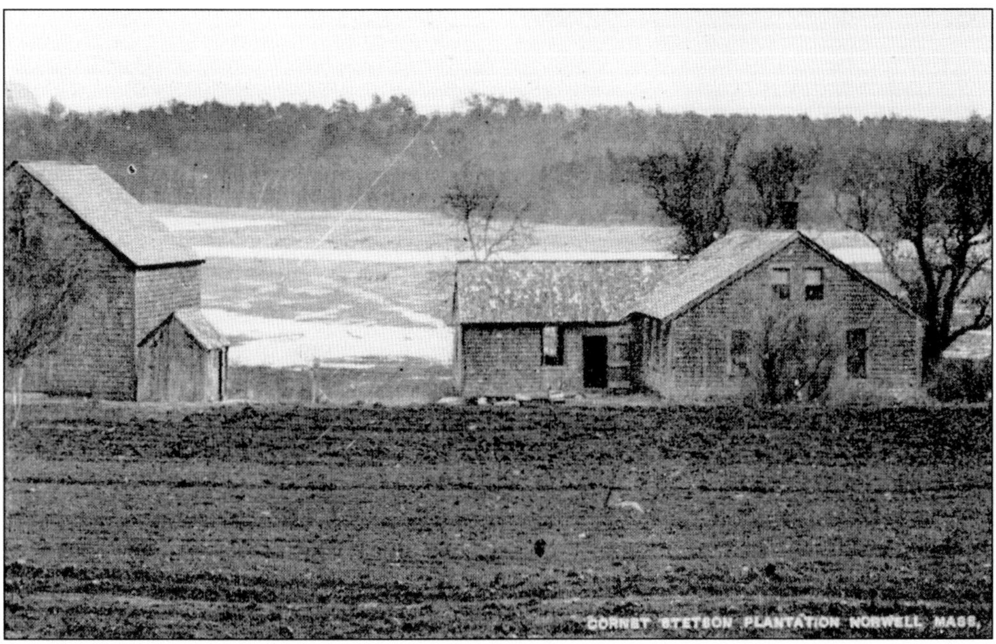

Cornet Robert Stetson was the first citizen of Norwell to arrive in the town that was then known as Scituate in 1634. The much bigger claim to fame is perhaps his descendant John B. Stetson, the maker of the Stetson cowboy hat. His hat was dubbed the Boss of the Plains (BOP), and it has been worn by illustrious trailblazers such as Buffalo Bill, Annie Oakley, Calamity Jane, and Wild Bill Hickok.

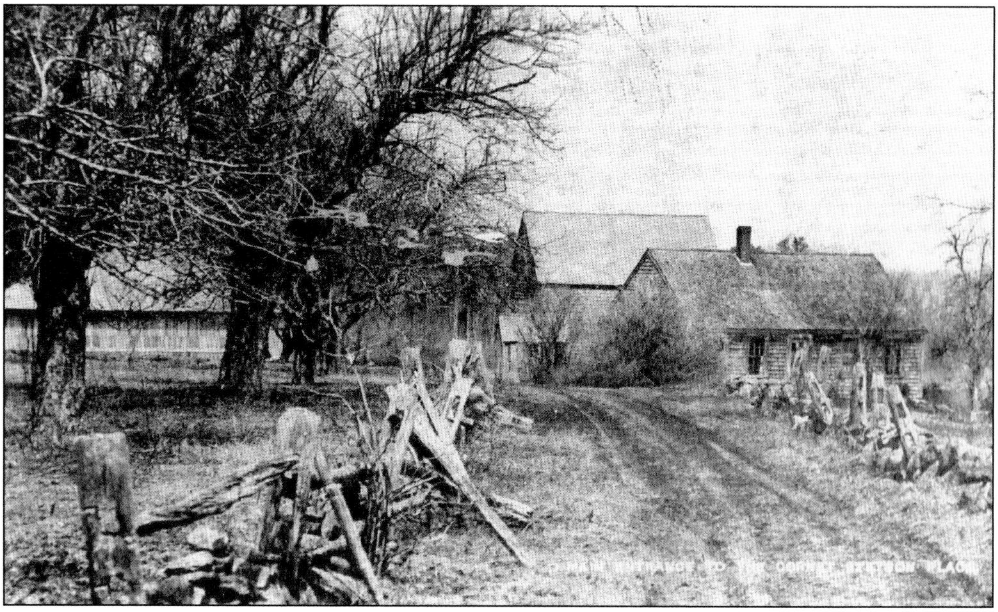

Established in 1905 for the descendants of Cornet Robert and Honour Stetson, Stetson Kindred of America Incorporated is a non-profit organization that owns the Cornet Robert Stetson Homestead. It is also known as the shrine. Cornet Robert Stetson passed the home on to his son when he died in 1702. Thus, it has never left the family. The Stetson Kindred meets regularly for reunions, and through charitable work, distributes scholarships to Stetson descendants.

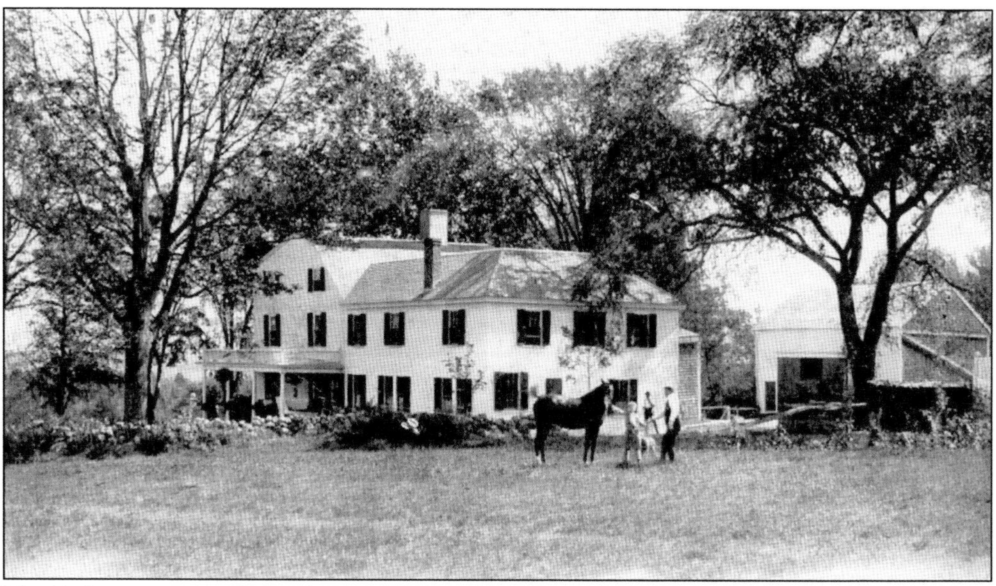

The Delano mansion located on River Street was built in 1803 by local shipbuilder William Delano. Delano was a descendant of one of the colonies' first settlers, Philip de la Noye of Leiden, Holland. At the age of 19, de la Noye arrived in Plymouth on the vessel *Fortune* on November 11, 1621. The *Fortune* was the second ship to arrive following the *Mayflower*.

William Delano married Sarah Hart and they subsequently raised four daughters and three sons at their mansion. The word mansion is supposed to mean that the home has more than one staircase. The Delano mansion indeed had several staircases. The mansion was located on what became known as Delano Hill. Attached to the home on the south side was a store that featured items from the China trade. Sarah received the items from her brother Capt. John Hart's travels.

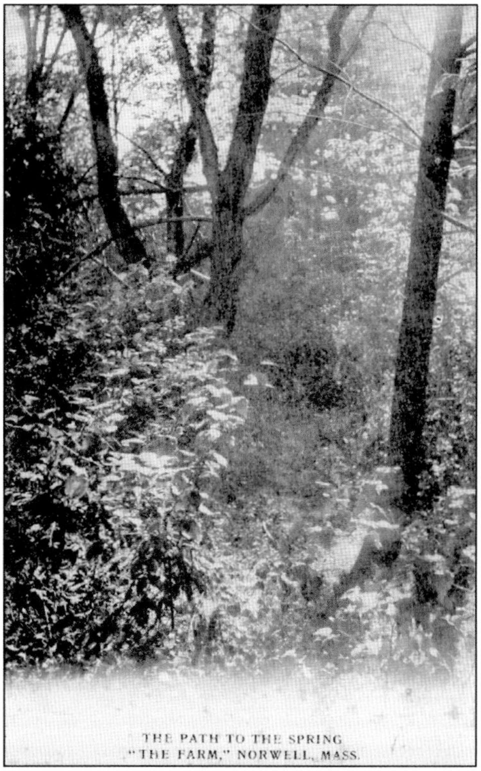

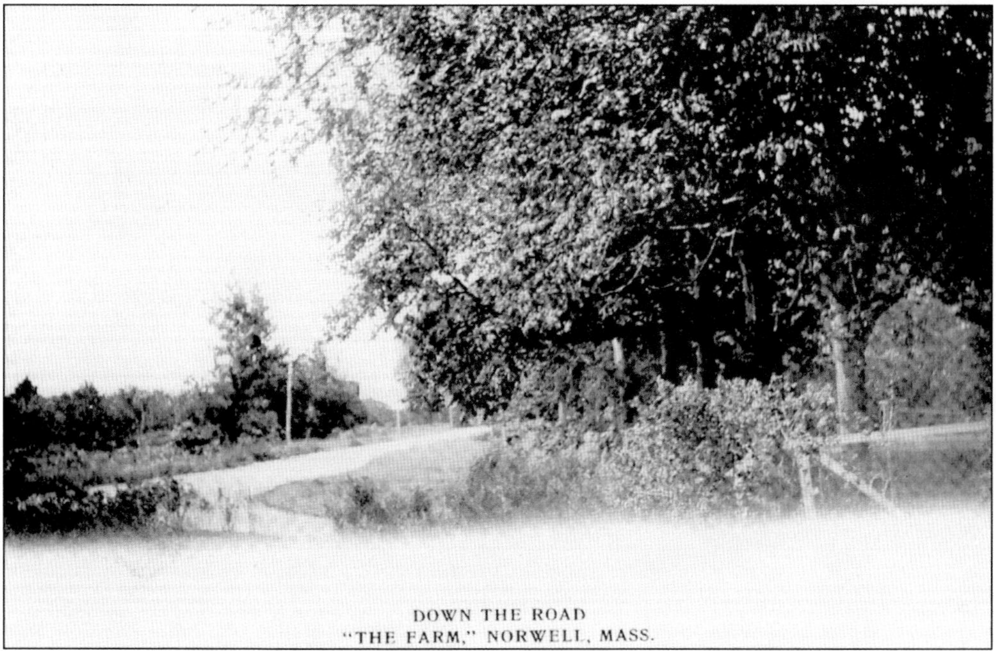

William Delano built his ships at the Wanton Yard along the banks of the North River. Delano built one of the largest ships ever built at the North River called the *Lady Madison*. It was 112 feet long and over 450 tons. It set sail in 1810, but was lost at sea in the English Channel five years later.

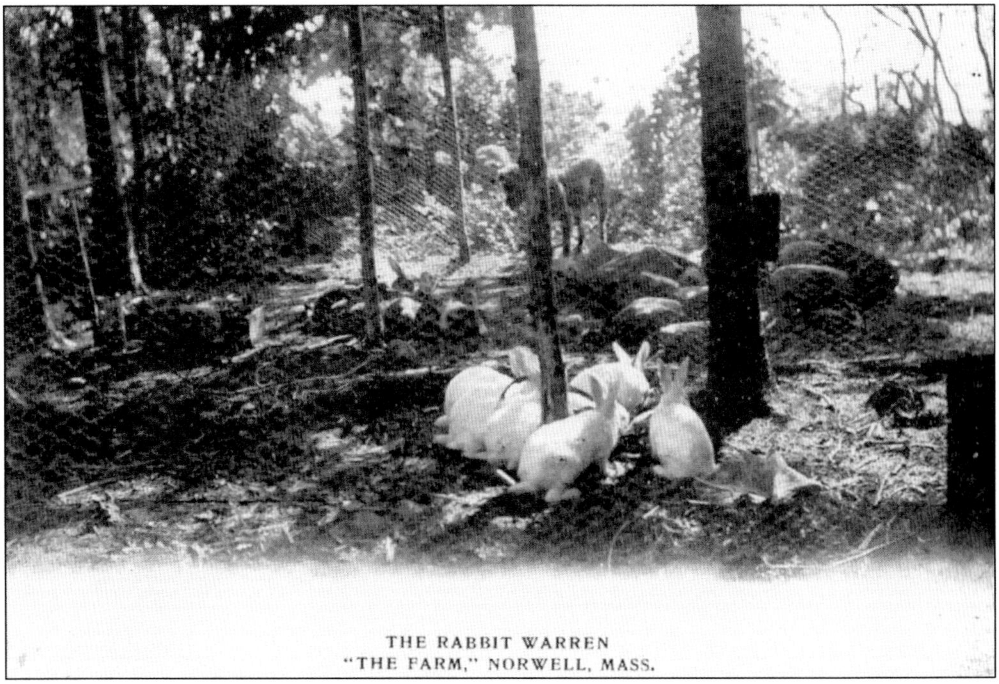

William Delano built his ships at the Wanton Yard beginning in 1770. Delano built ships called the *Topaz*, *Ganges*, *Augustus*, and the *Ida*. Two sons, William and Benjamin, followed in their father's footsteps in the shipbuilding business. William Delano's eldest son, William H. Delano, had his reputation grow in stature as he was often referred to as Lord North Delano.

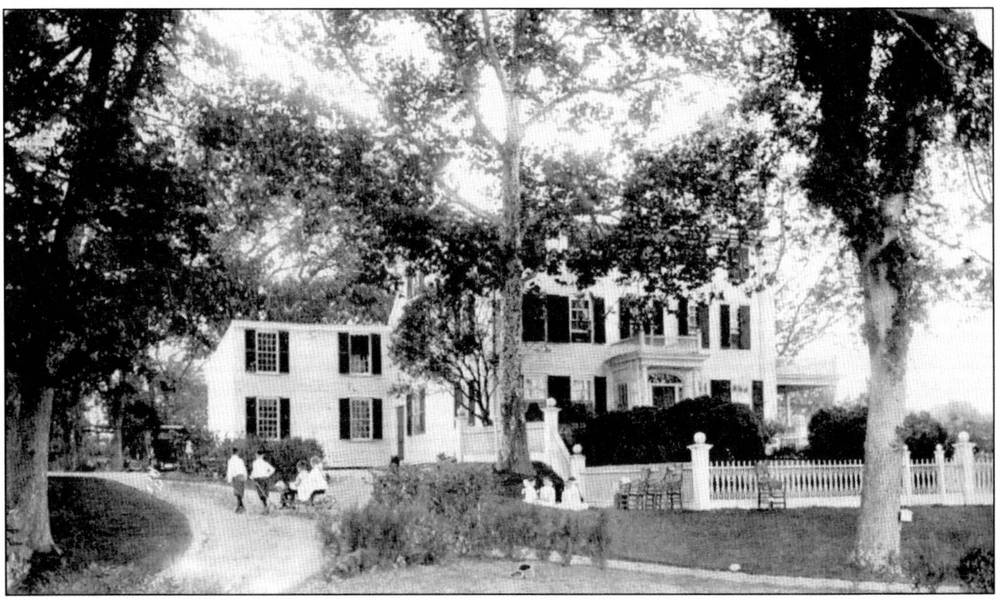

Three daughters, Lucy, Prudence, and Sarah, remained to keep up the large manse, but none ever married. When the last sister died, most items in the home went up for auction and others went for the benefit of Harvard University. Edward F. Delano, a grandson of William Delano, took over the mansion and eventually sold the property to Jon H. Gutterson in 1916.

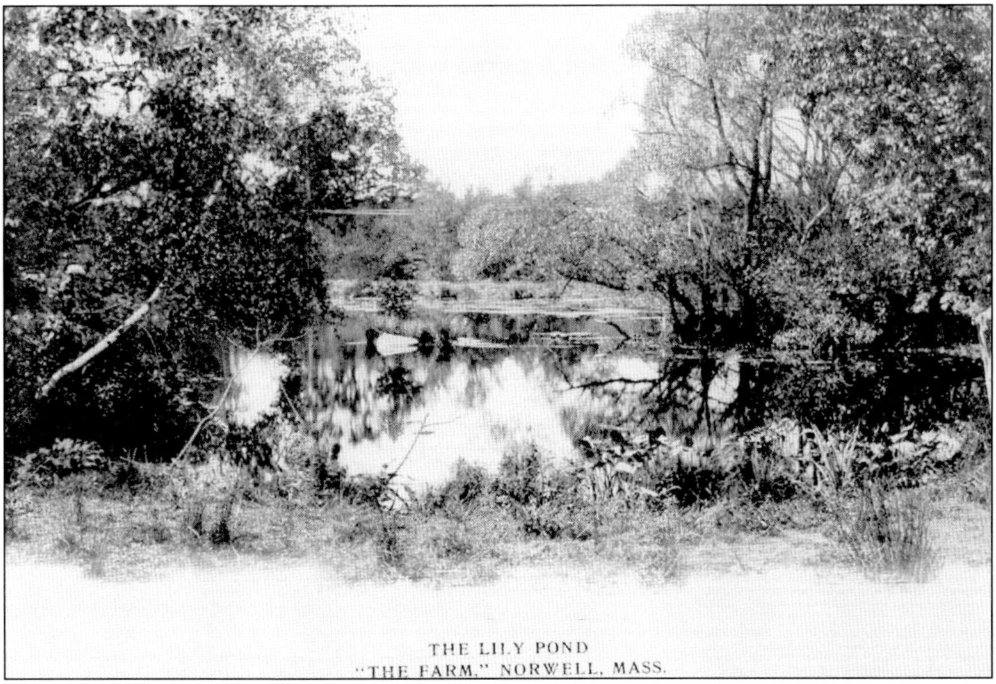

Since Philip de la Noye (changed to Delano) came to America in 1621, the Delano family has grown in stature and has a fellowship called the House of Delano or the Delano Kindred. One of its famous family members was the 32nd president of the United States. Sara Delano married James Roosevelt and had only one child named Franklin Delano Roosevelt.

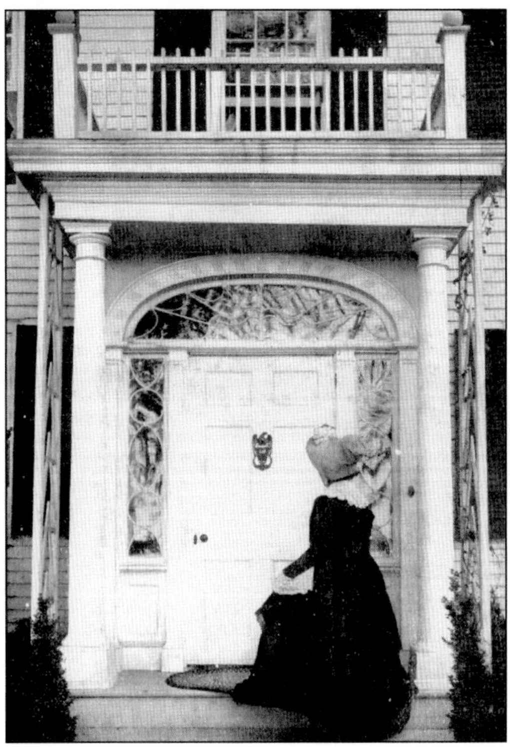

The home was turned into a country playground of sorts for Boston residents. Summer tourists would visit the "farm" and pay a nightly rate to enjoy country living in Norwell. The Delano farm was owned and operated by Alonzo Tolman. He advertised a "fine view of hill and dale" and a "good table."

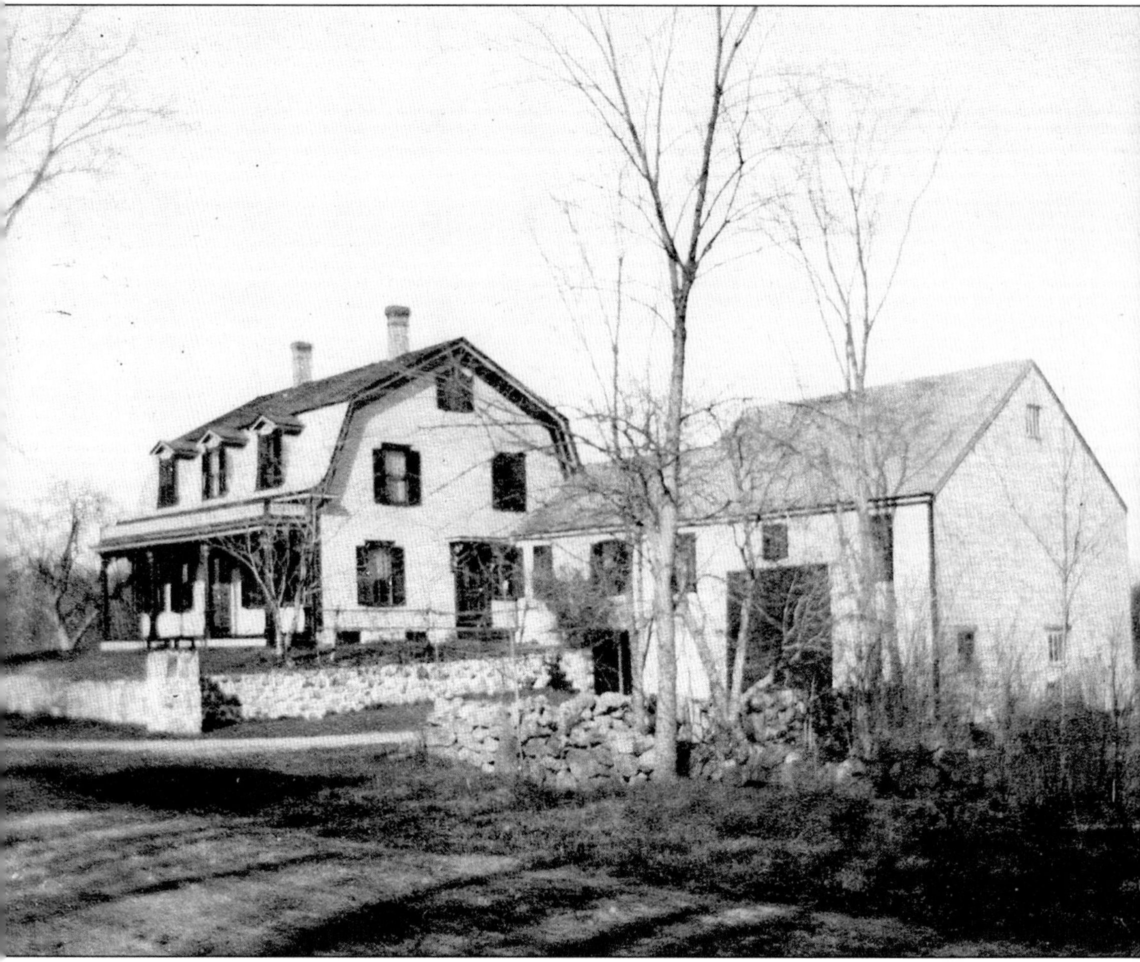

Across from Gaffield Park is a beautiful New England farmhouse located at 67 River Street, complete with a farmer's porch, stone wall, and attached barn. A large gathering of Norwell residents came together on Arbor Day in 1896. This day was proclaimed Gaffield Park Community Day in honor of Thomas Gaffield, who donated a large tract of land near River and Forest Streets. His gift to the town was to provide a place for children to enjoy a playground and a picnic. Gaffield Park was recently renovated, largely through the efforts of the Friends of Gaffield Park volunteers and a brick program donation from generous townspeople. This wonderful park was also made possible due to the efforts of Eagle Scout Brendan MacDonald. It was officially dedicated on July 1, 2000.

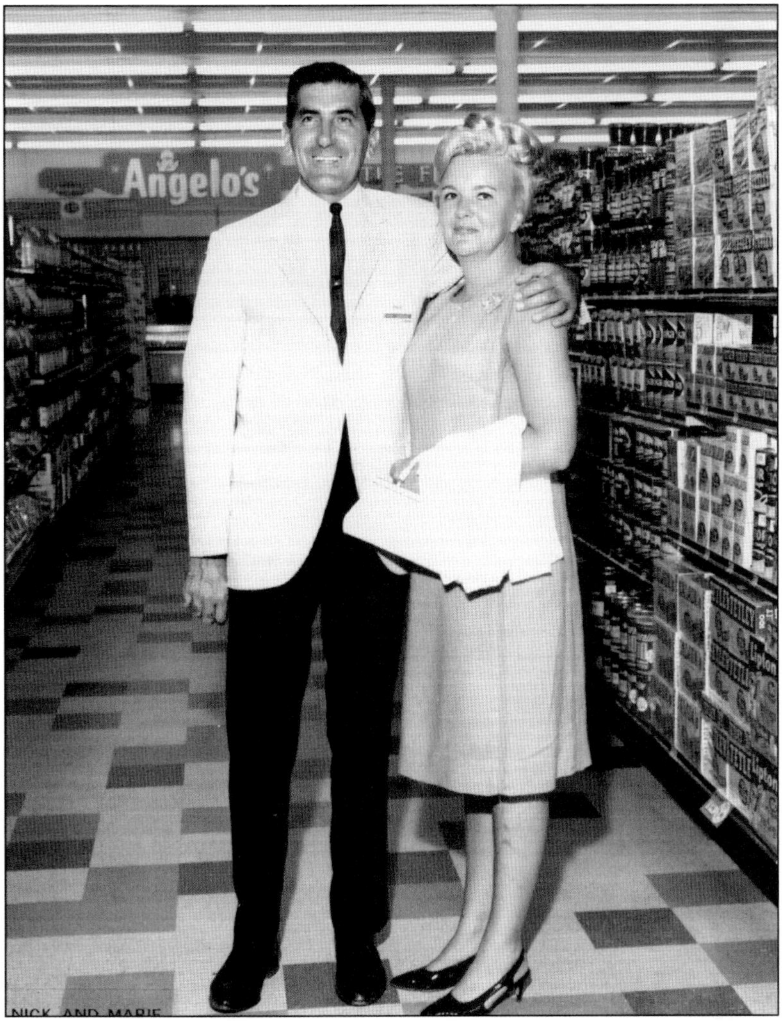

Longtime Norwell residents Nick and Marie Tedeschi are shown here at the grand opening of the new Angelo's Supermarket in Holbrook on Route 37. Many years later, Marie co-wrote a children's book, under the pen name Nora Wells, called *Stanley and Simons Big Adventure*, with another Norwell resident named "Captain Bob." The book was set in the town of Norwell, although actually never named, and featured many Norwell residents, such as Philly Joseph and police chief Nichols. Captain Bob Cottle had a television show named *Drawing From Nature*, where he taught children, for many years, how to paint a different animal each week. Nick and Marie have been happily married and living off River Street in Norwell for over 50 years.

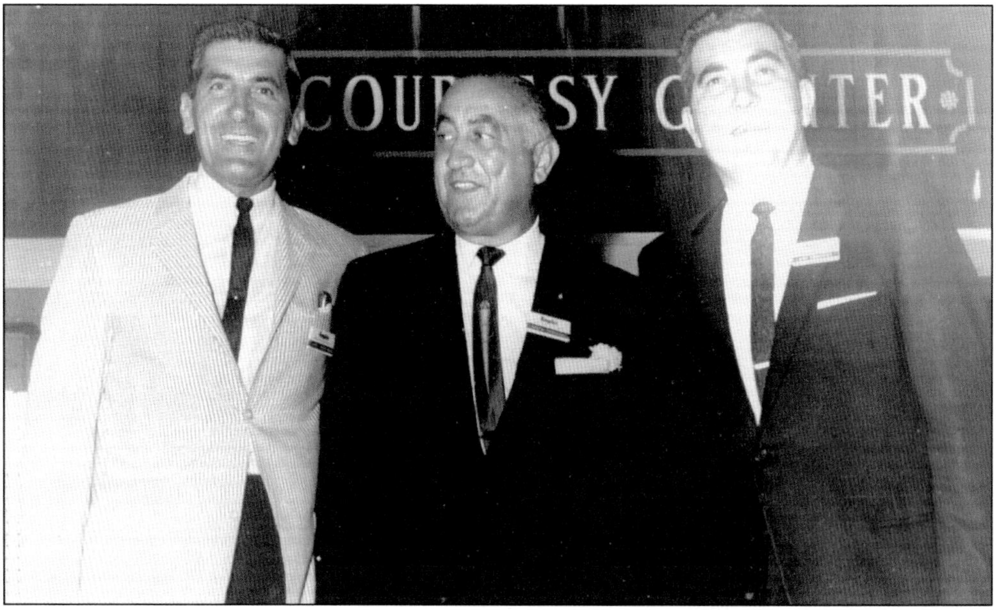

Seen here at the grand opening of the new Angelo's Supermarket in South Yarmouth in 1966 are, from left to right, Nick Tedeschi and his brothers Ralph and Bob. When the Tedeschi Supermarket chain was sold to Stop and Shop in 1960, the Tedeschi brothers went to work for their new suitors for a short while. In 1964, Stop and Shop sold the Tedeschi's the Holbrook supermarket and it became resoundingly successful under the new brand called Angelo's.

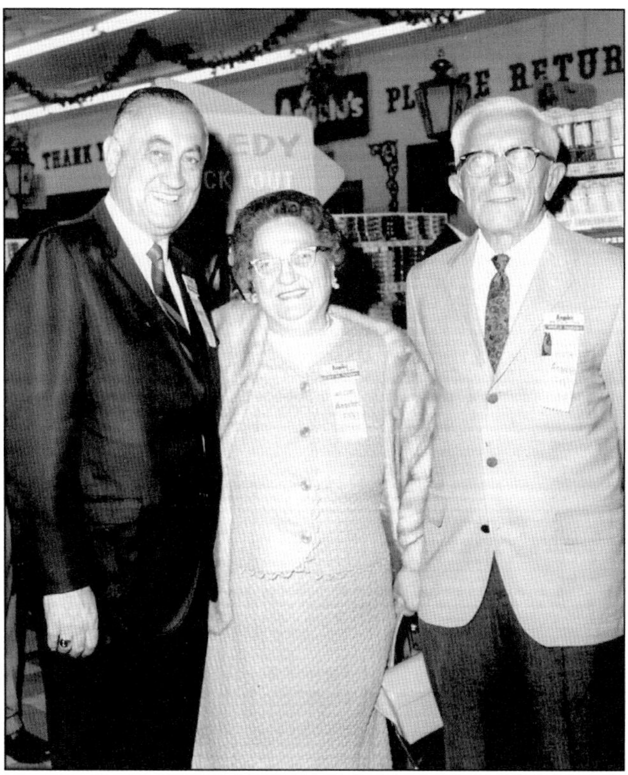

Longtime Norwell resident Ralph Tedeschi poses with his mother, Catherine, and father, Angelo, on the day of Ralph's grand opening of the new Angelo's Supermarket in Holbrook on Route 37. Angelo Tedeschi started a butcher shop in Rockland in the late 1920s. Ralph was a World War II war hero who returned home to build a supermarket empire on the South Shore that was admired across the nation by his peers.

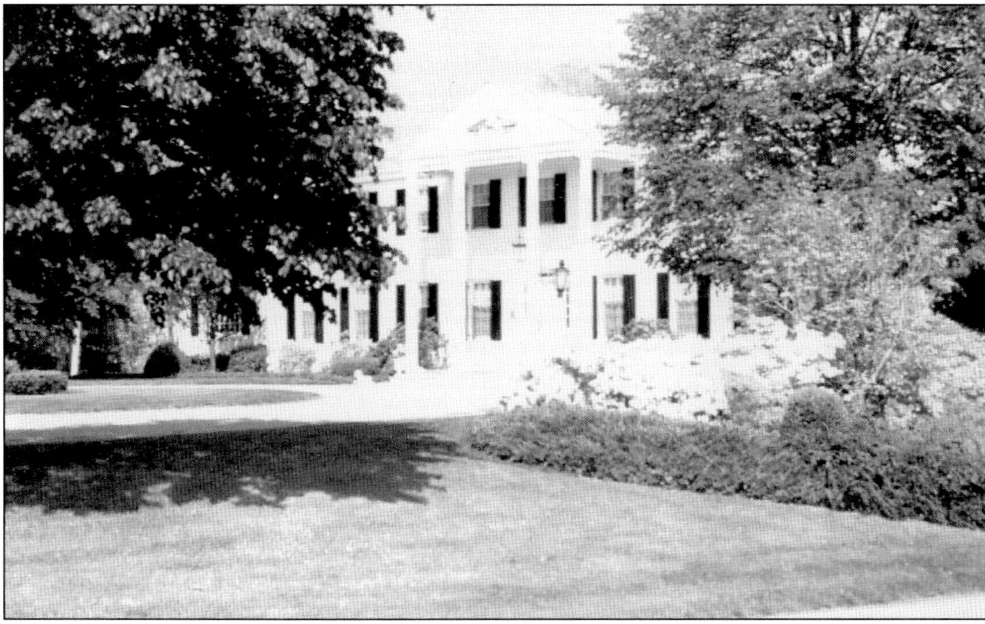

Ralph Tedeschi moved his family into a beautiful opulent estate off River Street in 1963 and called his home Tara. The home has wonderful memories for the townspeople of Norwell. Tedeschi opened his home to the entire town for the Independence Ball in 1976 and the Centennial Celebration Grand Dance in 1988. Today, the estate is a new development with several million-dollar homes on Tara Drive, one of the most sought after addresses south of Boston

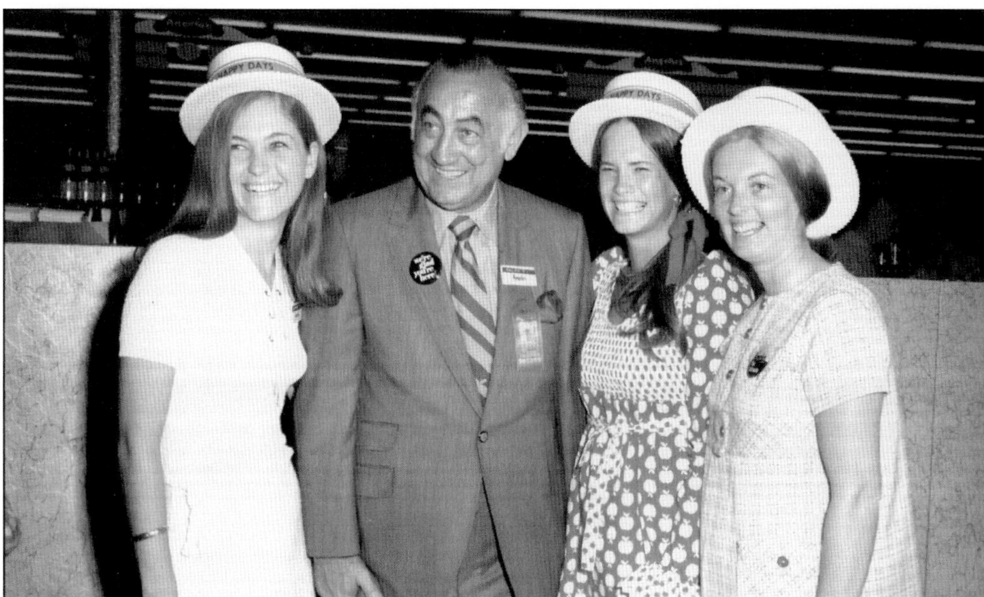

Pictured here is Ralph Tedeschi with family members, from left to right, Denise, Pam, and Joan Tedeschi at the 1971 grand opening of the Angelo's Supermarket at the Hanover Mall. Notice the theme "Happy Days Are Here Again" on the hats. At this time, Angelo's Supermarkets were growing rapidly and gaining national respect as a market leader in the Northeast. Today, there is an office supply store and a Chinese restaurant at this location.

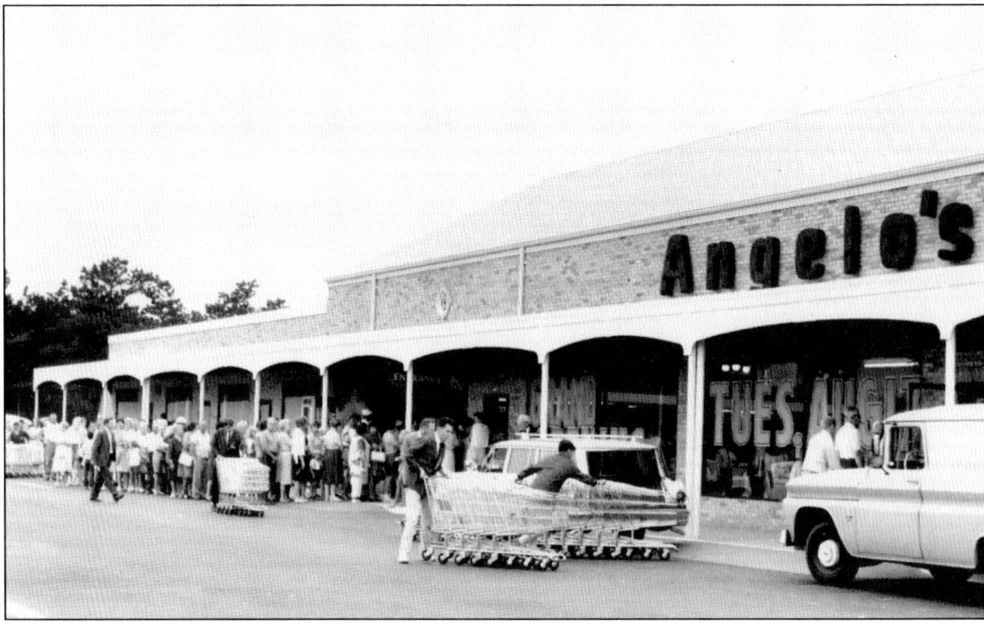

By the late 1950s, Ralph Tedeschi was a world renowned food merchandiser who had invented the modern supermarket. He had other companies across the United States come to visit his operations and study how he had revolutionized the grocery business. Pictured here is another grand opening celebration at the new Hyannis Angelo's Supermarket in 1965.

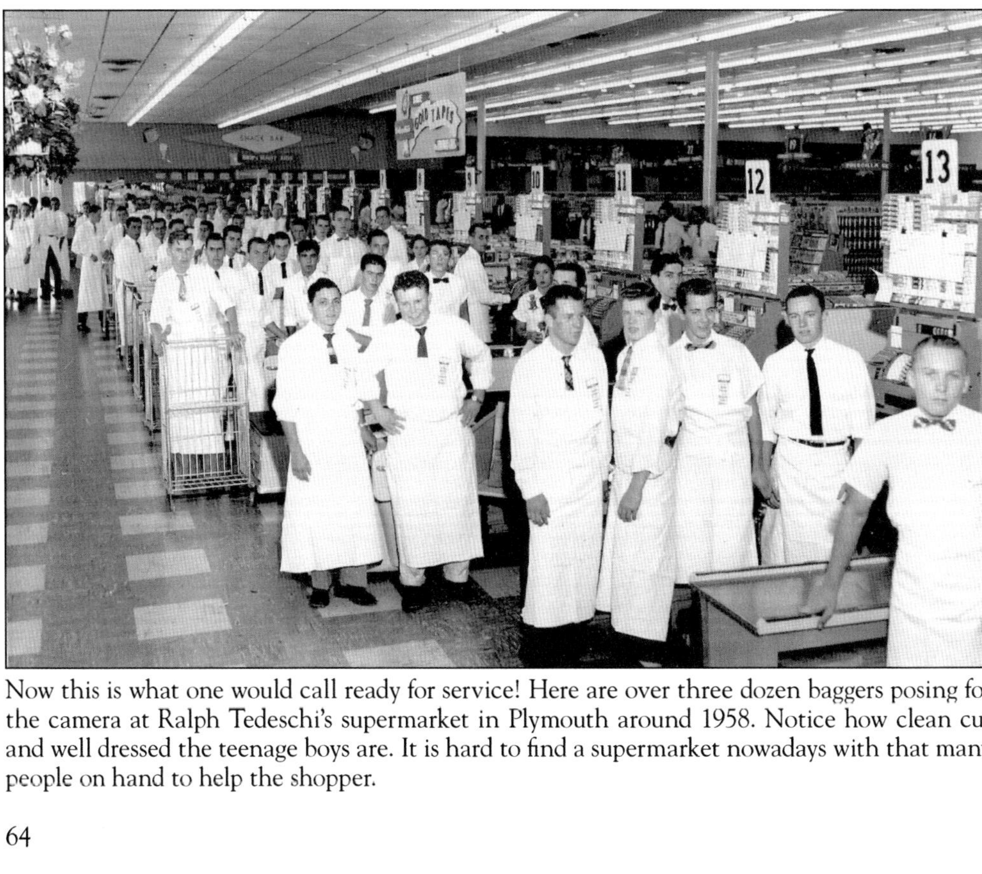

Now this is what one would call ready for service! Here are over three dozen baggers posing for the camera at Ralph Tedeschi's supermarket in Plymouth around 1958. Notice how clean cut and well dressed the teenage boys are. It is hard to find a supermarket nowadays with that many people on hand to help the shopper.

Ralph Tedeschi opened his home to the entire town of Norwell to help celebrate America's bicentennial. Hundreds of residents joined the festivities, which began with an 18th-century horse-and-buggy parade down River Street. The revelers wore period costumes form 1776. Among those leading the parade were Nick and Marie Tedeschi.

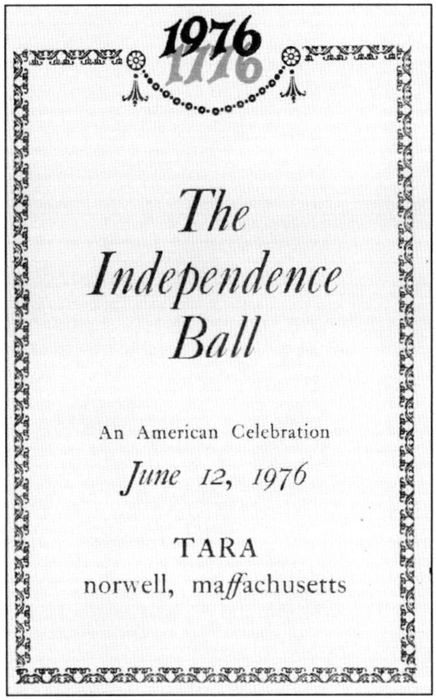

1976
1776

The Independence Ball

An American Celebration

June 12, 1976

TARA
norwell, maſſachusetts

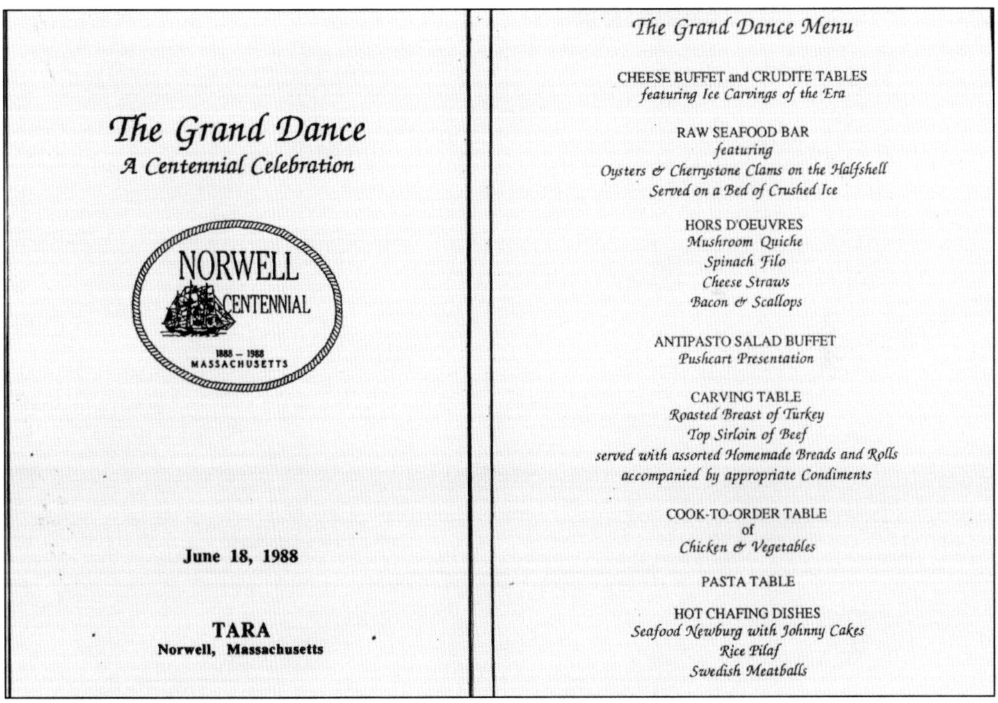

The Grand Dance
A Centennial Celebration

NORWELL CENTENNIAL
1888 – 1988
MASSACHUSETTS

June 18, 1988

TARA
Norwell, Massachusetts

The Grand Dance Menu

CHEESE BUFFET and CRUDITE TABLES
featuring Ice Carvings of the Era

RAW SEAFOOD BAR
featuring
Oysters & Cherrystone Clams on the Halfshell
Served on a Bed of Crushed Ice

HORS D'OEUVRES
Mushroom Quiche
Spinach Filo
Cheese Straws
Bacon & Scallops

ANTIPASTO SALAD BUFFET
Pushcart Presentation

CARVING TABLE
Roasted Breast of Turkey
Top Sirloin of Beef
served with assorted Homemade Breads and Rolls
accompanied by appropriate Condiments

COOK-TO-ORDER TABLE
of
Chicken & Vegetables

PASTA TABLE

HOT CHAFING DISHES
Seafood Newburg with Johnny Cakes
Rice Pilaf
Swedish Meatballs

Ralph Tedeschi threw another party at his estate, Tara, that Norwell residents would remember for years to come. The occasion was the Norwell Centennial Celebration, and the town went into a weeklong festive mode in the summer of 1988. Ralph Tedeschi's legacy of giving back to the town of Norwell lives on as Tara was recently opened to the town for a holiday house tour in which thousands of people were able to tour the home.

Programme

The celebrated Winiker Orchestra will provide fine Dancing Music from 8 P.M. until 1 A.M.. Additional pleasing Speciality Acts for your entertainment will include:

8:00 P.M. GILBERT & SULLIVAN REVUE

9:00 P.M. ELEGANT FOUR-PART HARMONY PRESENTATION

10:00 P.M. GRANDE PROMENADE

The Winiker Orchestra transports you to 1888 for this hour. Please note engagements on your dance card.

11:00 P.M. HISTORICAL TABLEAU TO SURPRISE AND DELIGHT

12:00 P.M. PARTICIPATORY MUSICAL PROGRAMME

All join in.

1:00 A.M. A CHORAL FINALE BY REVELERS OF:

"After the Ball"

DIVERTISSEMENTS

The recently developed Kodak Camera process is availab photographic portraiture in the billiard room of the Main Be astounded by this wonderful new invention and preser special moment for future generations to enjoy.

••••••

The horseless trolley will provide brief excursions on pictu Riverside Drive leaving from the Main Entrance eve minutes.

SPECIAL THANKS TO:

Mr. & Mrs. Ralph Tedeschi
The Anderson Family
Dave Armstrong
John Lunn
North River Electric
Joan Virta
Employees of Wearguard Corporation

CENTENNIAL BALL COMMITTEE

Susan Donahue, Chairman, Joan Ankner, Caroline Ca Carolyn Hogan, Susan Ingram, Connie Kieley, Judy Mitt Miriam Nelson, Nancy Ryan

CENTENNIAL COMMISSION

Bruce Donahue, Chairman, Joseph Carty, Jeanne Garsi Wilma Healey, Janice Litchfield, Bobbe Miner, Christine

Judging by the contents of the program, this was quite a party indeed. Hundreds of Norwell residents were invited to celebrate the 100th birthday of the name change of South Scituate to Norwell. In 1888, there were only 1,600 residents, but 100 years later, it grew to 9,100 people. The high school back in 1888 had only 32 students.

Five

ASSINIPPI

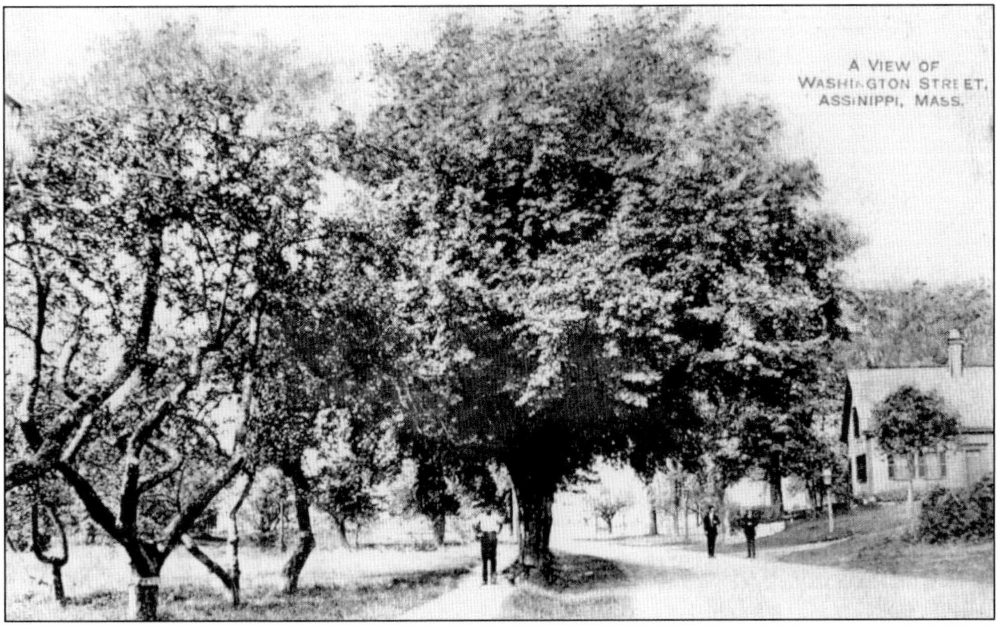

Because Washington Street was deemed a state road by the commonwealth, the Town of Norwell was required to upkeep the conditions of the road. Thus Washington Street was generally the best paved road in town and quite a well traveled one as it was the main road to Cape Cod from Boston.

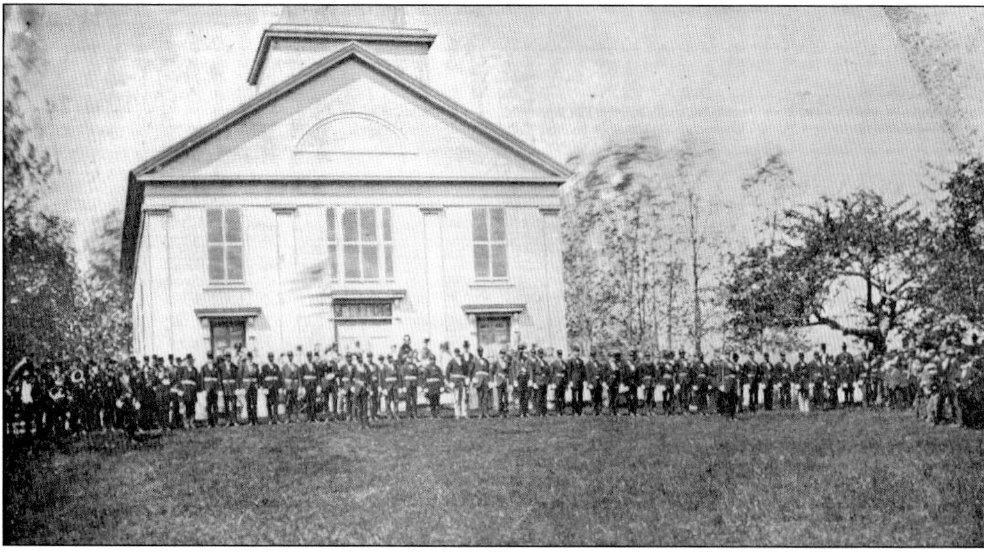

Civil War veterans of the Hanover and South Scituate Grand Army of the Republic (GAR) posts gathered on Memorial Day in Assinippi in 1878 at the Assinippi Church. The veterans would then march to Assinippi Cemetery and decorate the graves of their fallen comrades. The two GAR posts would honor the war-dead every year until the post memberships had passed on in the early 1930s.

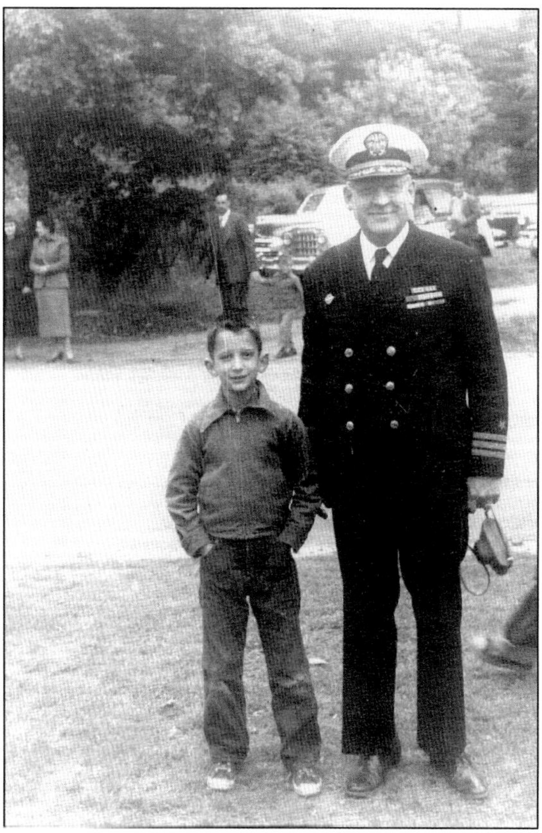

On Memorial Day, May 30, 1953, a young 8-year-old Jon Bond has his photograph taken with Com. John Chipman USN. Chipman lived in the May Elms Farm home on Main Street. On this day, there would be a parade and a cemetery plant distribution. Chipman was the president of the Norwell Historical Society. Bond is the proprietor of Bond Printing in Hanover. Bond is the past chairman of the Norwell Historic Commission and the past president of the Norwell Historical Society.

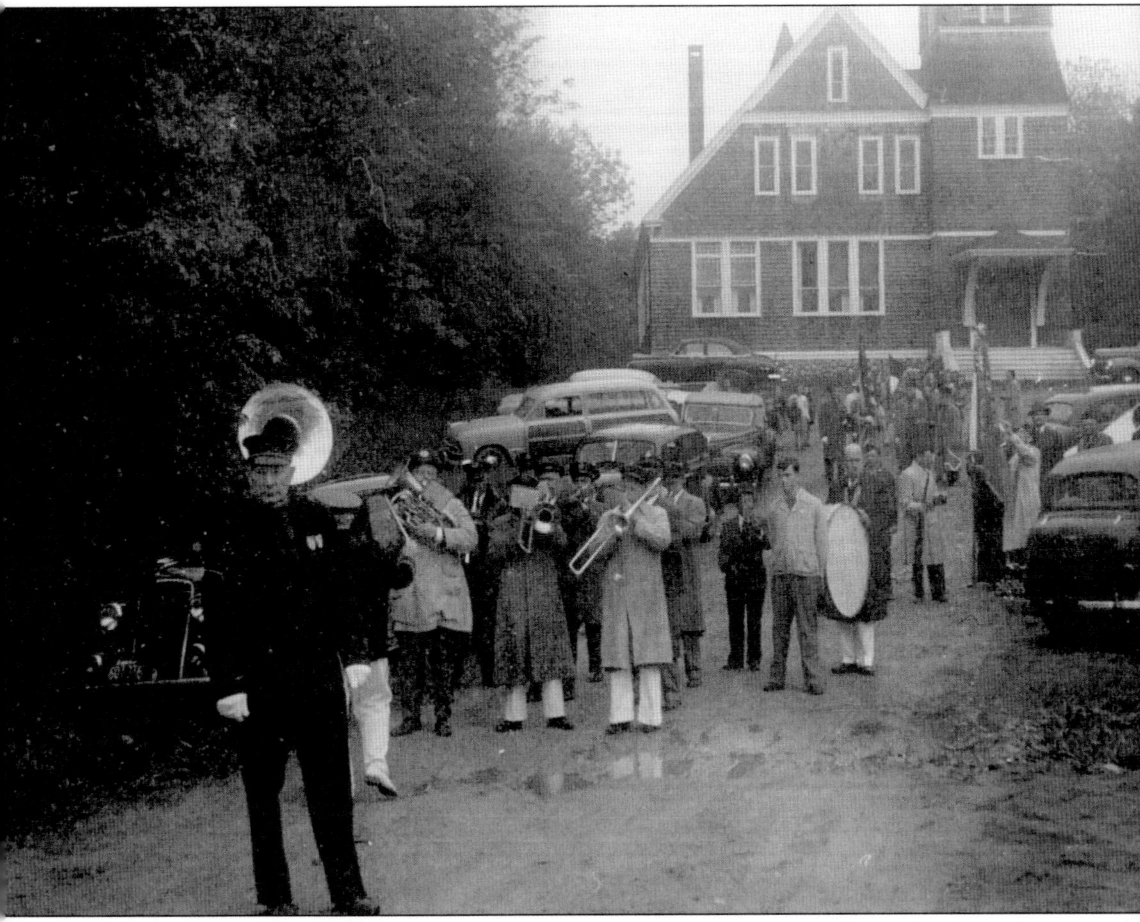

The band is getting tuned up and ready to march in the Memorial Day parade on May 30, 1950. Notice the large overcoats worn for the day's events. It must have been a very cold day indeed. The band is assembling in front of the Universalist church on Washington Street. The parade marshal is Donald Wilder, who was also the former Norwell tax collector. The church still stands today; however, it is located between modern day signs of progress. The Stop and Shop is on its right, and the Land Rover dealership is on its left.

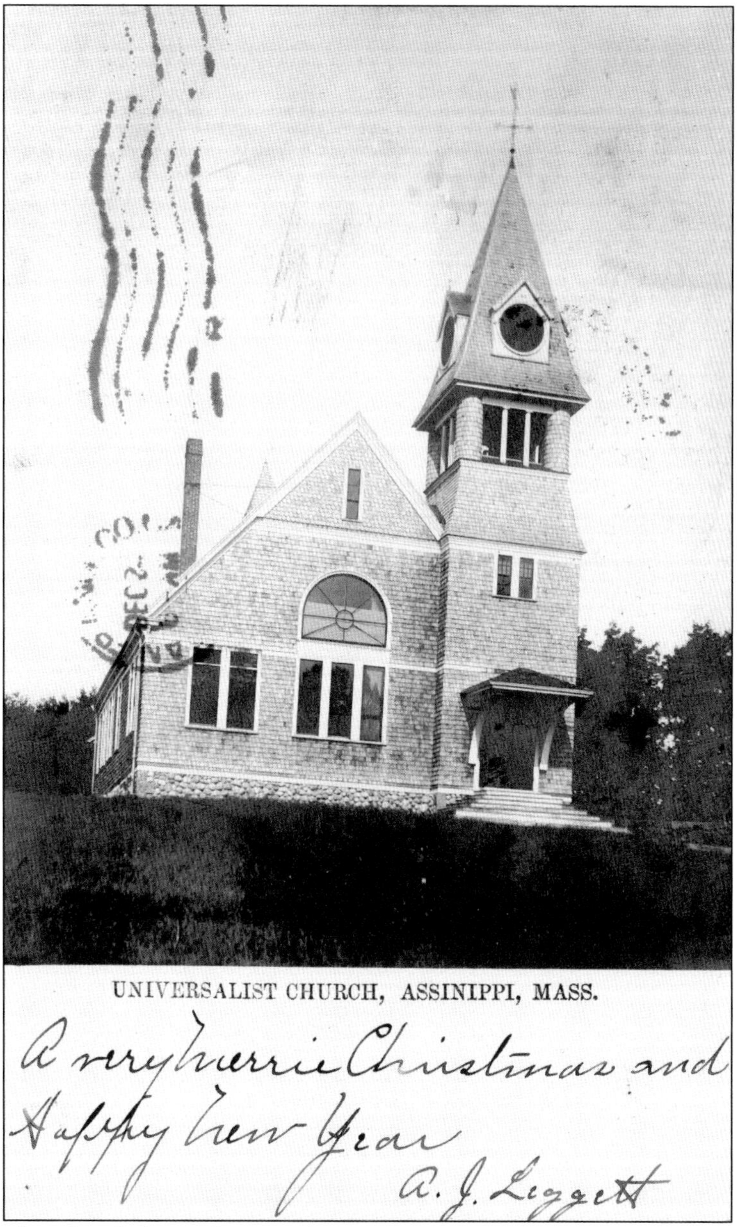

The Universalist church, located on Washington Street on Barstow's Hill in Assinippi, had a very auspicious beginning in 1812. The Second Parish Church in Scituate was quite upset that the Universalist church would become established because it feared that it would lose parts of its membership to the newly incorporated society. What the Second Church truly feared was losing its taxes that were paid by members of the congregation. These taxes supported the Second Parish Church, and a competing church would hurt its coffers. The Second Parish Church (known today as the First Parish) realized their fears indeed. Droves of members left the congregation and joined this new house of worship. The church building was used for 20 years, and then a new one was erected in 1832 which lasted for over 60 years until it burned to the ground. In 1894, the membership built a new church, which still is in use today. It can be seen on a knoll next to Stop and Shop.

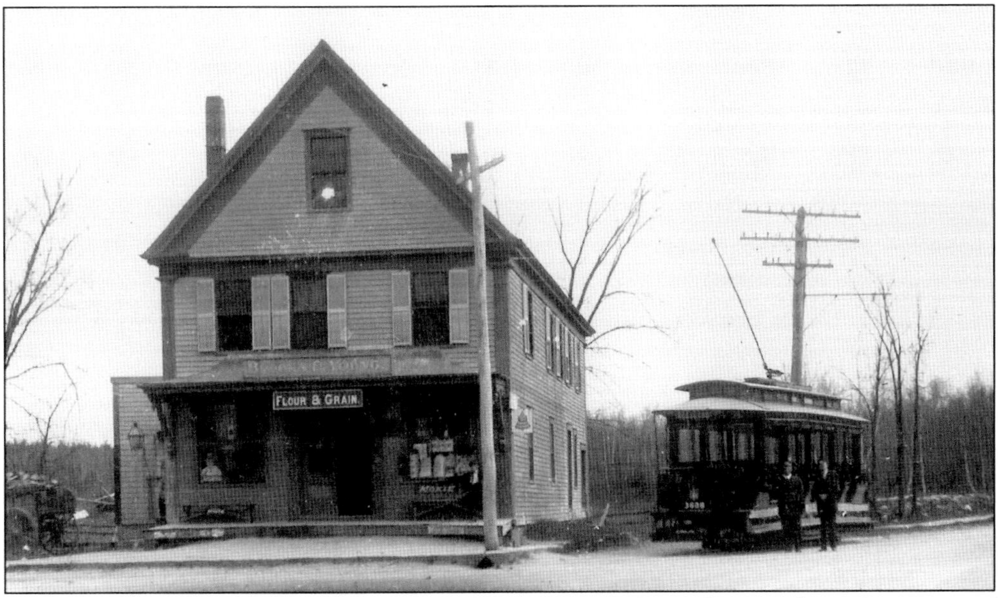

An "electric" is stopped with its train conductors posing for a photograph at the corner of Webster and Washington Streets in Assinippi. The electric would pick up its passengers here for the trip down Webster Street to Mann's Corner in North Hanover. The people riding the electric were skilled shoemakers headed to Rockland, Abington, and Brockton to work in the shoe factories.

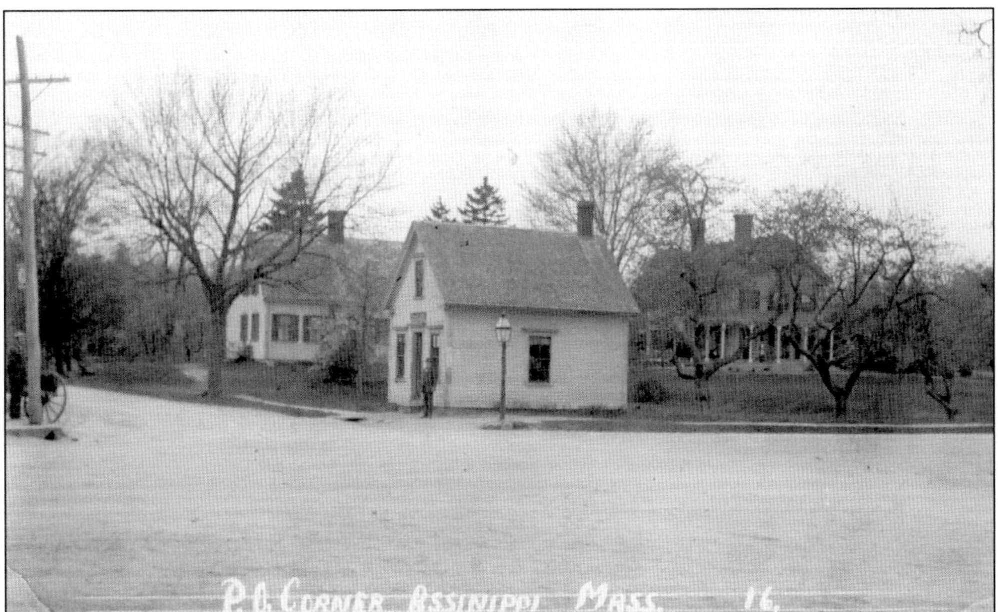

Shown here is the Assinippi Post Office, built in 1872, located at the corner of Webster and Washington Streets. It was situated opposite the Brooks and Young general sundries store. The homes in the background no longer exist, but this post office was saved from destruction and moved to Liberty Street in Rockland and expanded into a home. Today, there is a vacant lot upon which a gas station used to sit. The Land Rover dealership is now in operation there.

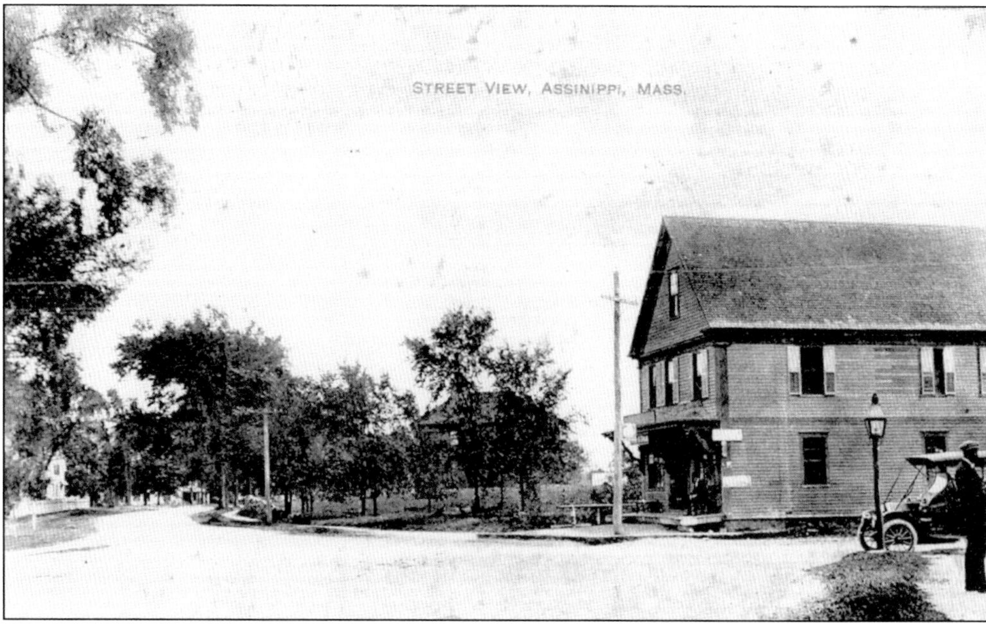

The building here was Brooks and Young, a general store that retailed sundries such as headache powder and Moxie. The bell sign indicated it was also a telephone exchange office. Passengers could take the electric to Mann's Corner in North Hanover and switch to another electric and travel to Nantasket via High Street or to Brockton by way of Webster Street. Today, the building has expanded with a garage, and it is known as the New England Mobile Auto Glass.

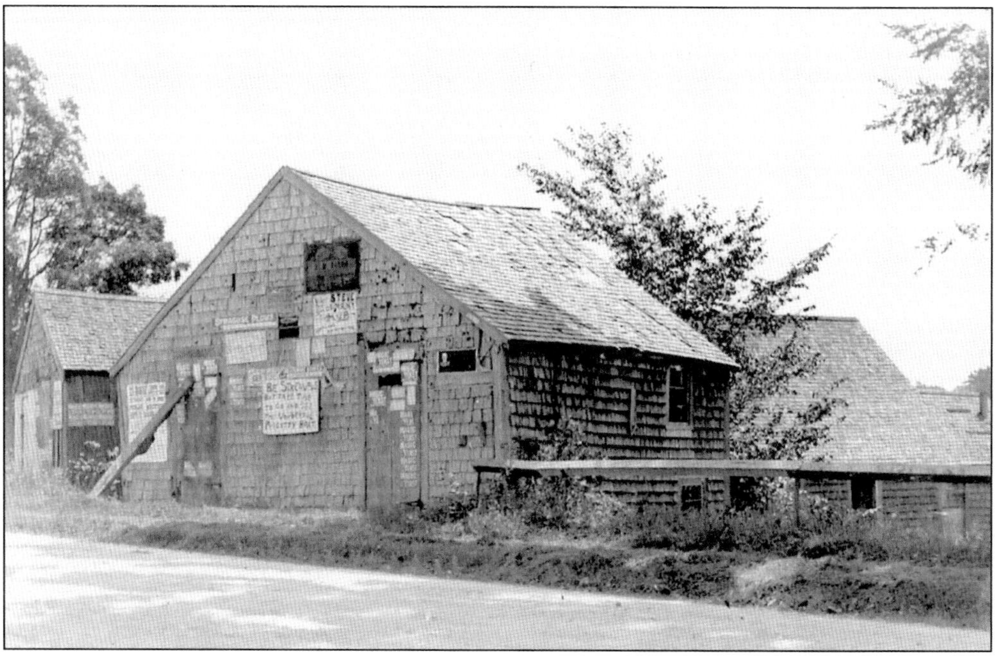

Joshua Jacobs and his older brother Dr. Joseph Jacobs were the builders and proprietors of the Jacobs Mill located by the Third Herring Brook. The mill burned down on July 4, 1920. The mill was located near the Jacobs Homestead, and today this property is the home of the Norwell Historical Society.

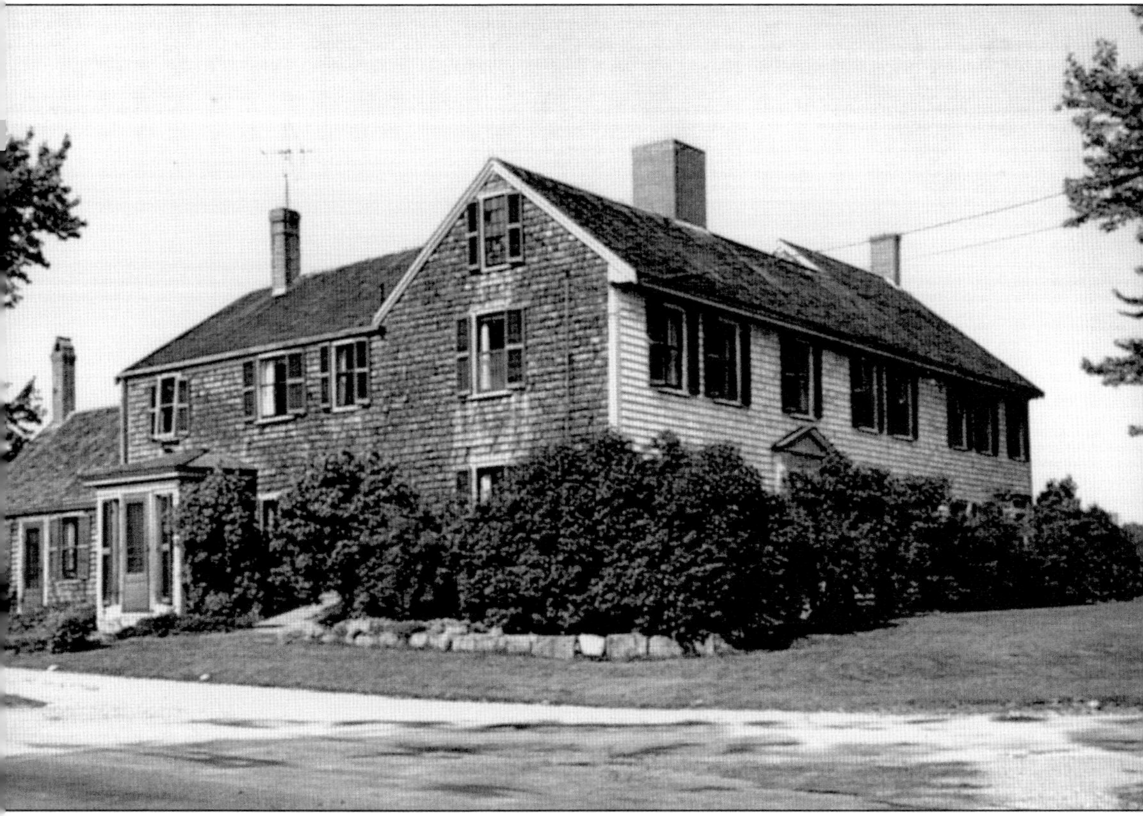

This large colonial home in the Assinippi area was built in 1726 by Joshua Jacobs. Jacobs was a prodigious landowner at the time, and he was quite successful at business too. He married Mary James of Scituate, and they had three sons who eventually all served in the Revolutionary War. The Jacobs boys later married all three sisters of the Richmond family from Little Compton, Rhode Island. Among the greatest achievements of the Norwell Historical Society (NHS) is the preservation of the Jacobs Homestead in Assinippi. It is there that the NHS keeps its archives and gives tours of the artifacts of the town. It also has a research room at the newly built Norwell Middle School. The NHS was formed in 1935 by a group of people who were interested in preserving the heritage of the town of Norwell. Some of the founding members of the society are a who's who of Norwell historians: Capt. Bill Vinal, Nellie Sparrell, Joseph Merritt, Mary Power, and George Turner.

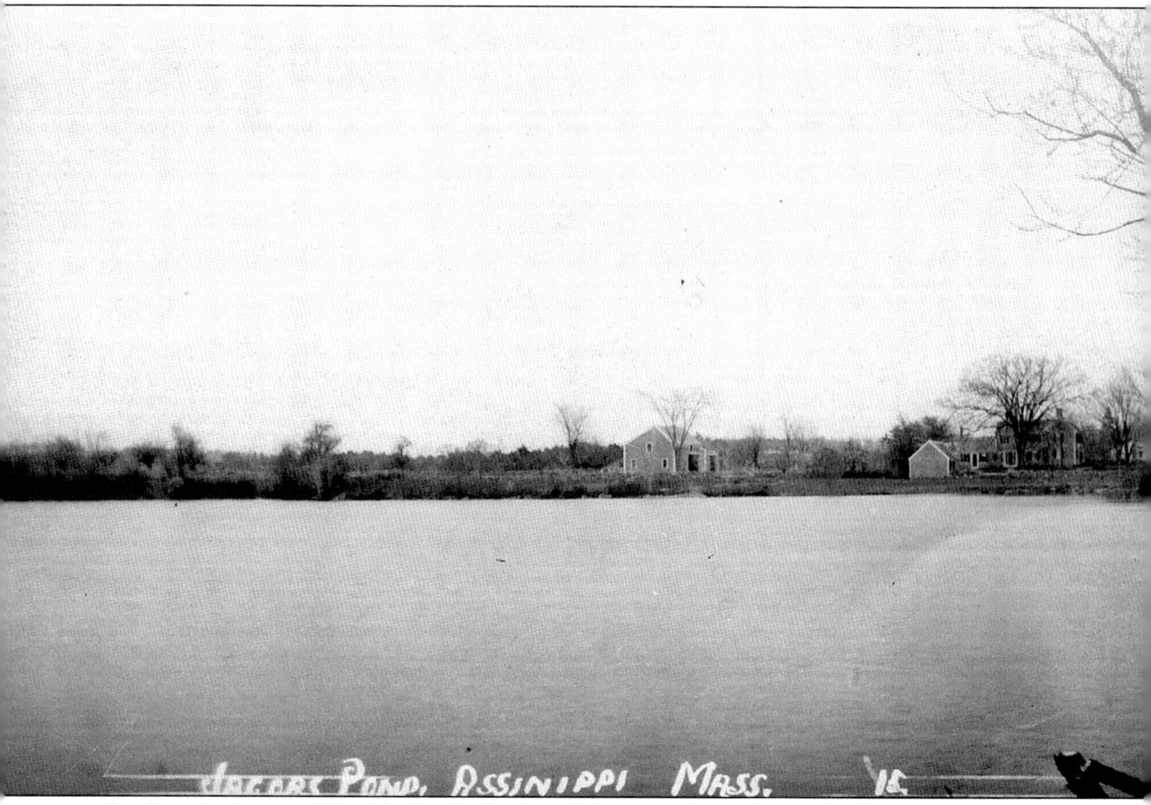

Brothers Joshua and Joseph Jacobs built a dam around 1730 on Third Herring Brook. The water was used to power a gristmill that remained until the early 1900s. This dam enlarged and deepened the Valley Swamp and created what is known as Jacobs Pond. Just before the pond, a very popular spot was Sargent's Restaurant, also called Barstow's. Customers would often stop there for a burger on their way to Cape Cod.

Located in Assinippi, this old oak tree was present at the time the pilgrims landed at Plymouth. This tree could be seen near the Jacob's Mill by Third Herring Brook. It has been reported that Native Americans would hold their treaties under this tree. Nearby the Old Oak Tree is the Union Cemetery in Assinippi.

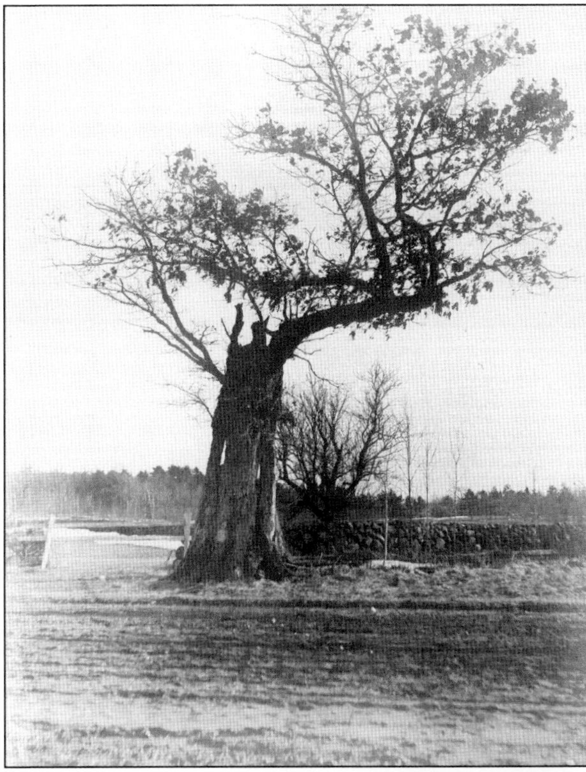

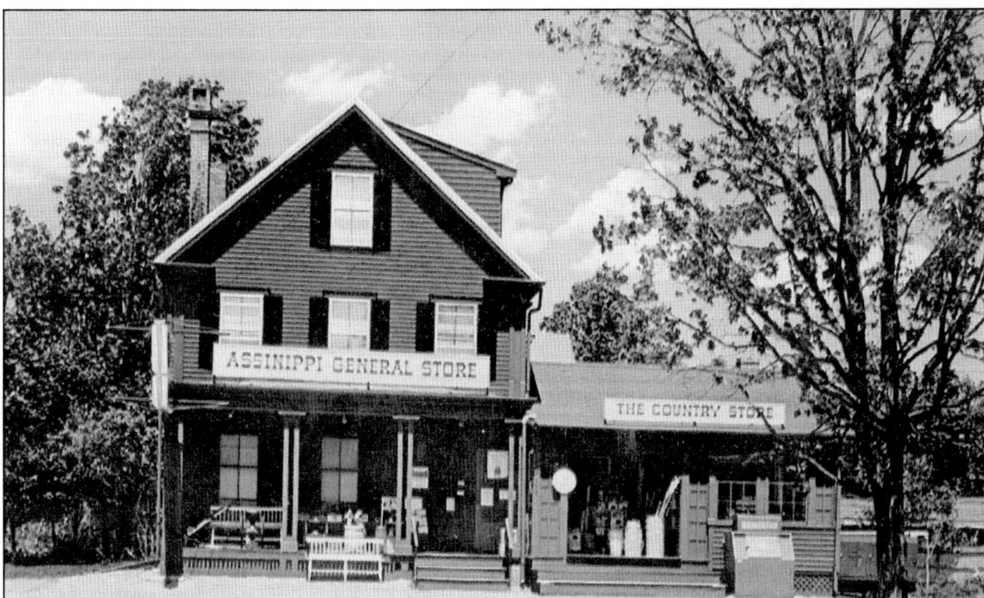

The name Assinippi was derived from the Native American name Hassen Ippi. It is said to mean "rocky water" because of the nature of the Third Herring Brook. This recognizable store is in the heart of Assinippi at the corner of Webster and Washington Streets. It has not changed much through the years. The village of Assinippi used to be strewn with local shops and farm stands all the way up to Accord.

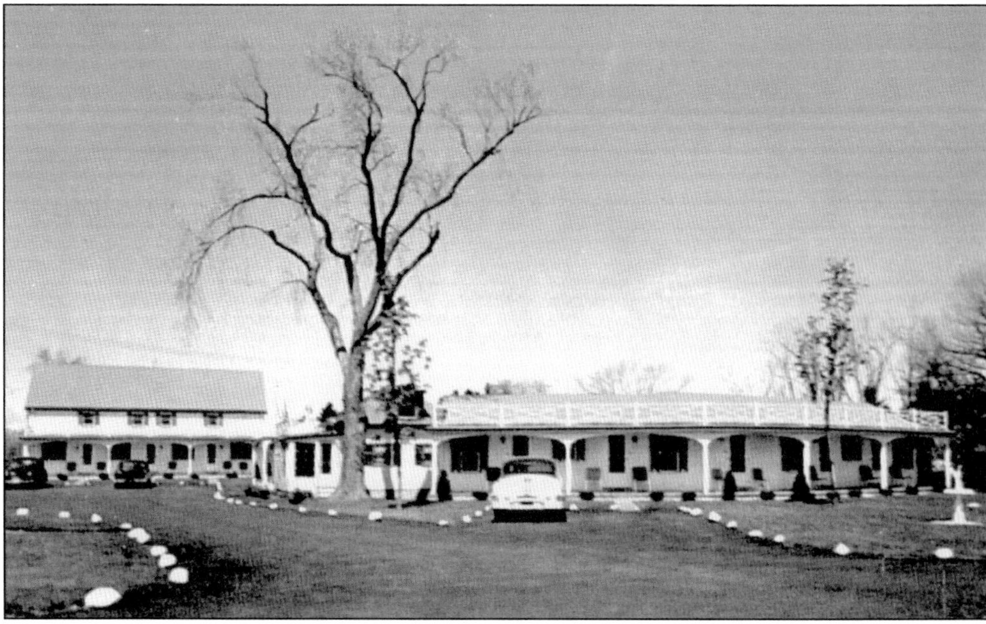

Weary travelers soon needed a place to stay. Many motels began to pop up on Route 3. When the current Route 3 was officially dedicated in 1960, the old Route 3 saw a dramatic decrease in traffic. As a result, the multitude of motels on this thoroughfare saw a decrease in visitors. Today, these motels are still in operation but are primarily used for families with low income. This motel, located near St. Helen Church, is still in operation.

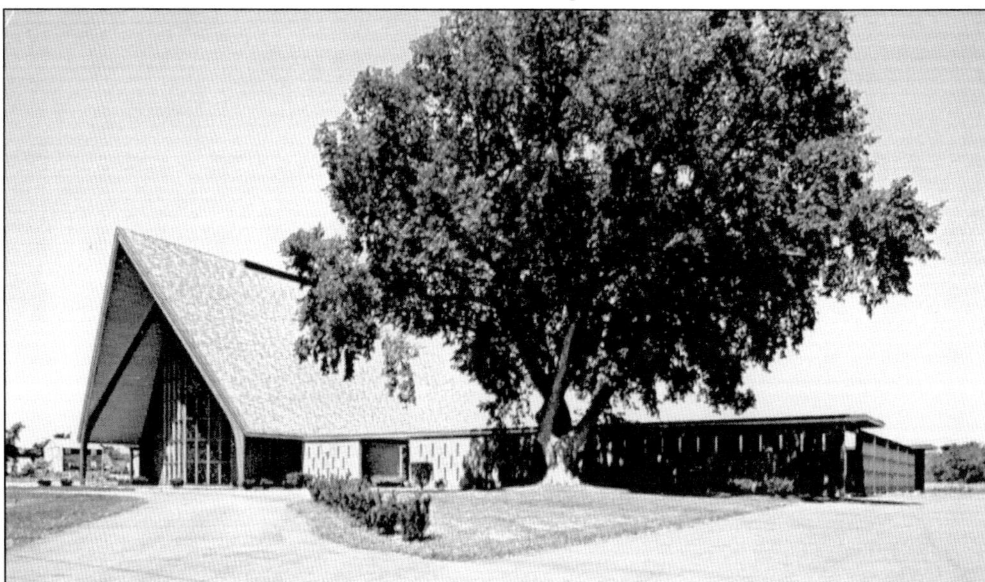

The first Catholic mass was celebrated at Fogg's Hall above the South Scituate Savings Bank in 1888. The Roman Catholic parish was established in Norwell in 1950. The church seen in this postcard was built in Assinippi on Washington Street in 1962. Several poultry farms operated in this area in the early 1900s. Walter Hall's poultry farm was located nearby. Because of the farm's proximity to the Washington Street Cemetery, chicken feathers would sometimes be seen flying around burial services.

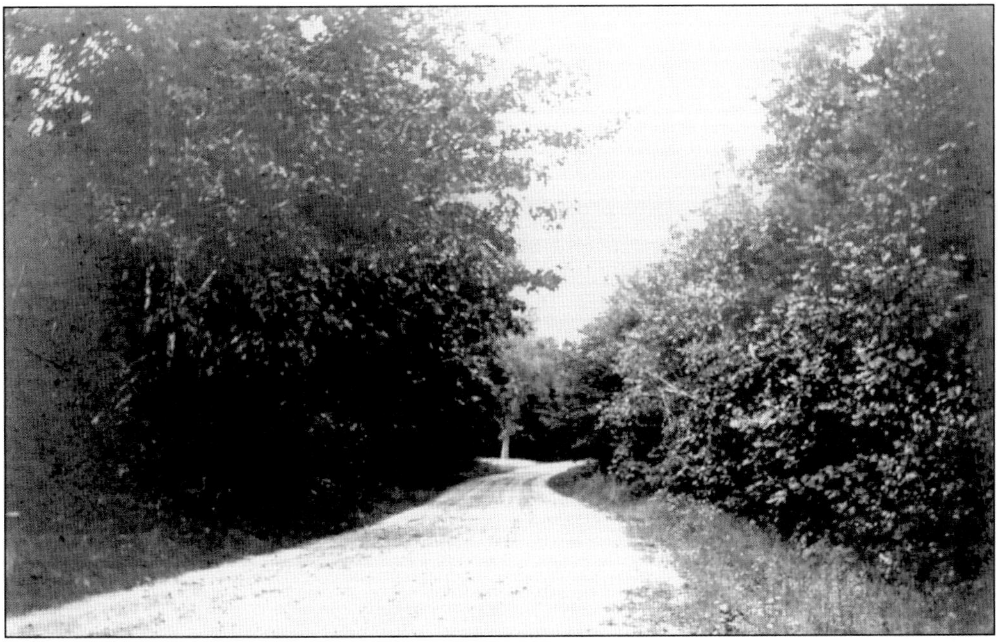

Three hundred years ago, Norwell had several swamps throughout the area. These tracts of land were considered quite valuable because of the unparalleled growth of cedar and pine. The early settlers had no way of knowing just where their land boundaries were because of the terrain. Each year, they had to go out and restake their territory. One such area was the Rocky Swamp in Assinippi.

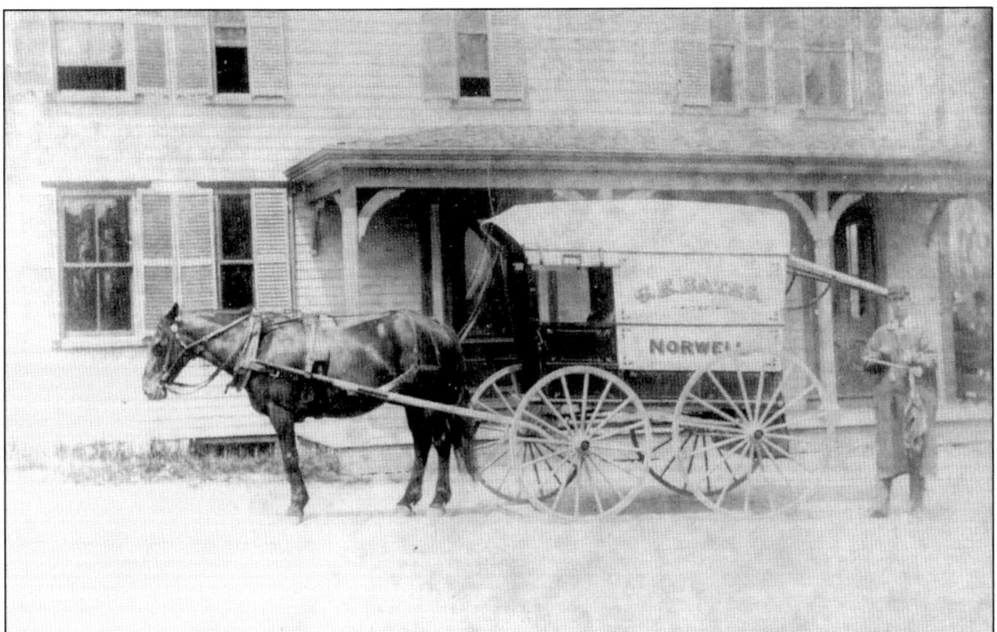

Seen here is a driver for the Bates Taxidermist located on High Street in the Ridge Hill section of Norwell. Bates preserved birds and animals and mounted them for his customers. He advertised in 1894 "Heads and Horns mounted in first class manner. Fur rugs made up in good style."

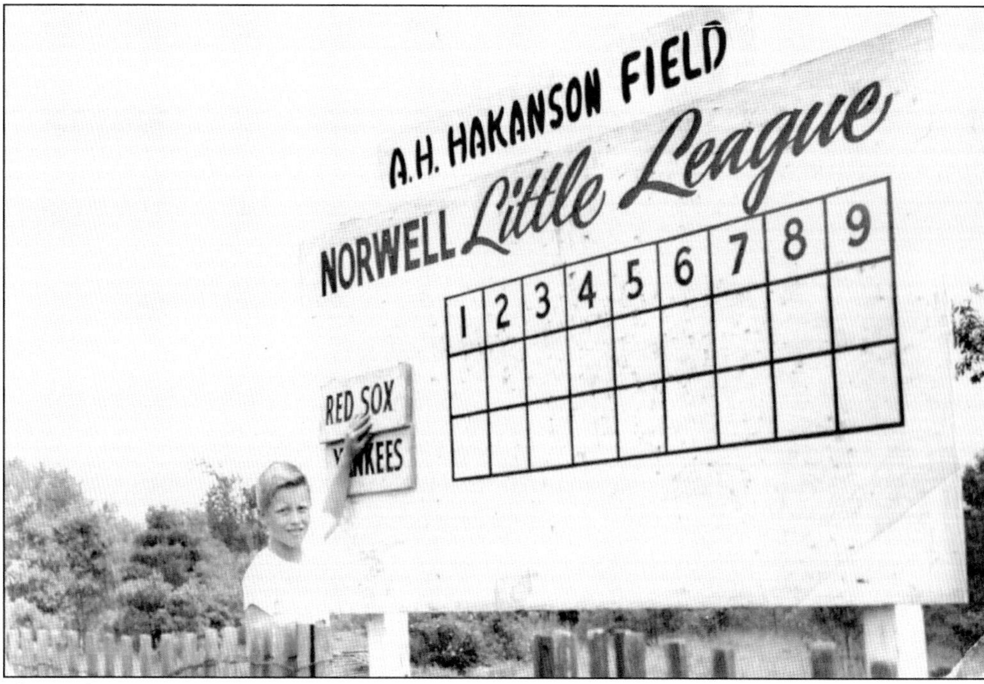

Shown here in 1958 changing the scoreboard is Alan Spradlin. He is at the Allan Hakanson Little League Field near Jacobs Pond in Assinippi. Hakanson was the founder of Norwell Little League and he served as its first president from 1950 through 1965. This photograph was submitted by Alan Spradlin's brother Don.

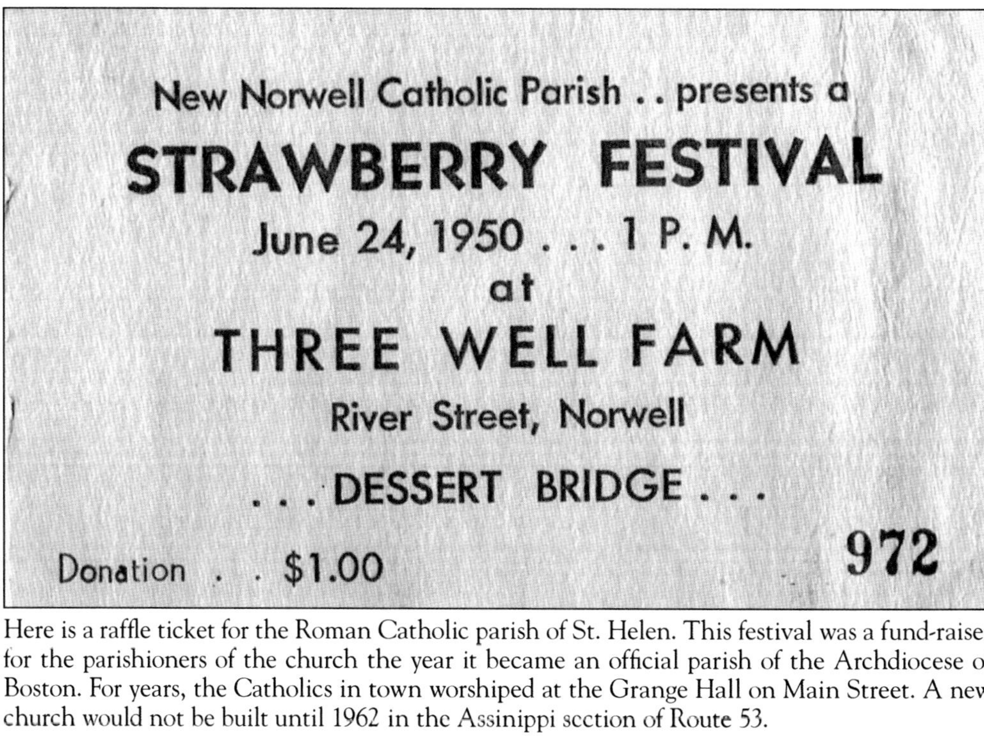
New Norwell Catholic Parish . . presents a

STRAWBERRY FESTIVAL

June 24, 1950 . . . 1 P. M.

at

THREE WELL FARM

River Street, Norwell

. . . DESSERT BRIDGE . . .

Donation . . $1.00 972

Here is a raffle ticket for the Roman Catholic parish of St. Helen. This festival was a fund-raiser for the parishioners of the church the year it became an official parish of the Archdiocese of Boston. For years, the Catholics in town worshiped at the Grange Hall on Main Street. A new church would not be built until 1962 in the Assinippi section of Route 53.

Six

Ridge Hill

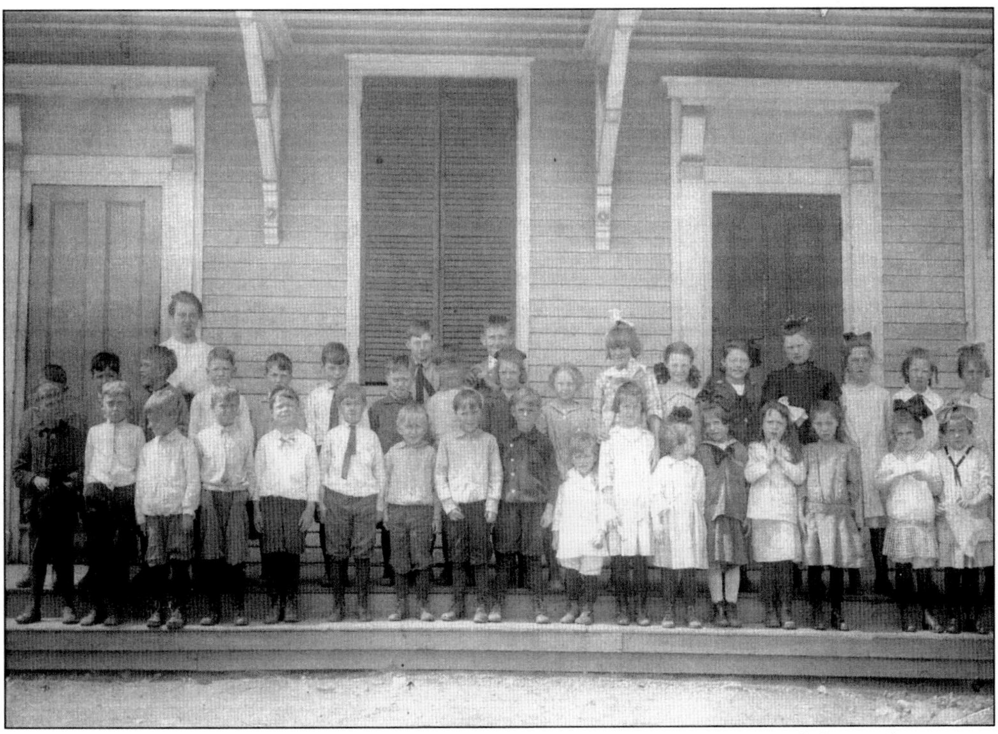

Schoolchildren are seen posing with their teacher around the beginning of the 20th century. They are standing on the steps of the District Number One schoolhouse, which was built in 1850. The building was erected to serve the students of Ridge Hill. All grades were taught in one room with one teacher who taught all the grades. The schoolhouse building was expanded with a second floor in 1933 to accommodate more students.

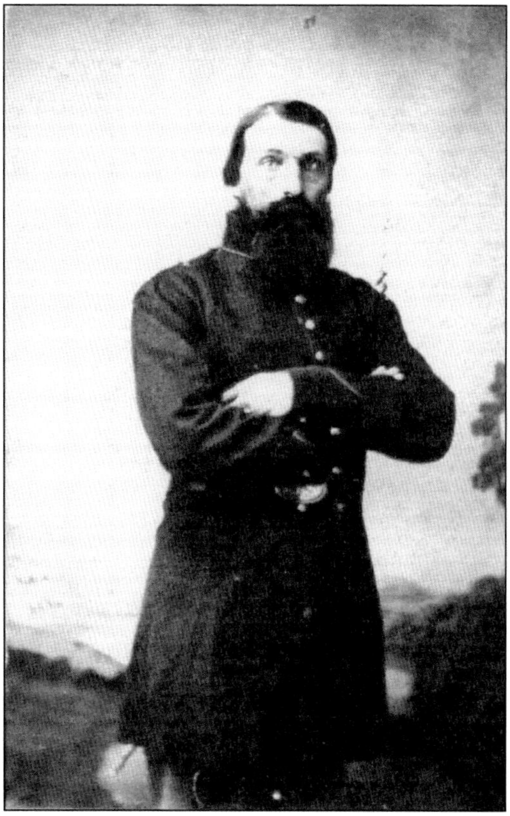

Charles Grose was born on June 15, 1828, in Hanover, Massachusetts, the second of 12 children of Ansel and Rebecca Wilder Grose. His brother Dexter and he began a shoe manufacturing business. Dexter and Charles and their older brother Henry enlisted in the Union Army serving in the Massachusetts 43rd Regiment, Company F. They were discharged after 10 months on July 30, 1863. Dexter and Charles continued their partnership until 1865, when Dexter moved to Abington and formed a business with W. E. Putnam.

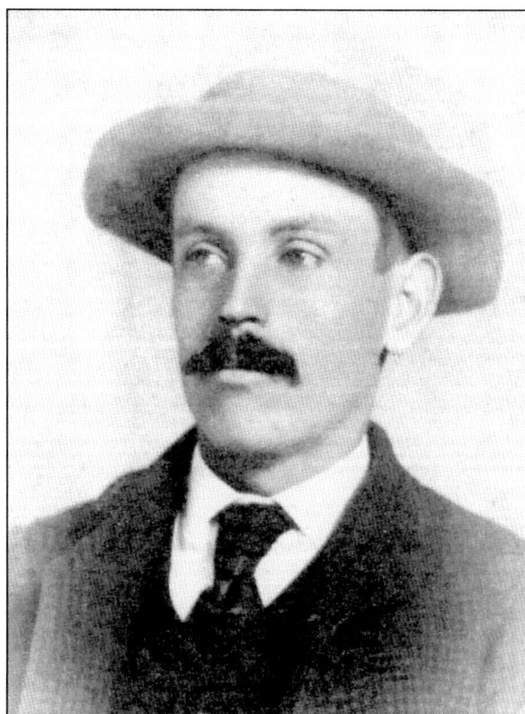

Pictured here is Charles Webster Grose, the son of Charles and Mary Grose. He was born on April 24, 1849, in Hingham, Massachusetts. Grose purchased from his parents in 1872 a home with a new French roof built on a half acre for $3,000. This home, situated at 122 High Street, stood across the street from the Charles Grose and Son shoe manufacturing business. Charles Webster Grose became a director of several mining companies out West. He was also elected president of the Hanover Street Railway Company in 1896.

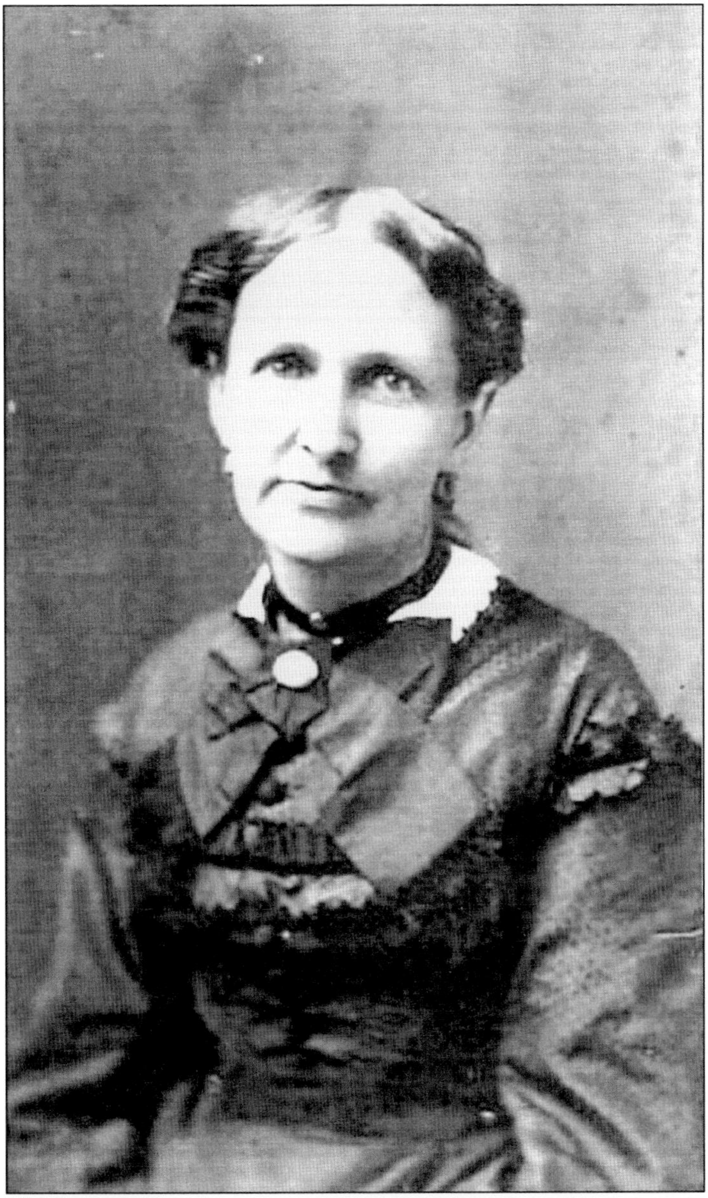

On July 11, 1847, Charles Grose married Mary Ann Hobart in a double ceremony in Hingham. Charles's brother Henry married Julia Curtis of Scituate. Rev. John Barry from Hanover officiated the wedding on this summer day. Mary Ann's ancestors were an illustrious family as Peter Hobart was the first settler of Hingham in 1634. In 1867, Charles and Mary moved to a new home at 116 High Street. The home still stands today and has several unique characteristics. There is an original lightning rod and weathervane on top of the barn that deflects the lightning from the home. Also, at one time, there was copper lined in one of the bathroom walls that was used to store rainwater. The water would funnel into a reservoir and be ready for later use in a bathtub. Another unique feature of the home is the two-hole privy which is another term for an outhouse. This particular privy was different because it was located between the barn and the home and not out in the yard. The present owner has kept his privy usable by chilling wine and beer in there!

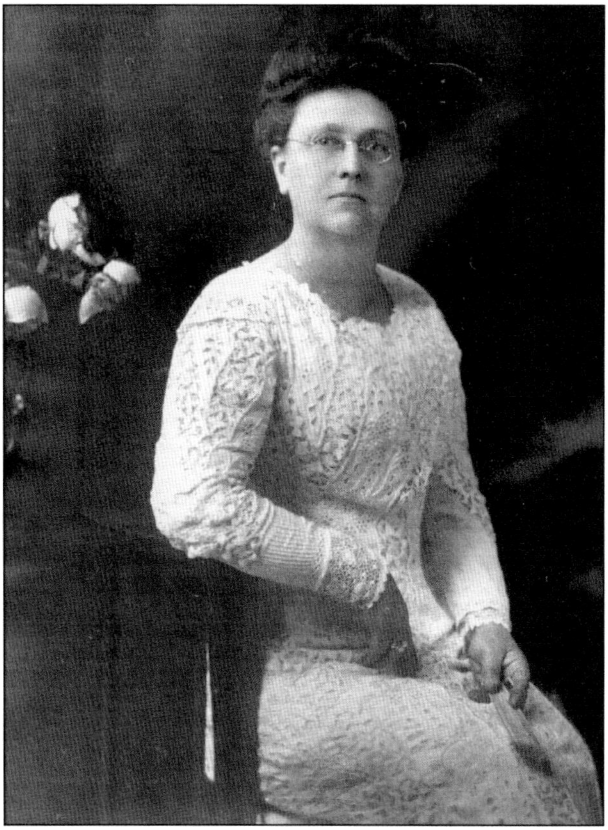

Mary Frances Grose was the second child born to Charles and Mary Ann Grose on Christmas Eve 1855. On January 22, 1874, at the young age of 18, Mary Frances married Elwin Temple Wright of Abington. Wright was a shoemaker who was in business with his father, Lorenzo, in what was then known as East Abington (Rockland).

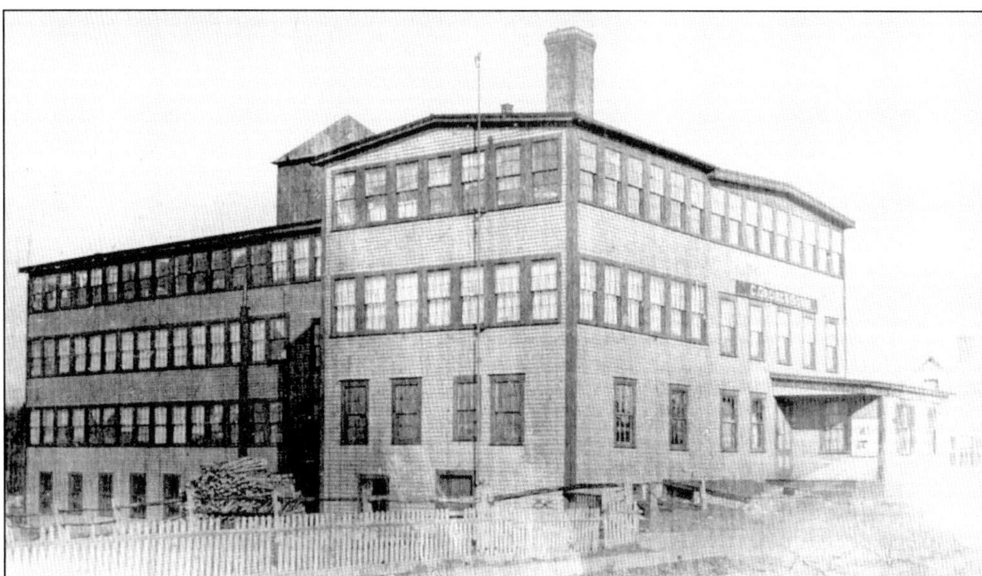

In 1872, Charles Grose and his son Charles Webster Grose begin manufacturing shoes and selling them at 111 Summer Street Boston. In 1884, Charles Grose and his sons Charles Webster and Ansel Hobart purchased the former shoe factory of Benjamin Young from the South Scituate Savings Bank for $1,625. The factory was located opposite 116 High Street in South Scituate.

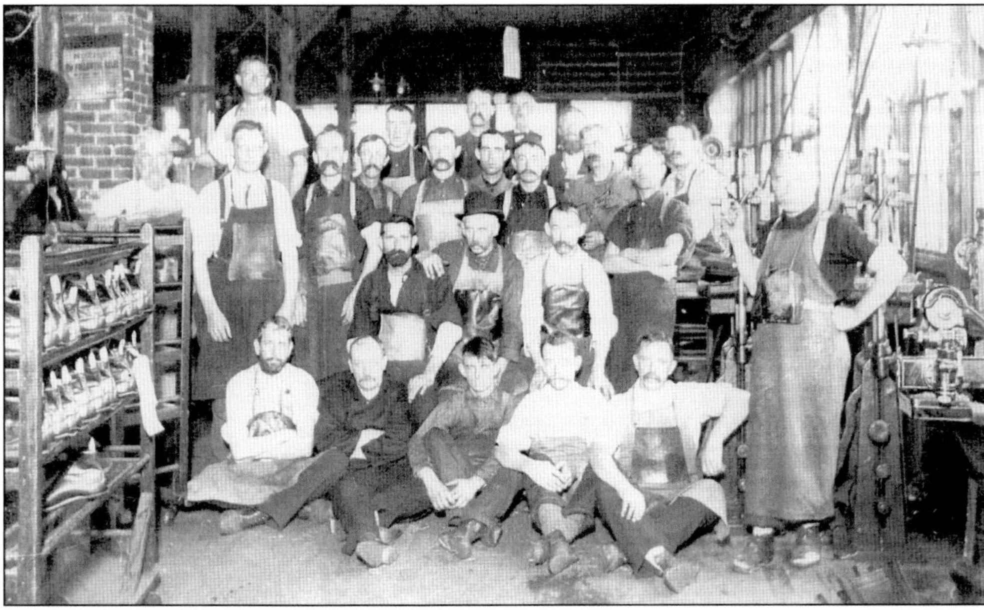

In 1884, the factory operations were renamed Charles Grose and Sons and continued under that name until 1898 when it was called the Ridge Hill Shoe Company. On October 12 of the following year, Charles Grose and Sons opened a wholesale store in downtown Boston at 86 Bedford Street. In 1888, Charles Grose signed the petition to the Massachusetts House of Representatives for the town name change from South Scituate to Norwell. His signature is the second one recorded.

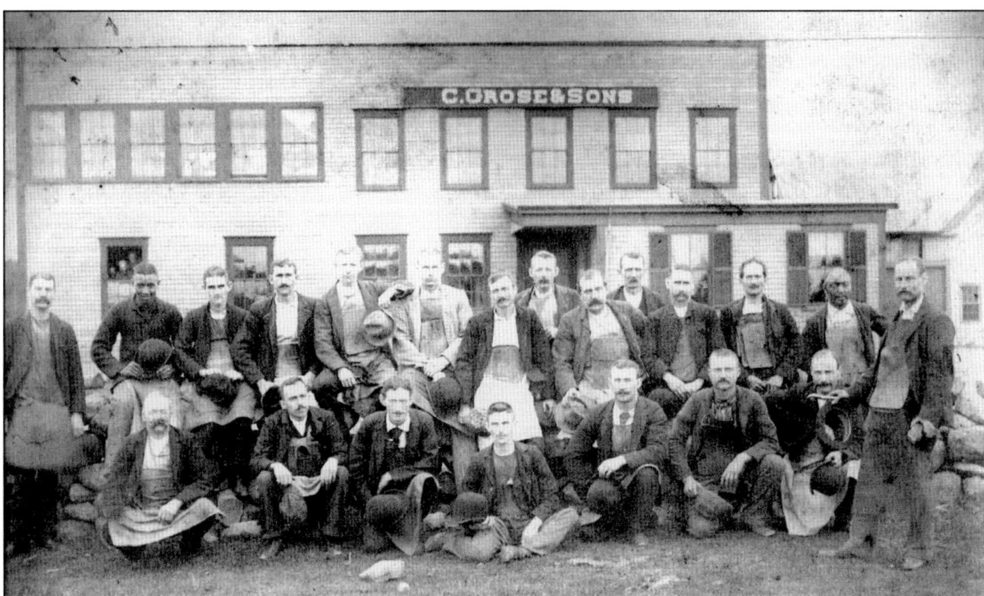

Pictured here outside Grose and Sons shoe factory is an ensemble of shoemakers. Charles Grose's son Charles Webster Grose is seen standing at the extreme right. His younger brother Ansel Hobart Grose is seated fourth from the left, holding his derby hat. Charles Webster ran the shoe manufacturing business after the death of Charles in 1892. His father left Mary Ann Grose $25,000 each quarter for the rest of her life.

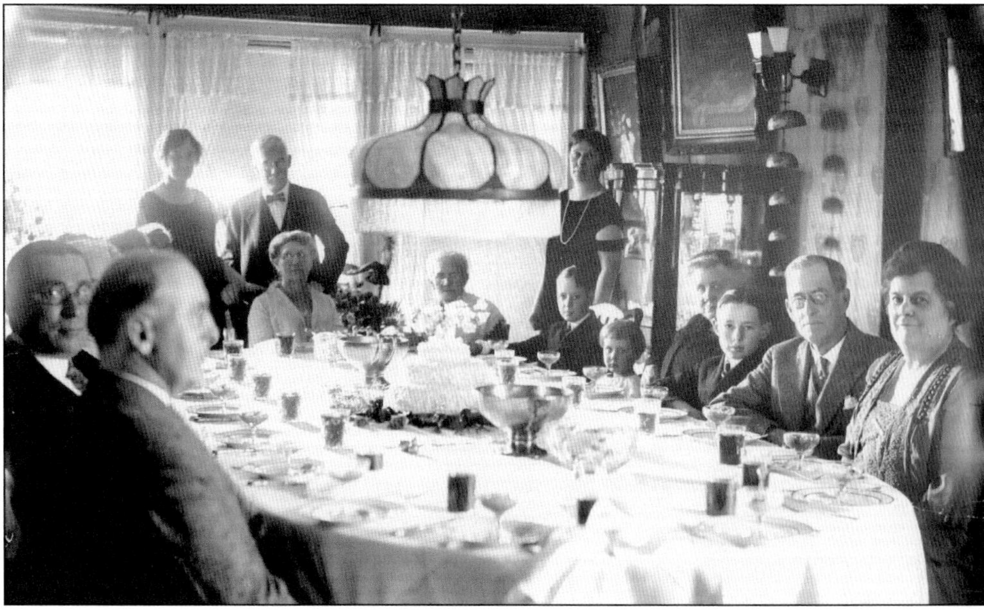

Seen here at the dinner table, this photograph was taken in the home of Elwin Temple Wright and his wife Mary Frances Wright. In 1876, Elwin and his 48 year-old father-in-law, Charles Grose, began a shoe company called Wright and Gross. Their partnership was solidified when Mary Grose paid a sum of $2,250 to Rockland Savings Bank on April 5, 1881, for the building. Today, E. T. Wright is among the nation's oldest and most respected shoe brands.

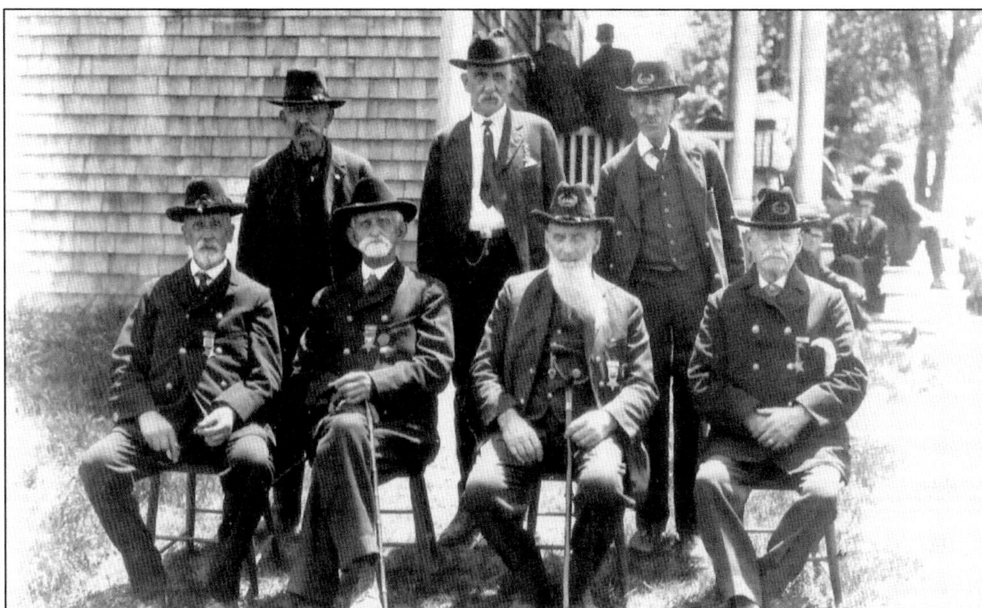

On Memorial Day in 1925, members of the Grand Army of the Republic (GAR) Post 112 posed for a photograph in front of the GAR Hall on High Street. The veterans seen here fought in the Civil War. Pictured here from left to right are (first row) Post Commander Alfred B. Litchfield, John H. Prouty, Edwin R. Studley, and Howard F. Mann; (second row) George A. Hatch, Frank Alger, and Benjamin W. French.

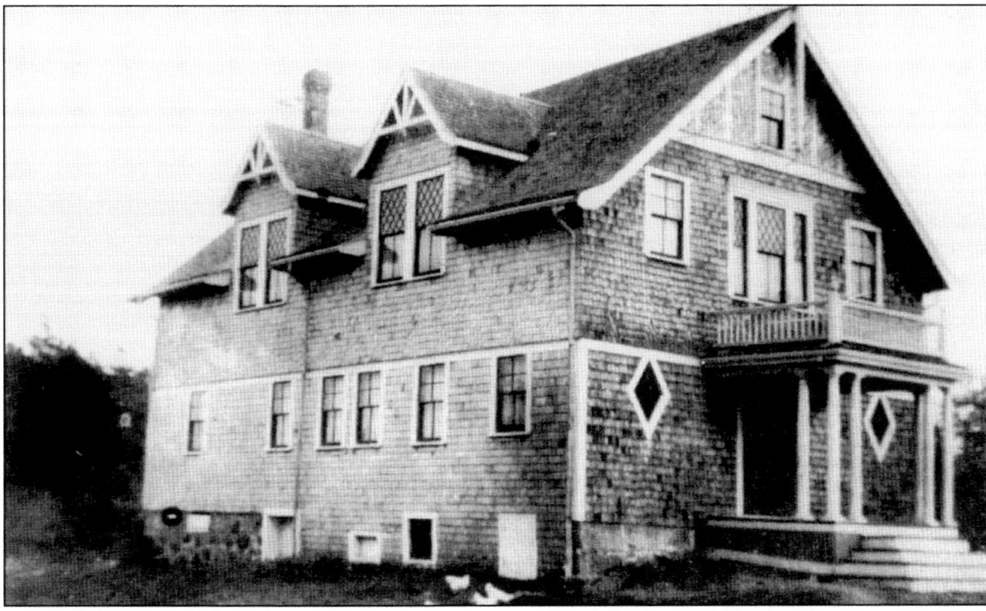

The GAR Hall is located on High Street in the Ridge Hill part of Norwell. Originally, this building was the Webster Cushing Shoe Shop. In 1900, it was remodeled by Norwell resident Fred Curtis and made into the town's new Memorial Hall. For the next four decades, the Memorial Hall, also known as the D. Willard Robinson GAR Post 112, would be used for refreshments after Memorial Day parades. Today, it is the site of the Ridge Hill Preschool. Prior to the Ridge Hill School operating out of this hall, a preschool was in business at the Yetman family home just down the street at 116 High Street. Frances Yetman ran a preschool in the downstairs area of the family home. Homeowner Jeff Keller still has visible chalk writing from the children over many parts of the walls in the barn.

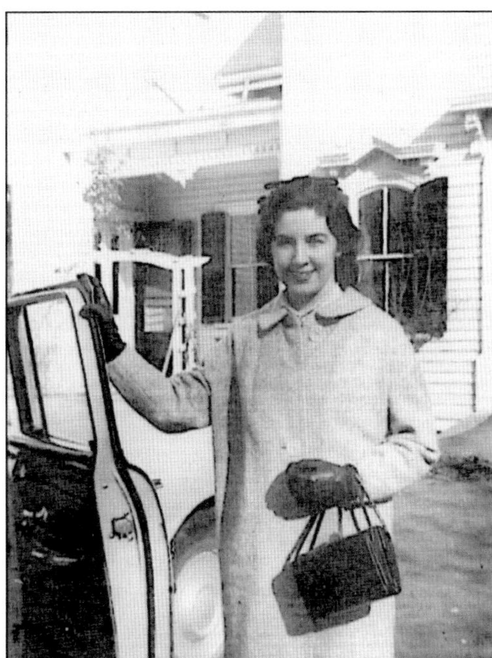

In 1947, William and Frances Yetman purchased the former Charles Grose home, numbered 116 High Street, from George and Marie Tuscan. Eighteen year old Joan Yetman, the eldest of nine Yetman children, is seen here in 1956 getting ready to ride to church on a wintry morning in the family Pontiac station wagon. William named his Ridge Hill homestead "Yesteryear," and the Yetman family would live in this home for over 32 years. Frances resides in northern California today.

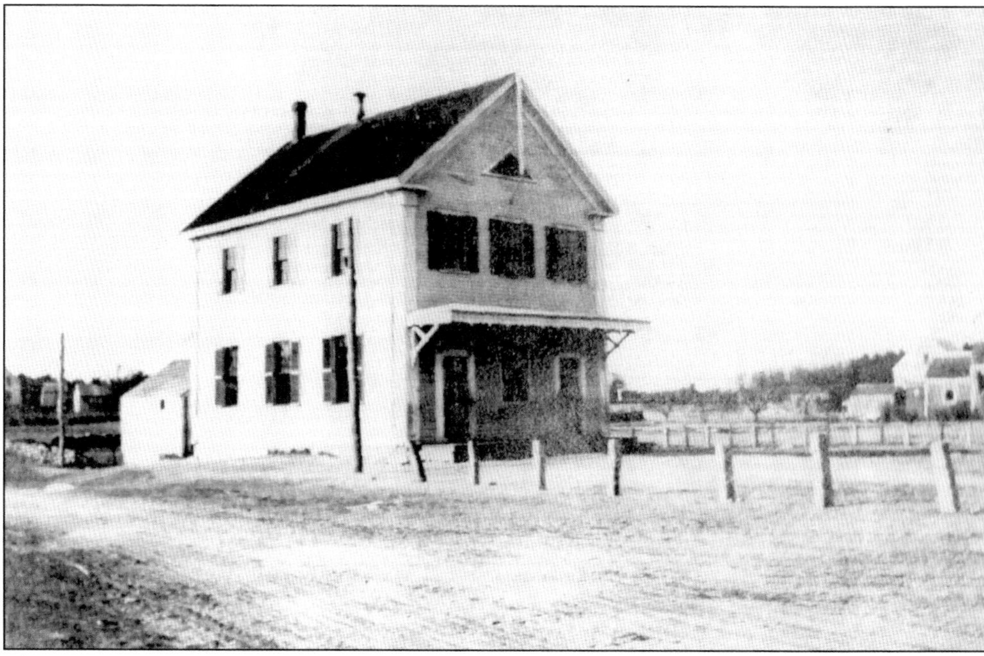

This is the District Number One schoolhouse located at the corner of Oak and Washington Streets. Located at what is now 164 Washington Street (Route 53), the building is part of an expanded commercial structure, housing an array of small businesses.

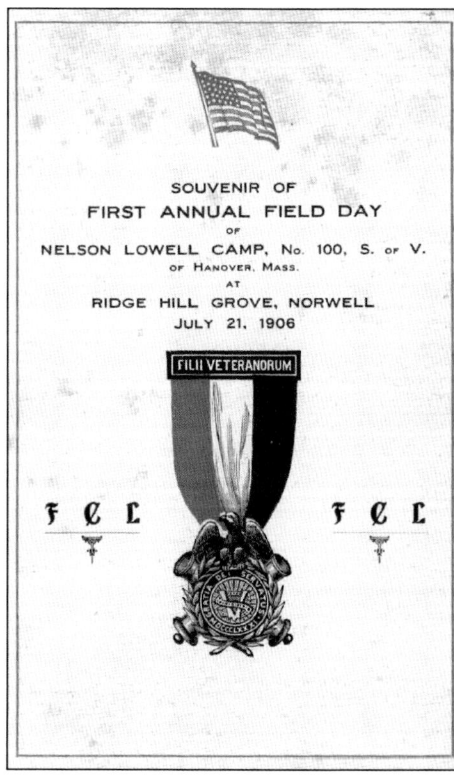

Oftentimes the organization renting out the Ridge Hill Grove would print souvenir cards for the participants. Among the many groups to use the grounds were churches, lodges, and school reunions. It was conveniently located on the "electric" street car line between Hanover and Nantasket. The grove had a large dance hall and a well-maintained baseball field. This one is from July 21, 1906, for the First Annual Field Day of the Nelson Lowell Camp of Hanover.

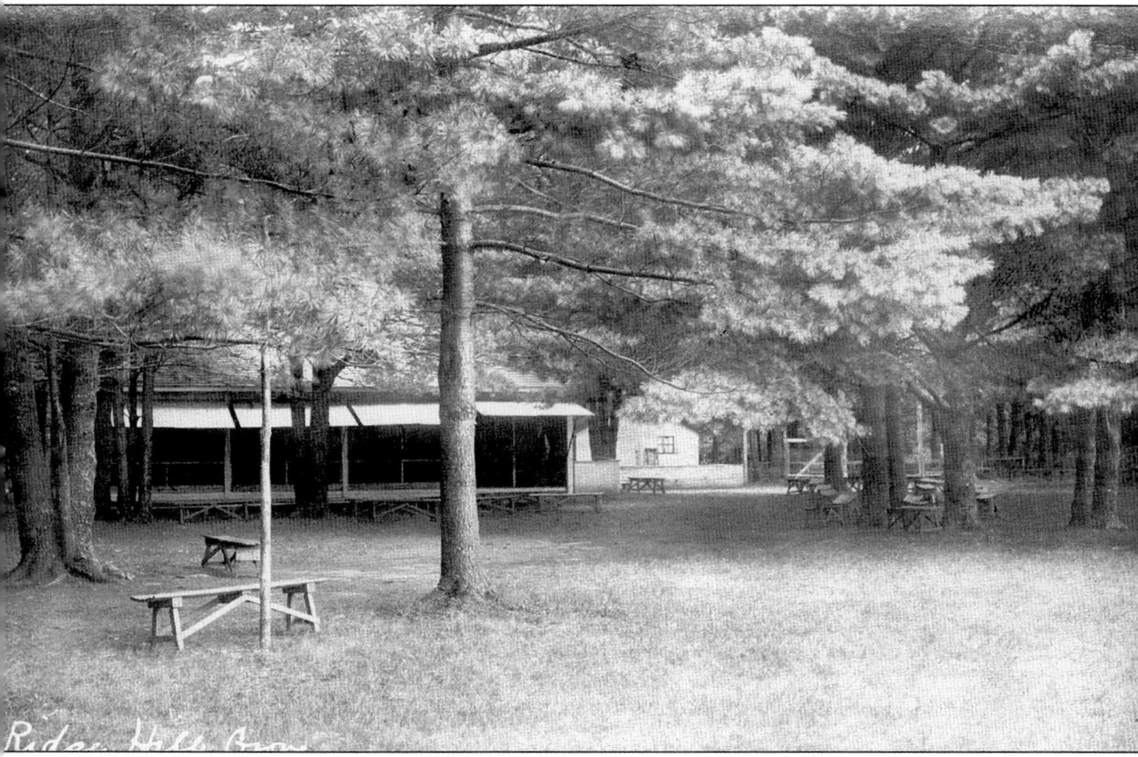

Along High Street at the present site of the Grace Farrar Cole Elementary School, a campground prospered for many years. It was called the Ridge Hill Grove, and it entertained legions of families from all over the South Shore. A group of men started to get together to play cards, football, baseball, and hockey as early as 1919. This group of interested members decided to formalize their organization and held their first formal meeting on May 2, 1923, at the home of Horace T. Fogg Esq., their legal advisor. The Union Athletic Association was incorporated as an organization in 1923, and they purchased the Ridge Hill Grove campground. The 122 charter members were comprised mainly of veterans from North Hanover and Ridge Hill. The Union Athletic Association disbanded in 1954 and gave the land to the town of Norwell with the stipulation that the town use the land for the children of Norwell. In 1956, the Grace Farrar Cole Elementary School opened at an estimated cost of $538,000. Cole was a former teacher and school committee member.

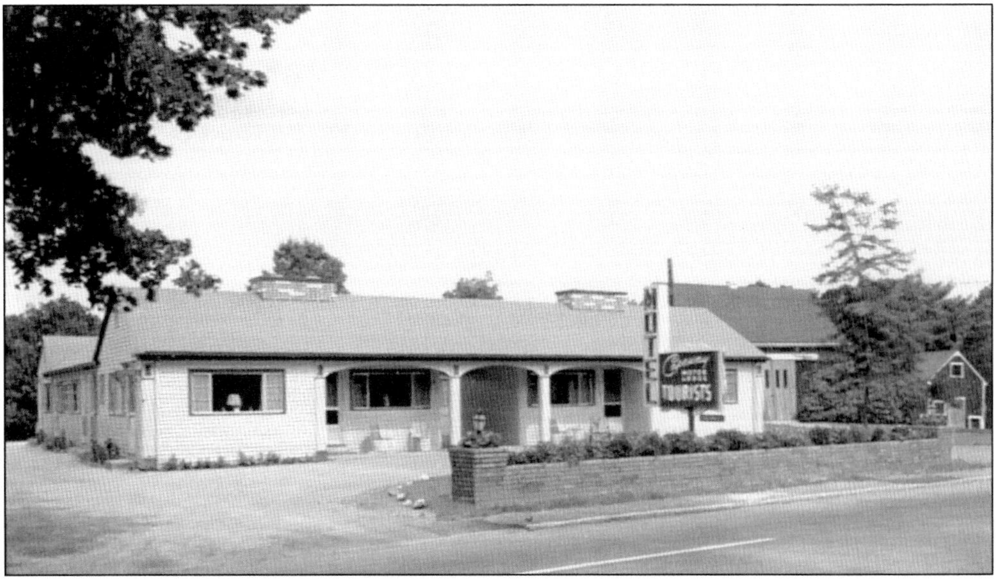

After World War II, there was a proliferation of new automobiles and therefore families began traveling more and more. One of the South Shore's most traveled routes was the modern day Route 53. This road has a long and storied history as it began as the primary stagecoach route to Plymouth. Back in the 1940s, it was known as Route 3. Motorists would travel to Cape Cod and stop over for a night in Norwell. This motel is still in operation today across the street from Webb's Fitness.

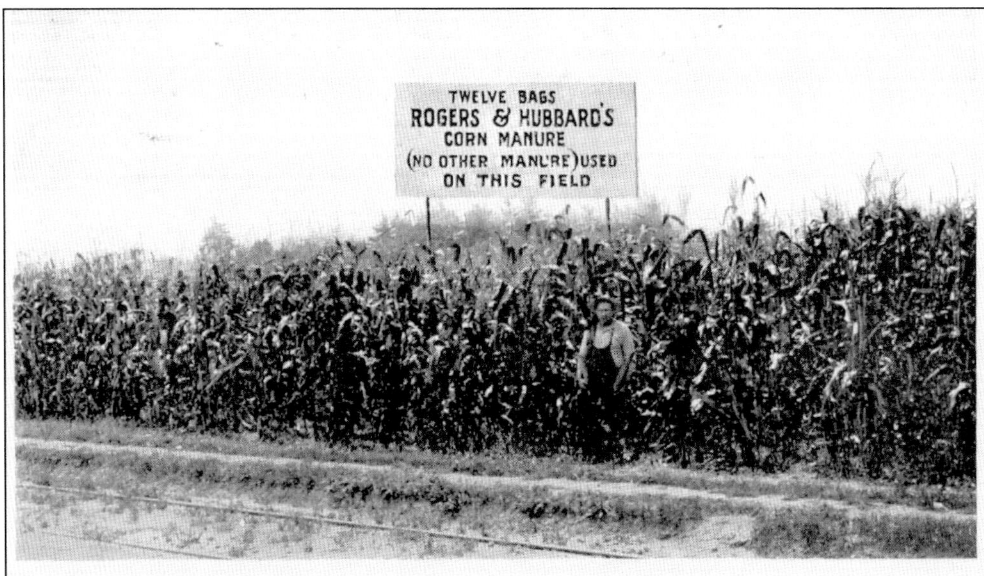

This corn farm was owned by Billy Wilder, and he is seen in this postcard with his large billboard behind him on 200 High Street. This sign was seen by many passengers of the Hanover Street Railway Company en route to Mann's Corner in North Hanover or Queen Ann's Corner in Accord. The property once stood where Route 3 now runs.

Seven

ACCORD

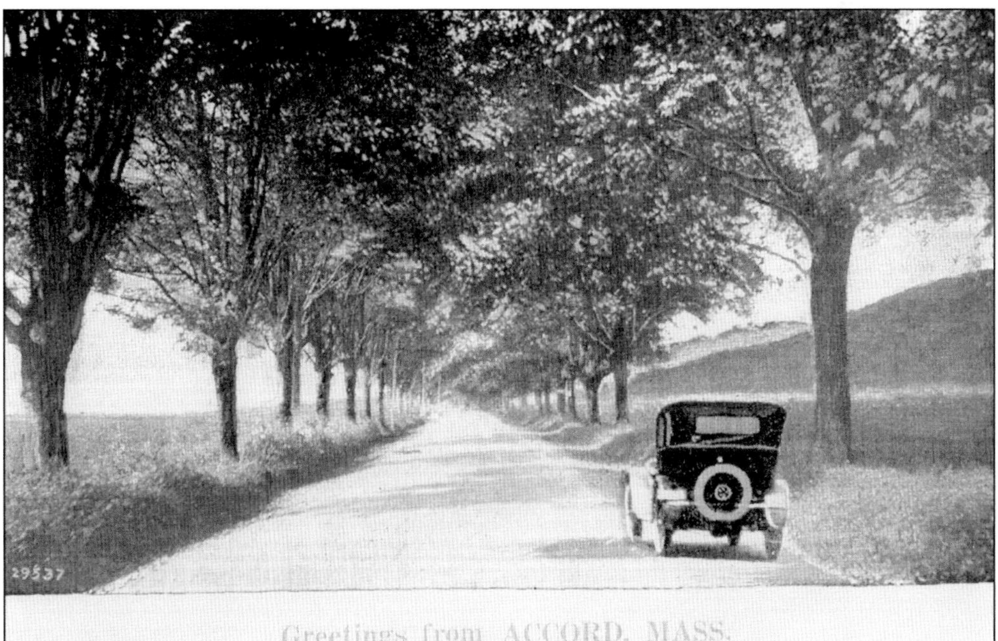

Accord is a village shared by the towns of Hingham and Norwell. It has its own post office (zip code 02018) just over the Norwell line in Hingham on Route 53. Accord is also known as Queen Ann's Corner, where thousands of people pass through each day. For over 100 years, Accord Pond was the locale for duck hunting, a very popular sport indeed. Different gun clubs operated out of Accord Pond. The fowl would migrate from Quincy Point to the salt water areas and thus Accord Pond became one of the most active ponds in Massachusetts for fowl hunting.

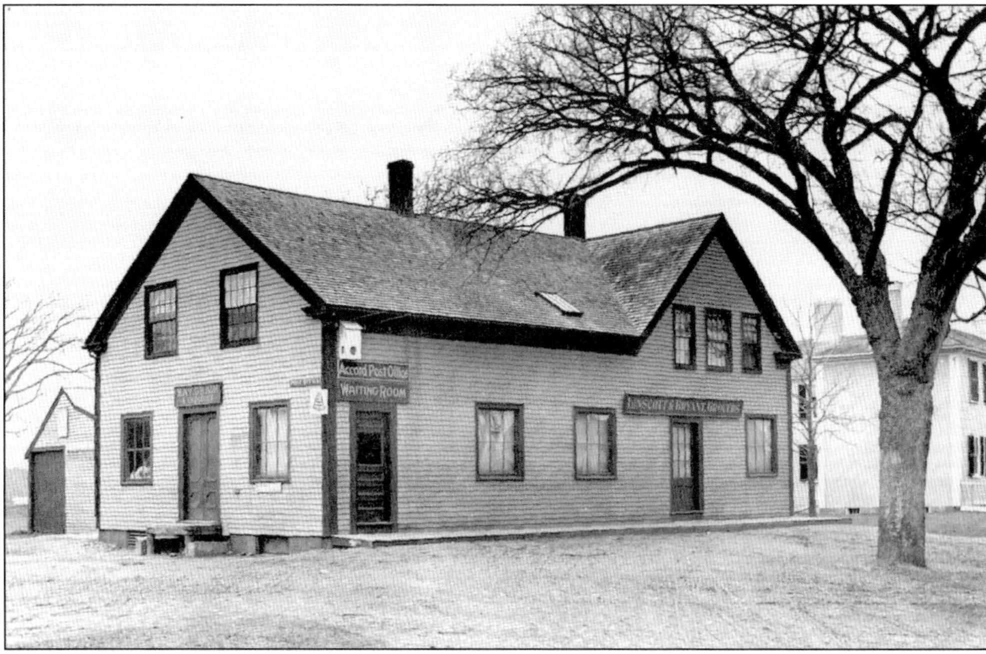

At the busy intersection of Washington and Main Street in Accord stands the Linscott and Bryant grocery store. This was a major staging area for the electric cars going to Hanover and Nantasket. The store sold sundries and gasoline along with telephone service. Its main function was to serve as a waiting room for the passengers of the Hingham Street Railway Company. Today, there is a liquor store at this location.

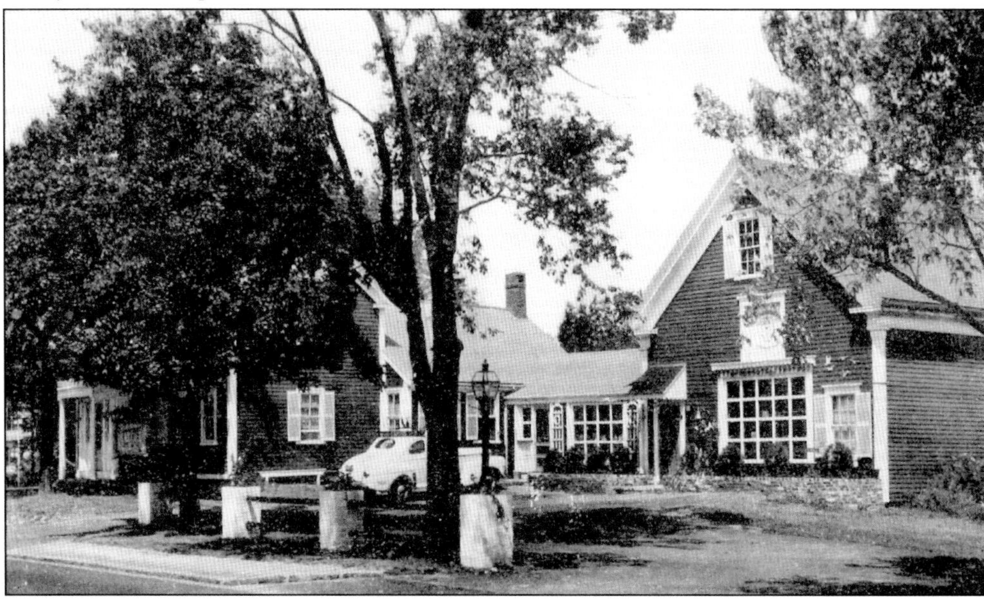

A century ago, Route 53 was the stagecoach road used to travel from Boston to Plymouth. Crossroads gift shop can be seen here in the 1940s. Today, it is part of the New England Real Estate Journal at 57 Washington Street. Among the businesses that used to operate nearby at the corner of High and Washington Streets was the E. W. Gardner Blacksmith. In 1894, Gardner advertised his business as a horse shoer and carriage smith.

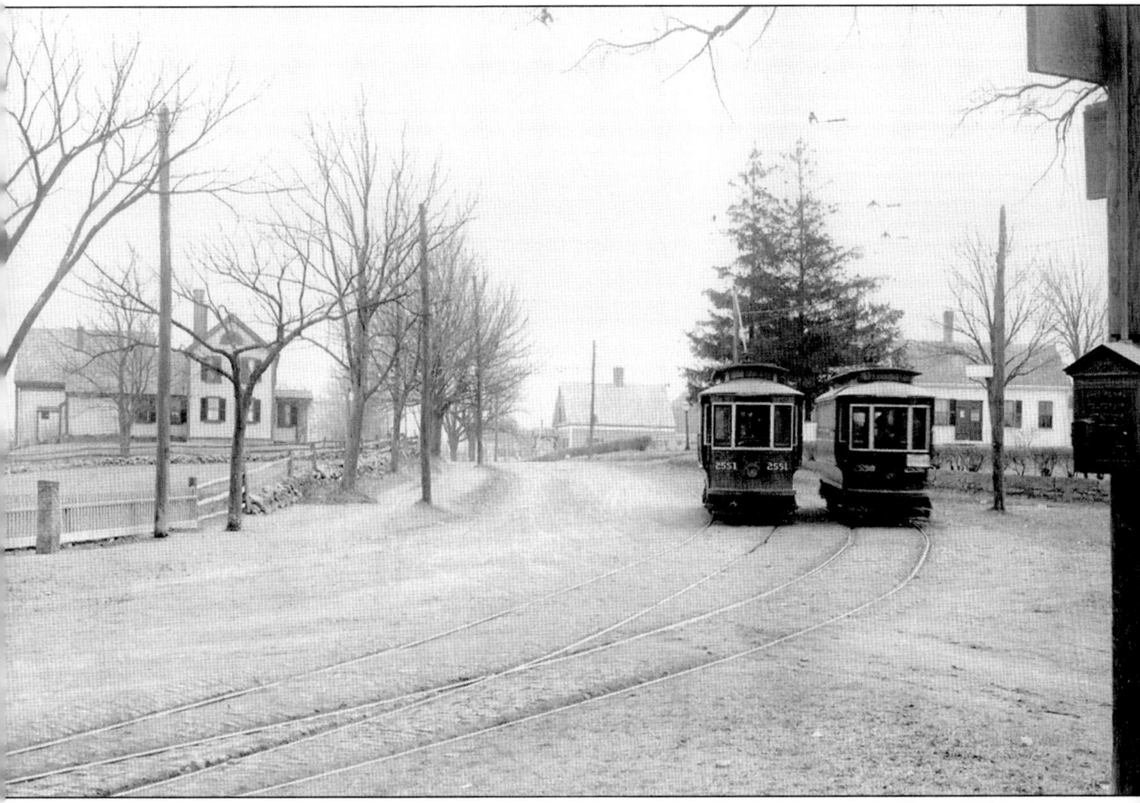

Shown here are two electrics passing each other on Washington Street near Queen Ann's Corner. The ride from Queen Ann's Corner to the Hingham Square Depot on North Street across from St. Paul Church took 21 minutes. Riders could switch to another electric for the ride to Nantasket Beach. This service ran from 1896 until 1920. With the advent of the automobile and improved roads, the need for the electrics was greatly diminished. Seen on the left is Charles "Clem" Thomas' home and ammunition shop. His shop was strategically located near the busy Accord Pond and on the main route to Cape Cod. Many hunters would stop by Clem's shop after a hunt to boast about their day's shooting. Today his shop and home would be near the Kentucky Fried Chicken in Queen Ann's Corner. Across the street are the Accord Post Office and Wilfred and Fannie Bowker's home. Eventually, the tracks were taken up and sold for scrap metal to the Japanese in 1931.

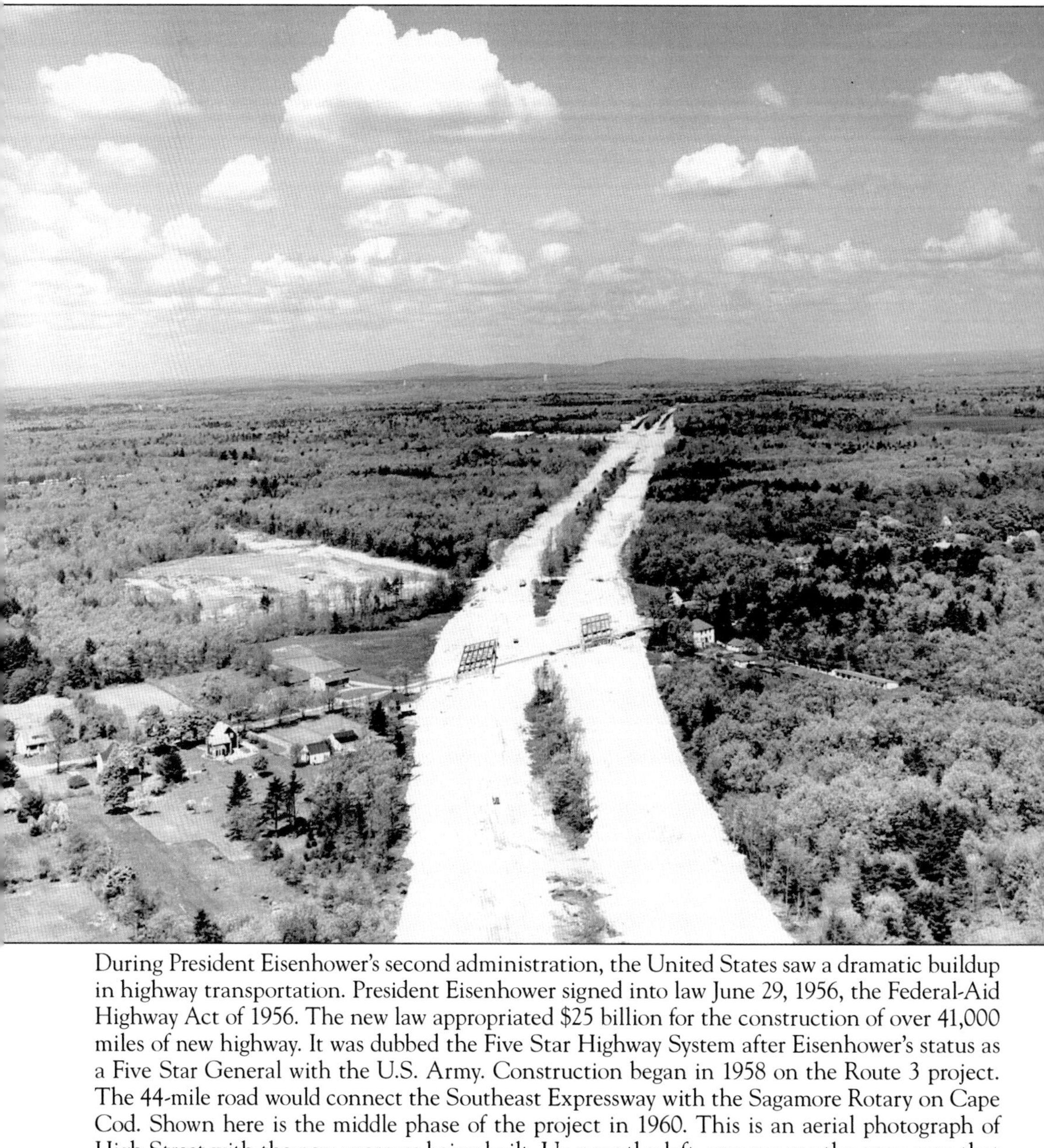

During President Eisenhower's second administration, the United States saw a dramatic buildup in highway transportation. President Eisenhower signed into law June 29, 1956, the Federal-Aid Highway Act of 1956. The new law appropriated $25 billion for the construction of over 41,000 miles of new highway. It was dubbed the Five Star Highway System after Eisenhower's status as a Five Star General with the U.S. Army. Construction began in 1958 on the Route 3 project. The 44-mile road would connect the Southeast Expressway with the Sagamore Rotary on Cape Cod. Shown here is the middle phase of the project in 1960. This is an aerial photograph of High Street with the new overpass being built. Up near the left, one can see the open area that became Assinippi Office Park. Further along, the Boston Whaler company can be spotted. Many South Shore residents are familiar with the Home Depot in Rockland. It operates on the former Boston Whaler site today. Among the homes displaced for the new highway was tax collector Don Wilder's home located on High Street. He moved his home to 483 Main Street.

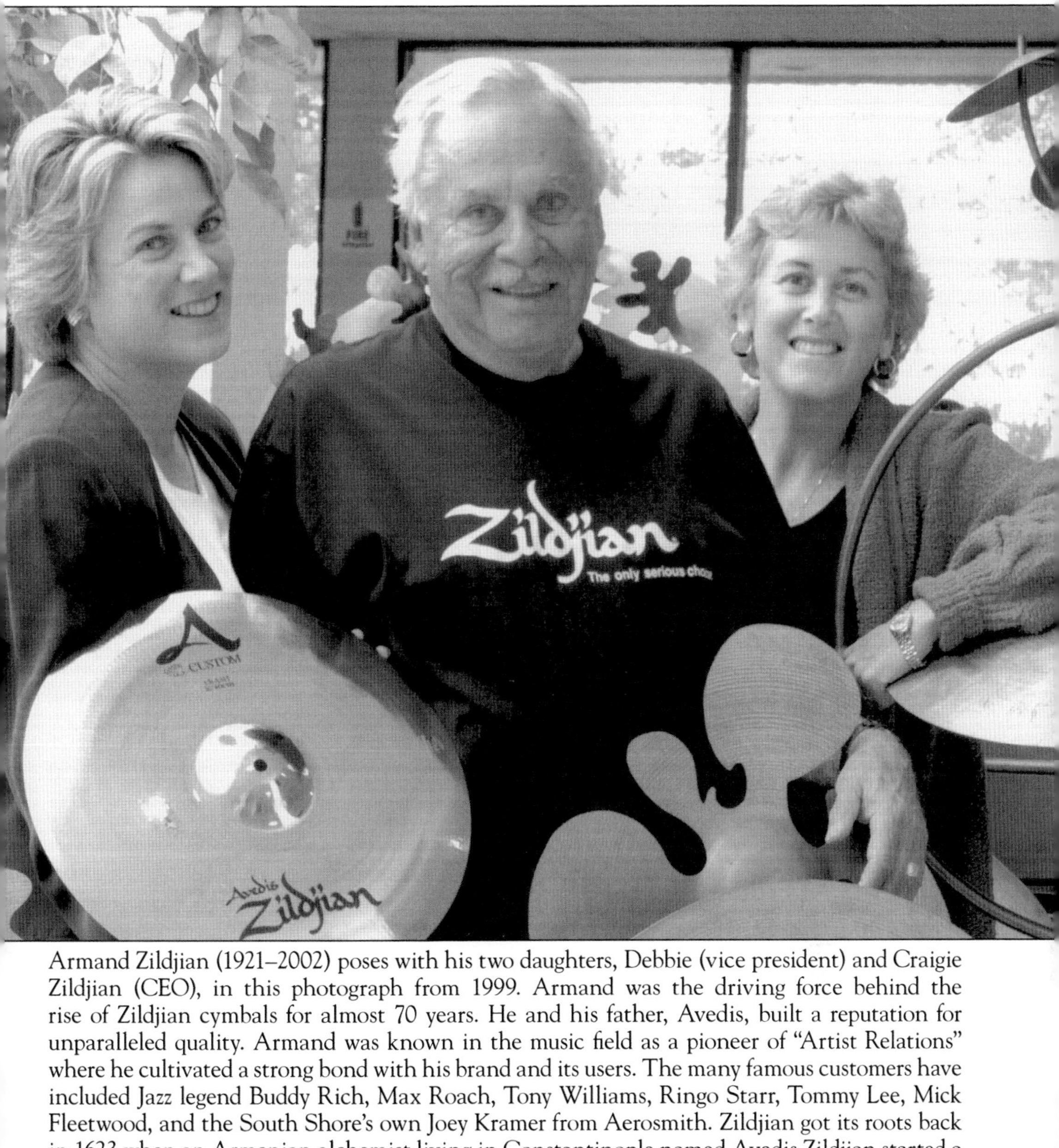

Armand Zildjian (1921–2002) poses with his two daughters, Debbie (vice president) and Craigie Zildjian (CEO), in this photograph from 1999. Armand was the driving force behind the rise of Zildjian cymbals for almost 70 years. He and his father, Avedis, built a reputation for unparalleled quality. Armand was known in the music field as a pioneer of "Artist Relations" where he cultivated a strong bond with his brand and its users. The many famous customers have included Jazz legend Buddy Rich, Max Roach, Tony Williams, Ringo Starr, Tommy Lee, Mick Fleetwood, and the South Shore's own Joey Kramer from Aerosmith. Zildjian got its roots back in 1623 when an Armenian alchemist living in Constantinople named Avedis Zildjian started a cymbal business. The secret alloy process is handed down generation to generation. In 1927, the Zildjian operations moved to America under the helm of Avedis Zildjian III. Zildjian has been officially recognized as the oldest continuously run family business in America.

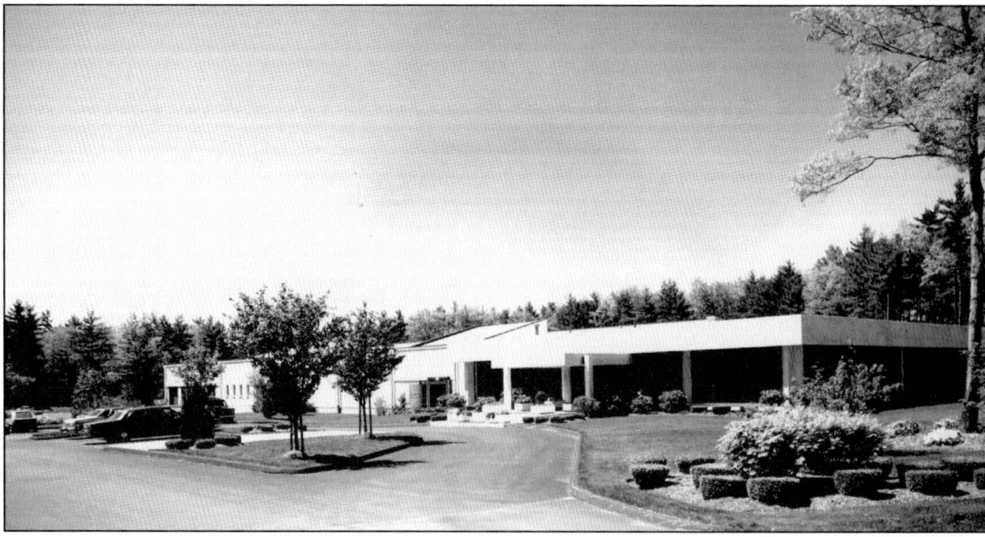

In 1973, Zildjian moved from its North Quincy plant to its current home in the Accord neighborhood of Norwell. This new home was opened in time to celebrate its 350th anniversary of manufacturing cymbals. The Zildjian factory has been constructed in many facets to ensure its standing as the premier cymbal maker in the world. Among the interesting attributes of the facility are a Drummers Hall of Fame, a drummer's lounge, and a performance center used primarily to educate local school groups.

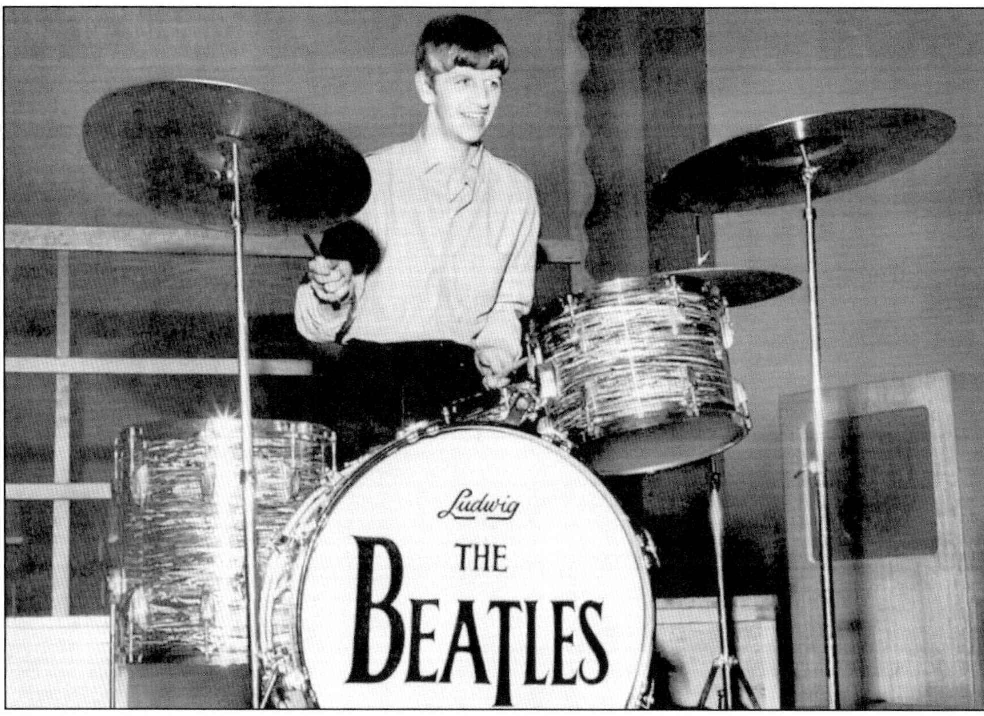

This 1963 photograph shows Ringo Starr, one of the Beatles, drumming on his Ludwig set and his 20-inch Avedis Zildjian Medium Ride cymbals. In 1964, the Zildjian cymbals became world famous after the Beatles appeared on the Ed Sullivan Show. This legendary drummer of the Fab Four is still a major proponent of the Zildjian brand to this day and uses them on his current tours.

Eight

Mount Blue

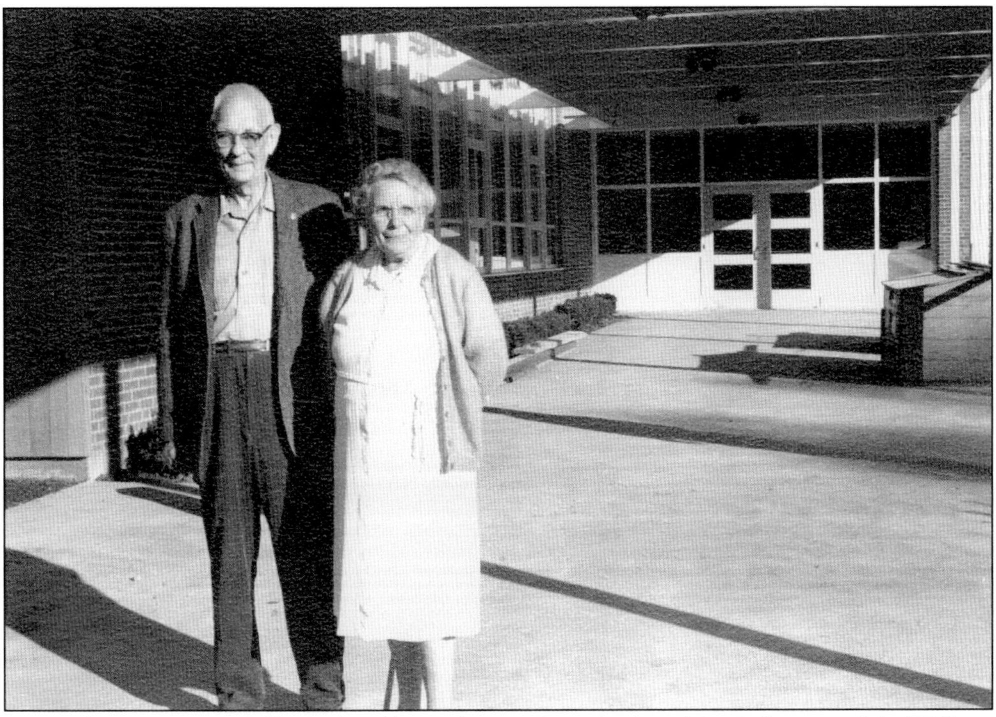

Pictured here are Capt. Bill Vinal and his wife in 1967 on the day of the dedication of the William Gould Vinal Elementary School. Vinal Elementary is located on Old Oaken Bucket Road near Norwell Avenue. "The Old Oaken Bucket" was a poem written by Samuel Woodworth, who lived in Scituate. The school was named for Captain Bill because of his generosity to the town of Norwell. The dedication speech was given by school committee member John C. Bond.

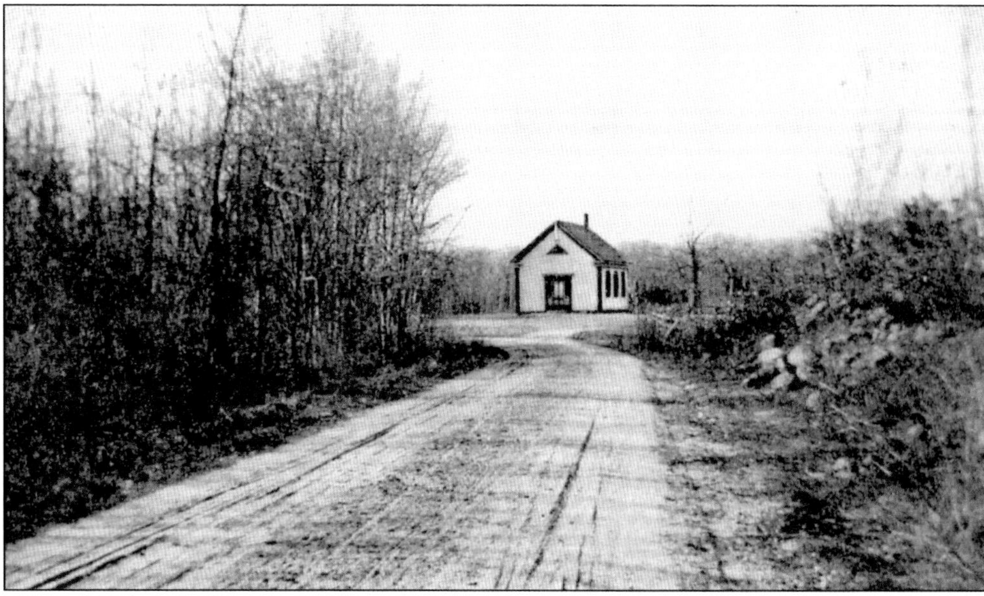

Situated back from the main roads stood Schoolhouse District Number Three. It was located in the Mount Blue section of Norwell at the junction of Grove and School Streets. The town had in total seven district schools for its residents. This particular school district was closed in 1901 due to the dwindling numbers of students. The town sought to consolidate the schools to better serve the needs of its students. The school District Number Three building was sold and moved to a private residence in Hingham on Hersey Street in 1919.

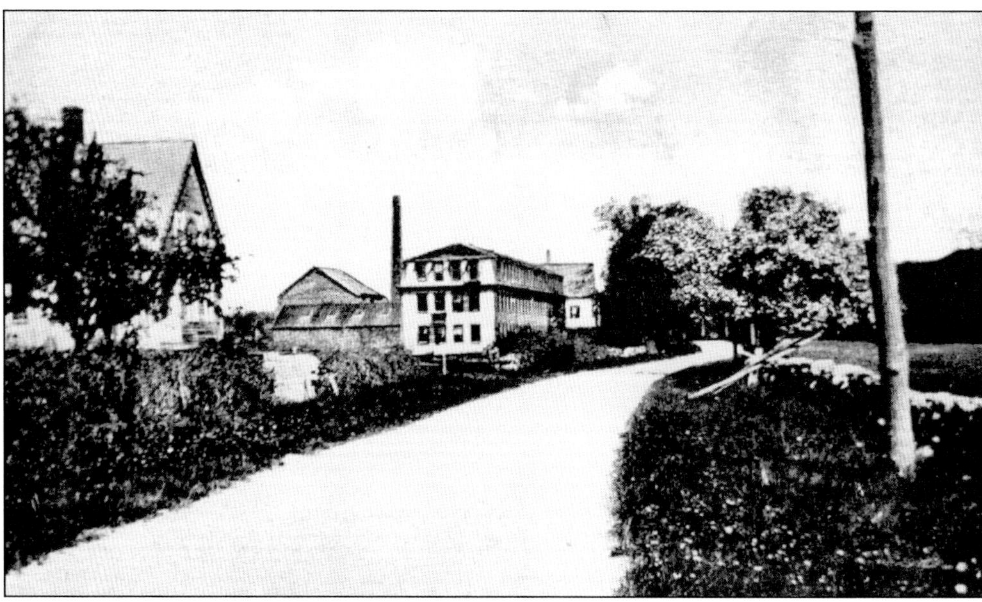

This large building located in the Mount Blue neighborhood of Norwell was the Litchfield Shoe Factory. This business situated at 35 Norwell Avenue was established in 1870, and by the time Norwell was officially named in 1888, there were over 100 shoemakers employed there. John Litchfield started the business, and his son George took over in 1889.

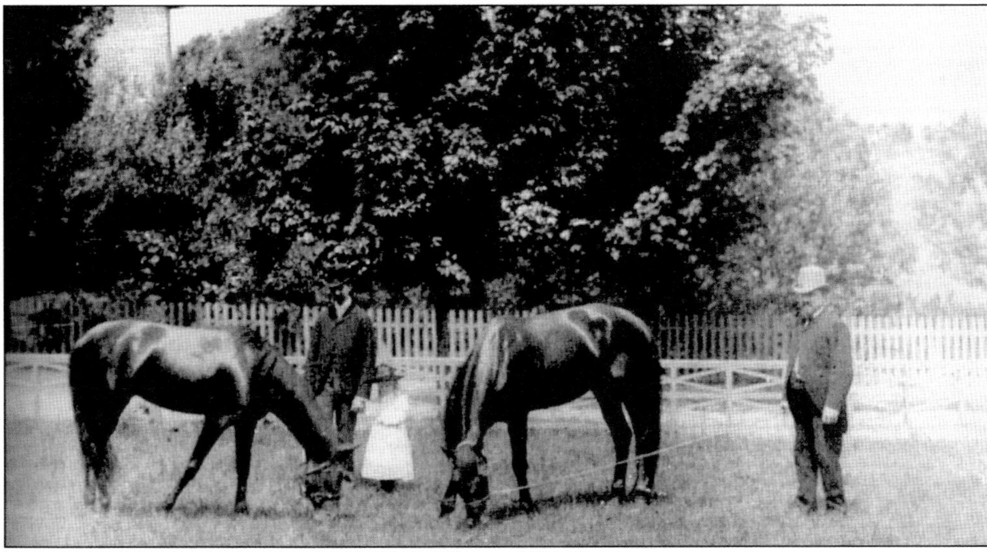

This photograph was taken in 1890 and shows, from left to right, Edward Cole, Bella Farrington, and Henry Norwell. Norwell was a successful dry goods merchant who immigrated to New York from Scotland in 1855. He ran a large operation on Winter Street in Boston, and he summered in South Scituate.

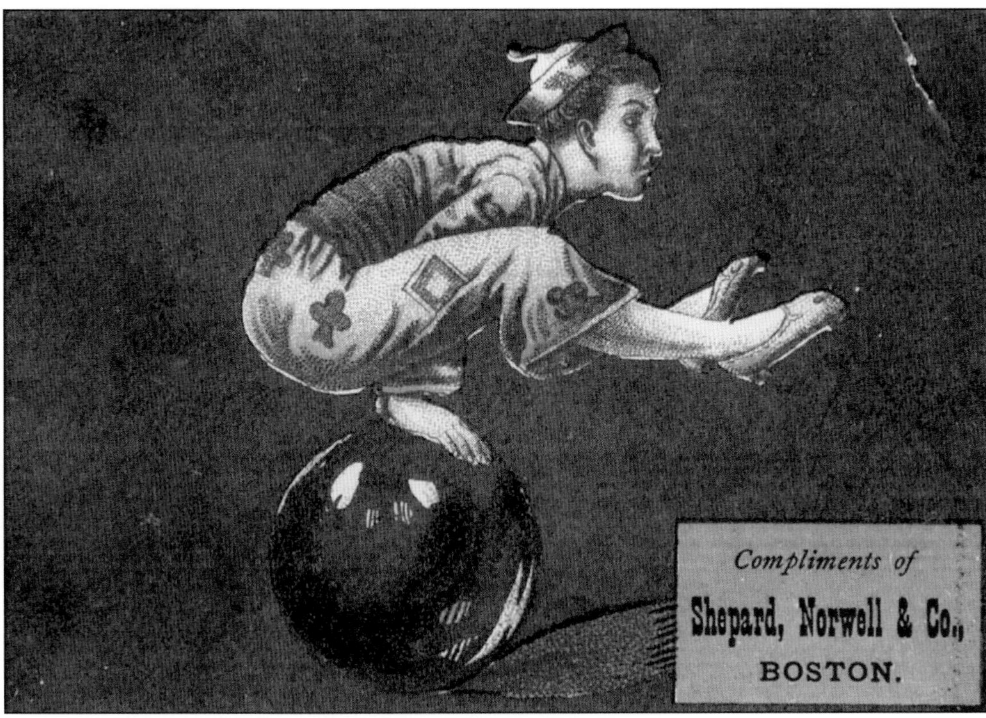

This is a 19th-century advertising trade card from Henry Norwell's Boston-based business. The advent of trade cards began after the Civil War as an effective national advertising medium. New consumer markets were rapidly opening up at the time, and manufacturers and retailers used these cards as a means to communicate their extraordinary variety of goods to the American public.

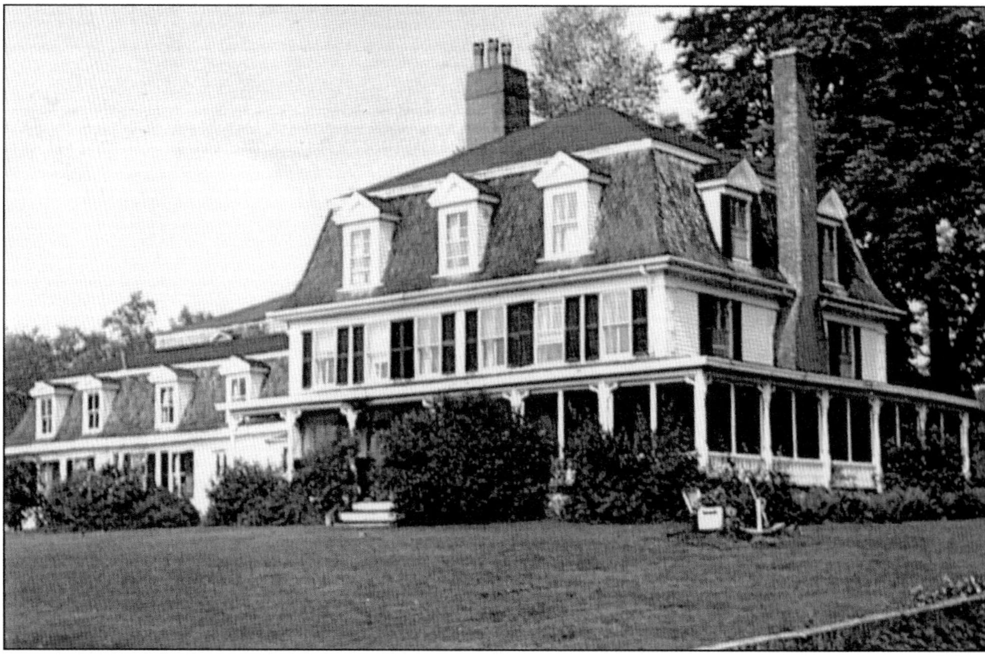

Henry Norwell's summer residence is shown here. Because of his wealth, a committee of South Scituate residents asked him to endow a school. He was not interested in giving funds for a school named after him. He instead contributed $25,000 to the upkeep of roads over a 10-year period. In 1888, the South Scituate Town Meeting voted to change the name of their town to Norwell.

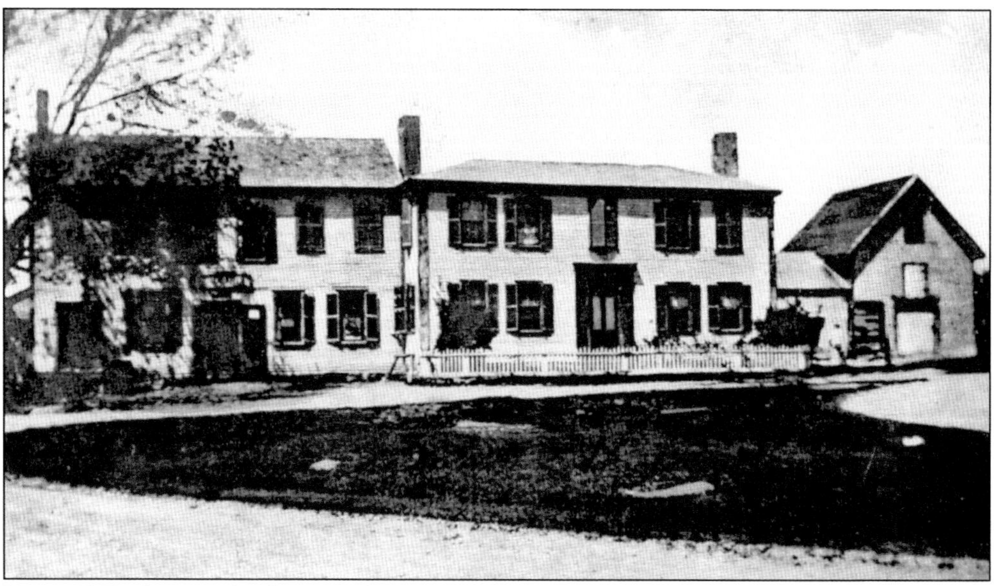

Henry F. Ford was a shopkeeper who ran a store and post office at Bryant's Corner in Mount Blue. Many years later, his nephew Atwood continued on the store operations until the early part of the 1920s. Several families subsequently conducted business at Ford's Store until 1930. There are no signs of Ford's store on Norwell Avenue as it was torn down in the early 1930s

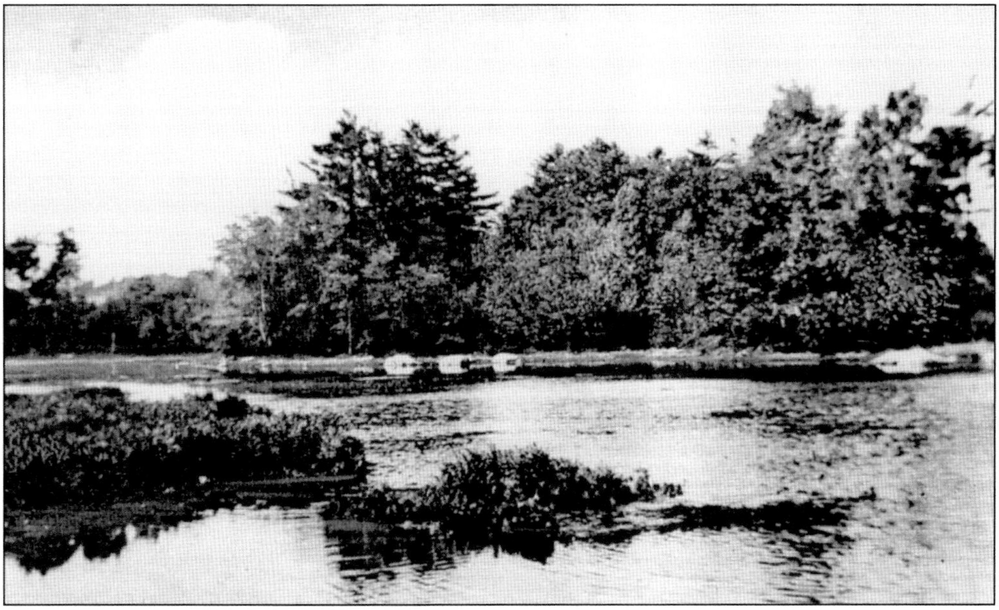

This pond is situated in Mount Blue and is located off of Mount Hope Street. Jon Bond remembers driving by the pond in a school bus when he was on his way to the Osborn Elementary School. The pond is mainly filled in now. The pond was named for Joseph Hackett, who was a Maine lumberman. He and his son Wallace purchased the Stockbridge Mill and operated it for the latter part of the 19th century.

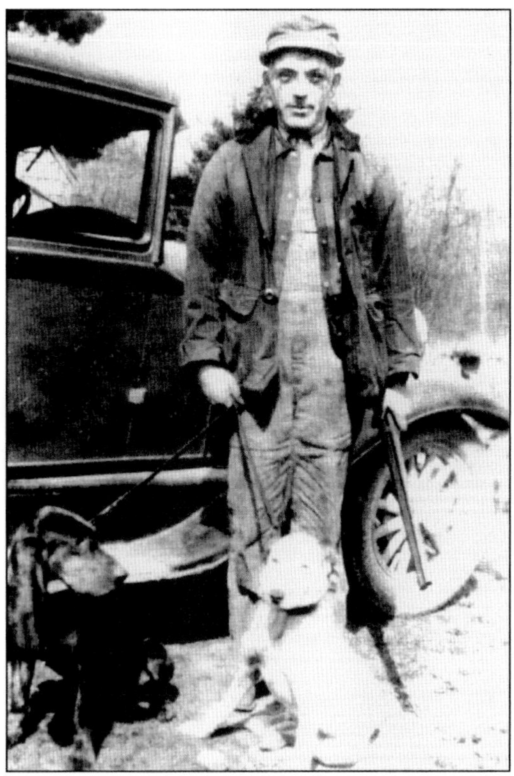

Pictured here is Eddie Winslow with his hunting dogs Spud and Tut in 1935. Known as an expert marksman by his fellow Norwell residents, Winslow hunted fox. He also tended to five acres of gardens at his Bowker Street home. Most popular of his vegetables was the peas on July 4. It was said at the time that all of Norwell would come to Winslow's house to buy his peas for their traditional salmon dinner on the Fourth of July.

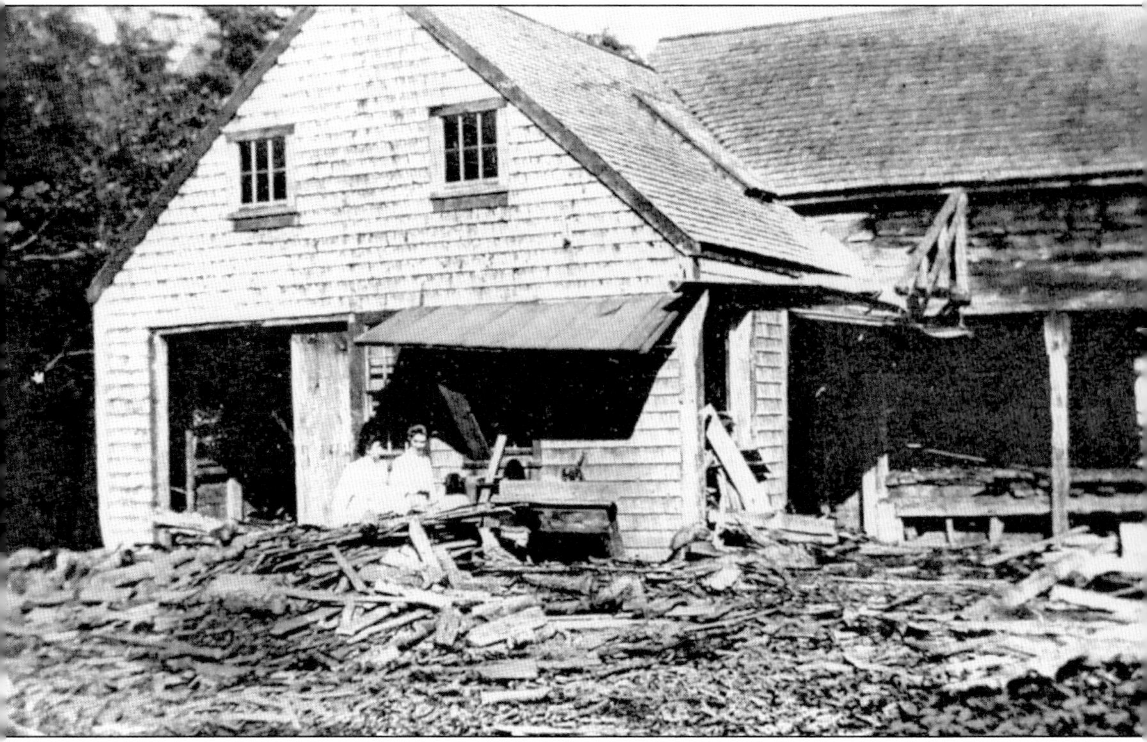

Located in the Mount Blue neighborhood of Norwell was Richardson's Mill. Mount Blue was originally called Groundsell Brook. Mount Blue is considered a glacial hill, and to reach its summit one has to climb the grounds of Stockbridge Cemetery near the junction of School and Mount Blue Streets. At the top, one is afforded a view of the ocean and the towns of Hanover and Hingham. This particular mill had a long history dating back to 1752 when Samuel Stockbridge opened his mill near a pond off Mount Hope Street. The mill was situated in an area that is difficult to decipher whether it was operating in South Scituate or Scituate. It was generally considered to serve both towns. The Richardson brothers were the last owners of the mill and manufactured boxes there. The mill was closed in 1917.

Nine

North River Theater

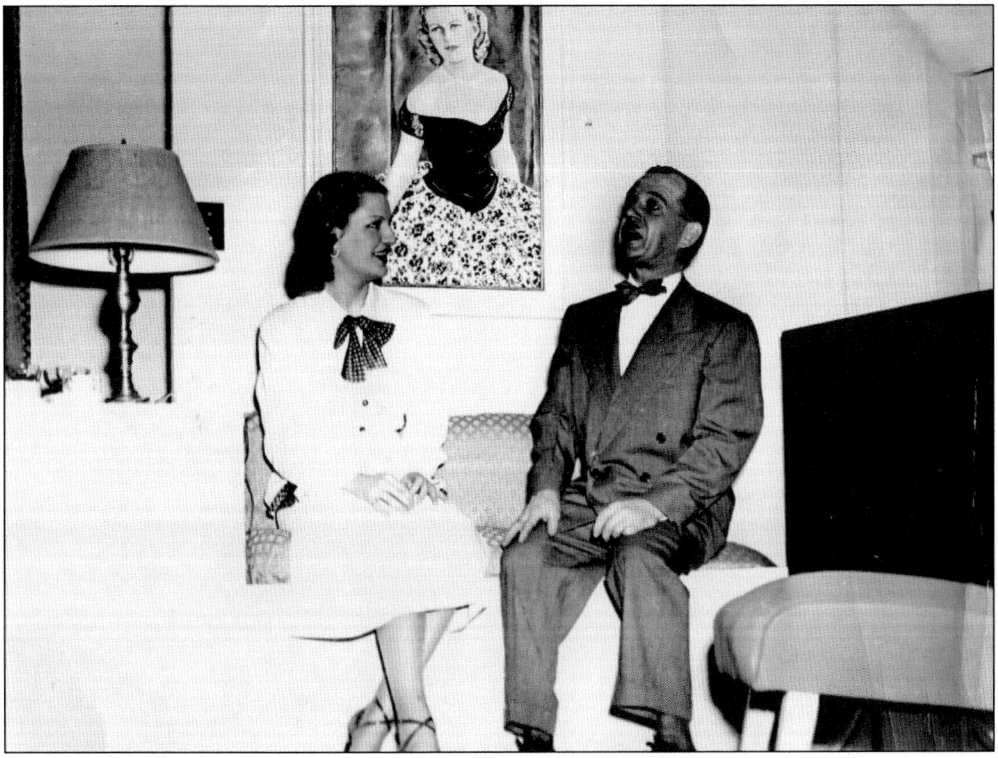

Located at 513 River Street is the venerable North River Theater. This community theater operates as a non-profit organization and has been putting on performances since 1927. Originally, the theater was a schoolhouse, built in 1865, which was used for the residents of the Church Hill neighborhood of Norwell. It was known as the Schoolyard District Number Seven. Seen here is a photograph of Ruth Chipman Bailey and Emery Leonard acting in the 1952 production of *Laura*.

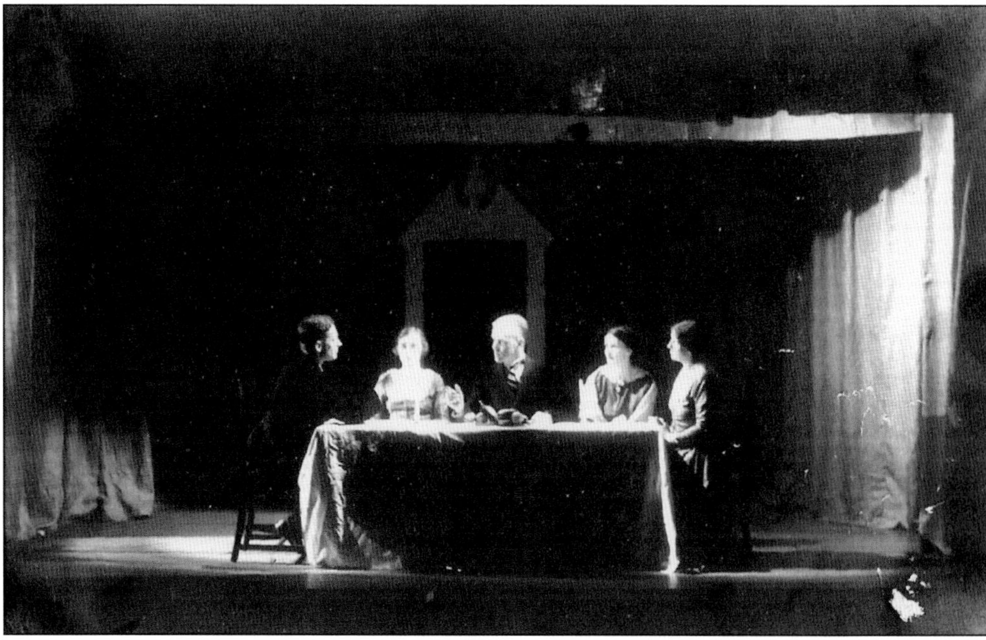

The North River Theater has wonderful detailed archives, and this photograph is a relic from its storied past. Shown is a scene from *The Long Christmas Dinner* in June 1932 starring Homer Snow, Martha Whiting, Gentry Clark, Alice Weeks, and Lillian Clark. *The Long Christmas Dinner* is a one-act play first performed at the Yale University Theatre on November 5, 1931.

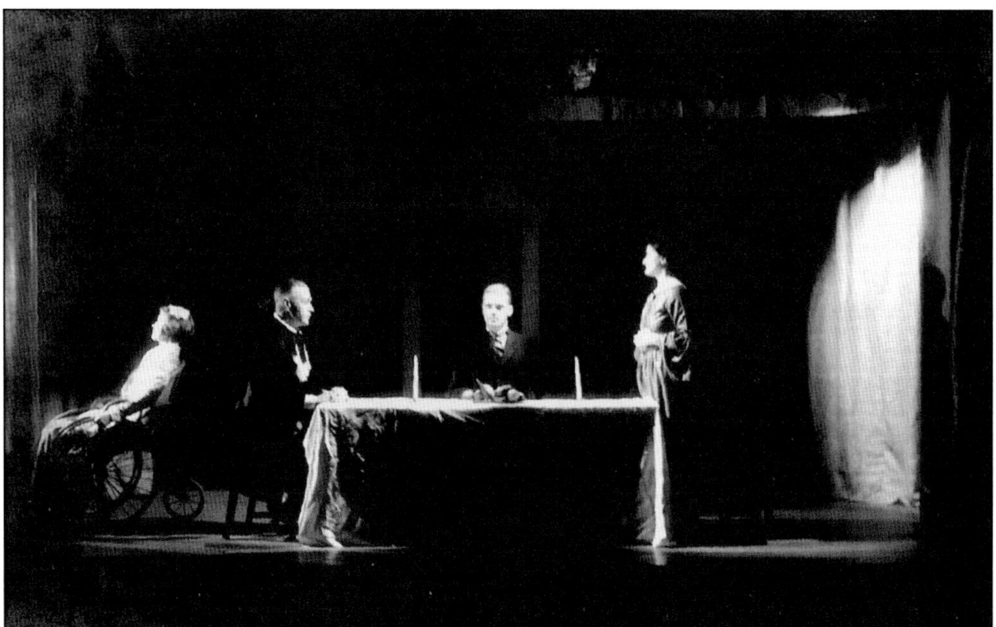

The play is about the interaction of four generations of the Bayard family and its annual Christmas dinners set over the course of 90 years. The play was written by well known American playwright Thornton Wilder, who was also responsible for other famous works such as *Our Town, Matchmaker,* and *The Skin of Our Teeth.*

This is a playbill for the Gilbert and Sullivan comic opera called *The Yeoman of The Guard.* This musical comedy was written by the legendary English playwright W. S. Gilbert in collaboration with composer Sir Arthur Sullivan. This production was staged at the Cushing Memorial Hall in Norwell Center to accommodate the large crowds expected for the musical.

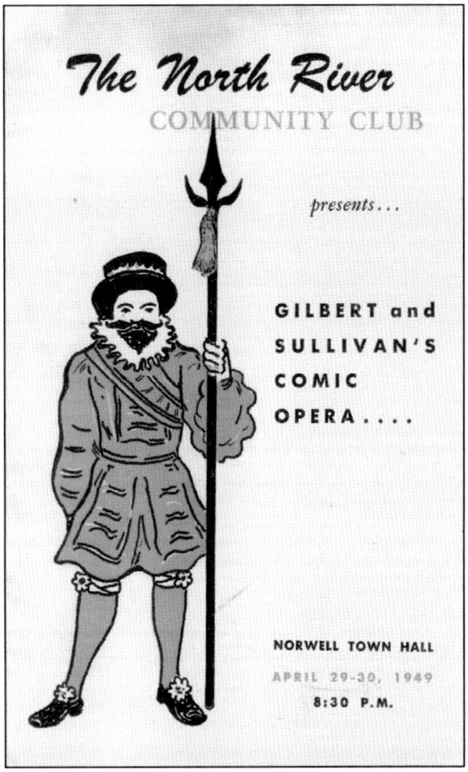

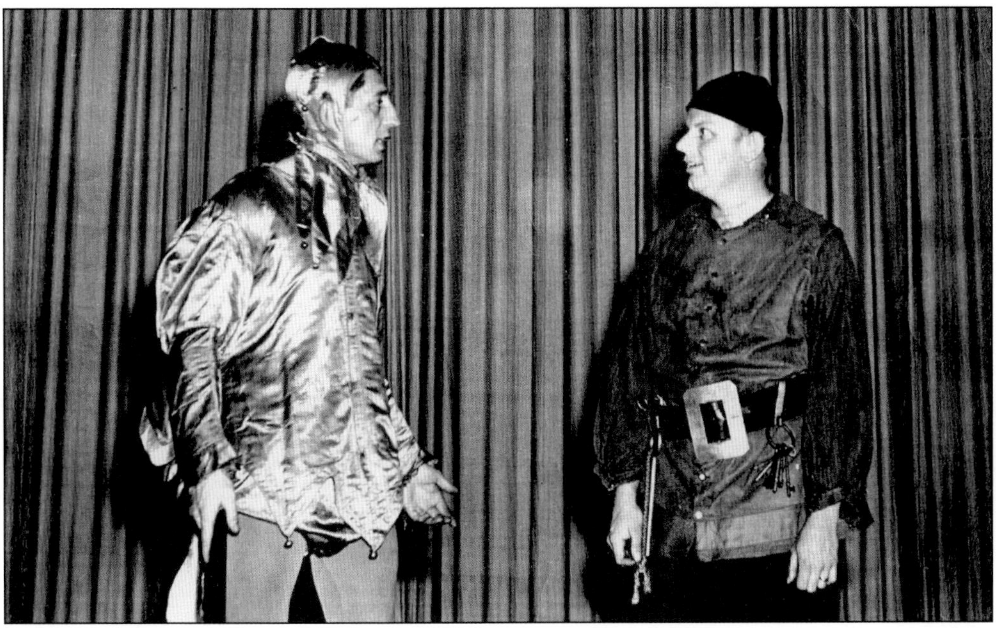

Written in Victorian England, the musical centers around a 16th-century strolling jester who finds himself embroiled in a risky intrigue at the Tower Of London. The musical premiered at the famed Savoy Theatre in London on October 3, 1888. Playing the jester is Jackson Bailey, and opposite him in this scene is J. Leonard Arnold. The photographs of the show were taken by Lloyd West.

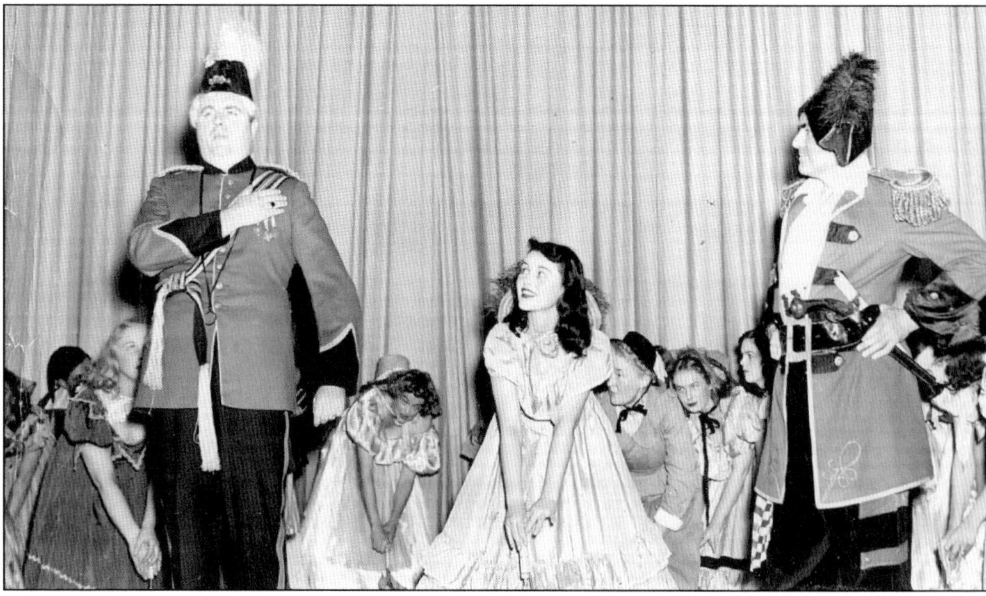

This musical was Gilbert and Sullivan's favorite work but has not been as popular as the other works. Sir Arthur Sullivan surmised that perhaps it is the tragic ending. Identified here are Priscilla Merritt Spradlin, Doug Reilly, Eleanor Causer, Joan Wallace, Kay Conant, and Ralph Gordon. Ushers who worked at the musical included Mrs. James Shearer, Mrs. Charles Rounds, Mrs. Thomas Barstow, Mrs. T. Curtis Power, Miss Joan Cruff, Miss Hope Poor, and Mrs. Hobart Wright.

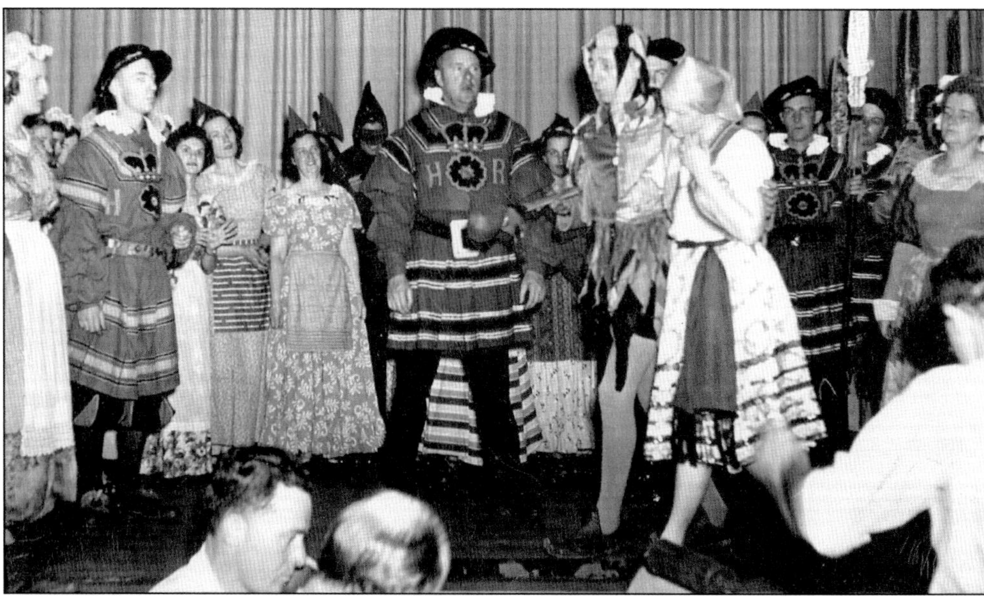

Gilbert and Sullivan's creative stable of musicals included *Pirates of Penzance*, *HMS Pinafore*, *the Mikado*, and *the Sorcerer*. In a pivotal scene of the *Yeoman of The Guard*, the jester played by Jackson Bailey is led off stage. The orchestra members for the play included Mrs. Arnold Weeks, Arthur Carlson, Richard Berry, Jane Mitchell, Evan Bailey, Jesse Story, Roberta Lehr, David Quinlan, John Prouty, and Ruth Lincoln. Identified here are Ruth Chipman Bailey, Alice Wadsworth, Pauline Hanson, and Bea West.

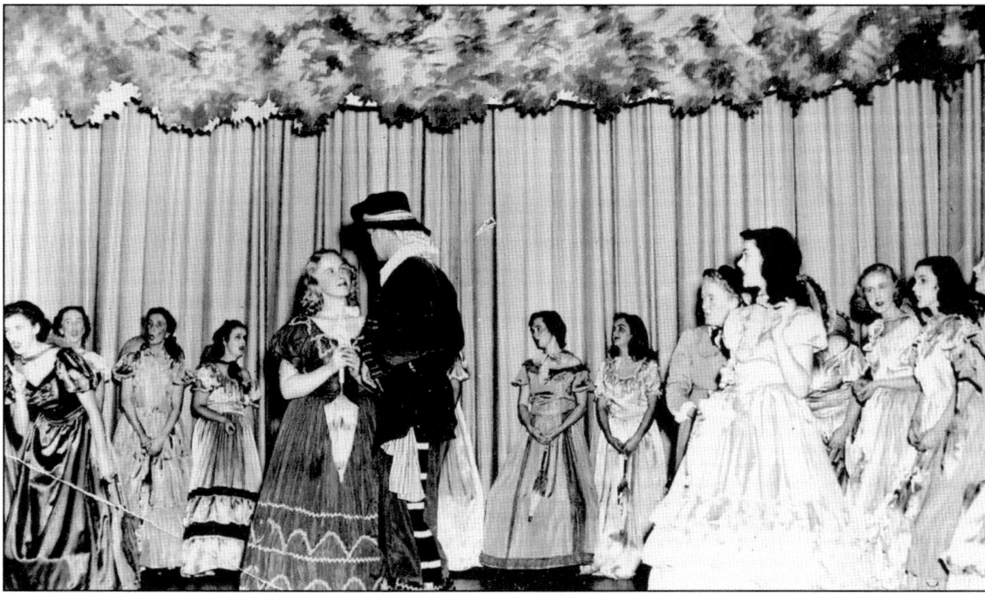

The Yeoman of The Guard was written with the intent to be a showcase of W. S. Sullivan's trademark satire of the times. North River Committee Chairmen included J. Lee Turner, Mrs. James MacDonald, Mrs. Alden Wells, Mrs. Ray Wallace, Mrs. Stearns Poor, Mrs. A. Ralph Gordon, and Mrs. Robert Currie. Priscilla Merritt Spradlin is featured prominently in this scene with Clark Atwater, Alice Davis, and Joan Wallace. Priscilla was current Norwell selectman Richard Merritt's aunt.

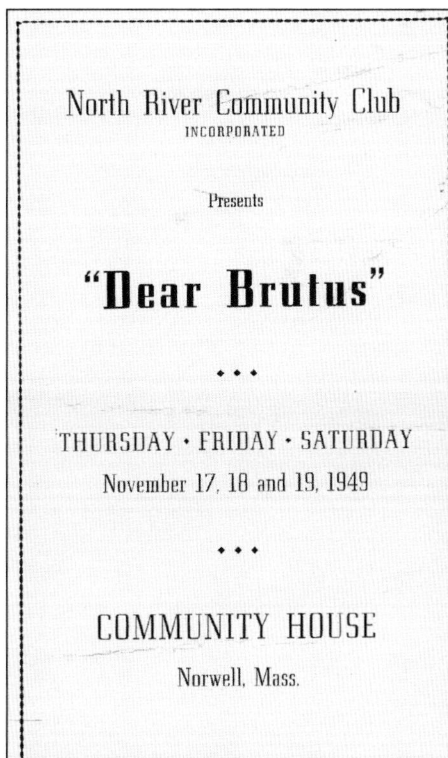

North River Community Club
INCORPORATED

Presents

"Dear Brutus"

• • •

THURSDAY • FRIDAY • SATURDAY
November 17, 18 and 19, 1949

• • •

COMMUNITY HOUSE

Norwell, Mass.

Shown here is the playbill for the production of *Dear Brutus* by famed Scottish playwright Sir James Matthew Barrie. Barrie is better known as the creator of *Peter Pan*. *Dear Brutus* was written in 1917, and the story centers around eight people who enter into a magic wood and come out of these woods as markedly different people.

"Dear Brutus"

A Comedy in Three Acts

By

J. M. Barrie

Cast of Characters

MRS. COADE	BEATRICE C. BAILEY
MRS. DEARTH	ESTELLE GORDON
MRS. PURDIE	BARBARA FORD
JOANNA TROUT	BARBARA LEONARD
LADY CAROLINE LANEY	BETTY WALSH
MARGARET	MARTHA BAILEY
MATEY	FRANK ROUNDS
LOB	EMERY LEONARD
MR. PURDIE	ROLLIN BAILEY
MR. COADE	CLINTON V. MacCOY
MR. DEARTH	FRANK SWEETSER

Synopsis of Scenes

Act. 1 Lob's House
Act. 2 The Wood
Act. 3 The same as Act 1.

Director	Sylvia Bigelow
Business Manager	John D. Davis
Production Manager	Louise Gordon

Staging and Sets

Mrs. Emery Leonard, *Chairman*

Dr. & Mrs. Charles Rounds	Mrs. Richard McMullan
Mr. & Mrs. Richard H. Rice	Mr. Donald DesGranges
Mr. & Mrs. H. P. Causer	Mr. G. H. Repass
Mrs. W. Clarke Atwater	Mr. Emery Leonard

Mr. William Ford

Publicity
Mrs. Richard McMullan

Hand Properties
Mrs. Alden Wells

Lighting
Mr. Lee Turner

Make-up
Mrs. Peirce Fuller

Prompter
Mr. James F. Barron, Jr.

Sound Effects
Mr. Neal Gray

Tickets

Mrs. Schuyler Dillon	Mrs. Ernest Sparrell
Mrs. Ray H. Wallace	Mrs. John D. Davis

Dear Brutus was a comedy that transforms people into what they might have become if they had not entered the magic wood. The play is set in a wood-paneled drawing-room of an English country house, to which a group of guests have been invited by a mysterious old man called Lob played by Emery Leonard.

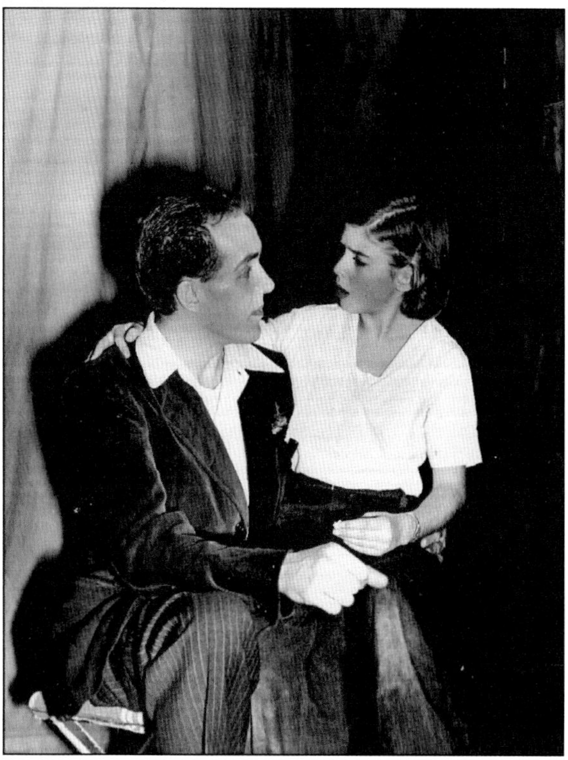

The play's title is taken from the lines in William Shakespeare's play *Julius Caesar*, "The fault, dear Brutus, is not in our stars, but in ourselves, that we are underlings." Shown here is Frank Sweetser playing the part of Mr. Dearth with Martha Bailey playing Margaret.

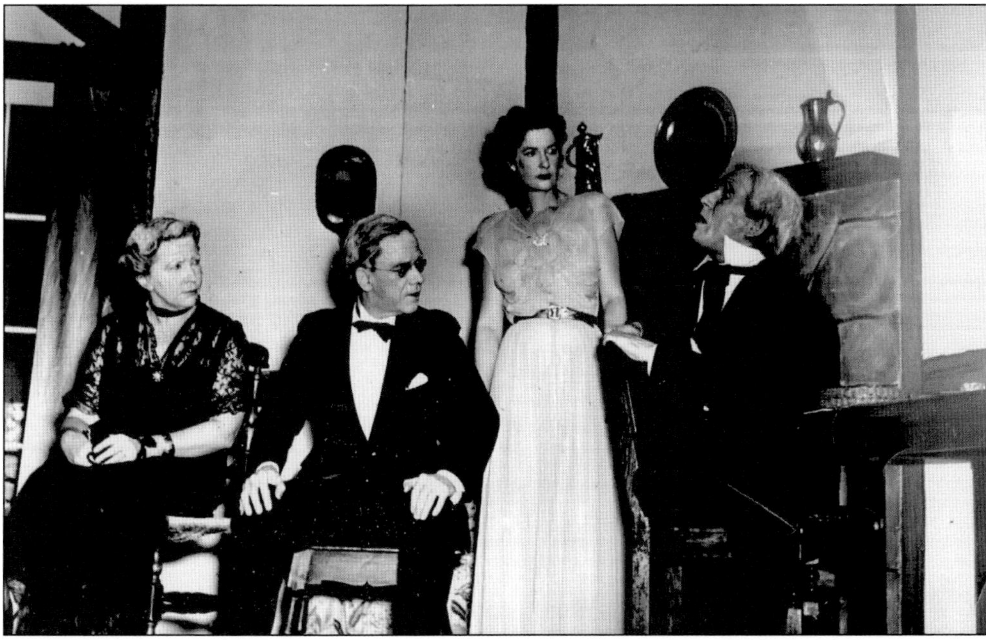

The characters are supposed to disappear into the woods and live a different life for one night. When they emerge, they see each other in a totally different light and begin to question themselves. Shown in a scene from *Dear Brutus* are, from left to right, Bea Bailey, Clinton V. MacCoy, Betty Walsh, and Emery Leonard.

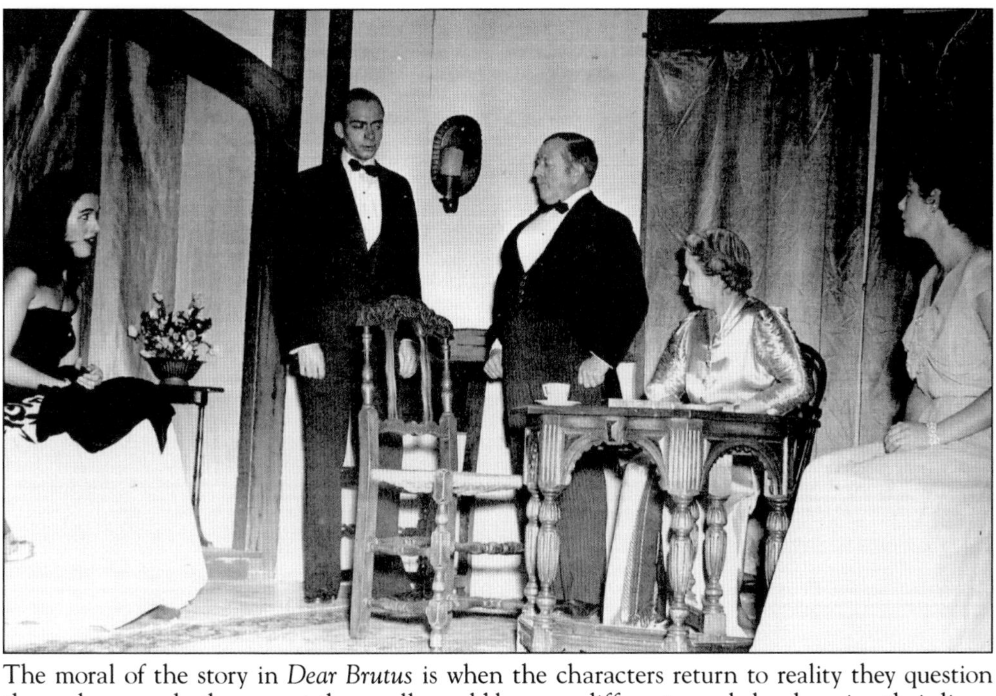

The moral of the story in *Dear Brutus* is when the characters return to reality they question themselves on whether or not they really could become different people by changing their lives. Pictured in the first act, from left to right, in Lob's House is Barbara Leonard, Rollin Bailey, Frank Rounds, Bea Bailey, and Betty Walsh.

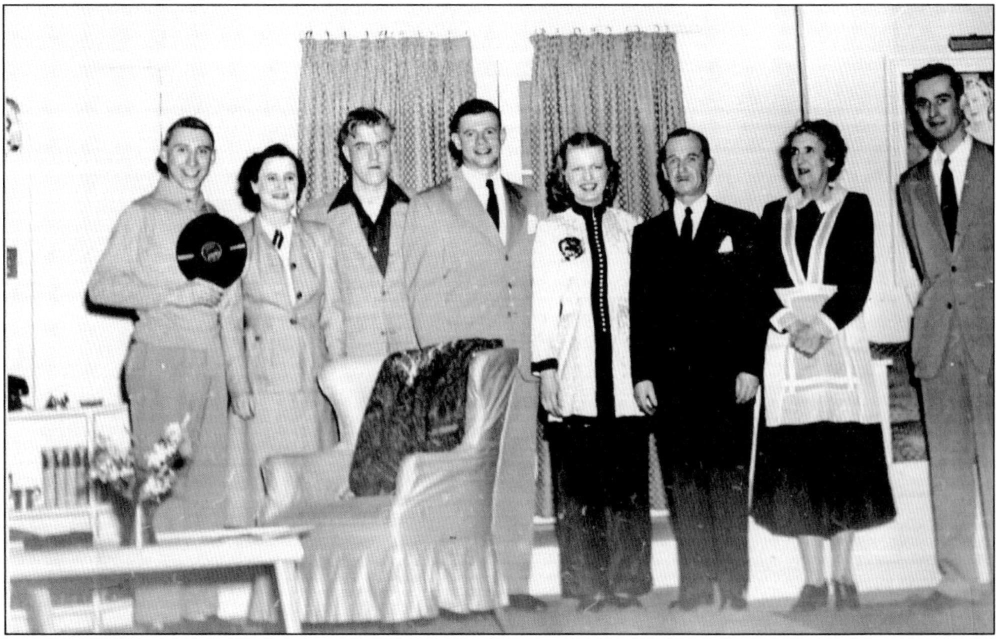

Laura is about a detective who investigates the murder of a young woman. While conducting the investigation, he becomes fascinated by her portrait and soon everyone becomes a suspect. Identified here for a curtain call are cast members David Turner, Barbara Sweetser, James Leonard, Gibbons Warren, Ruth Chipman, Emery Leonard, and Lillian Clark.

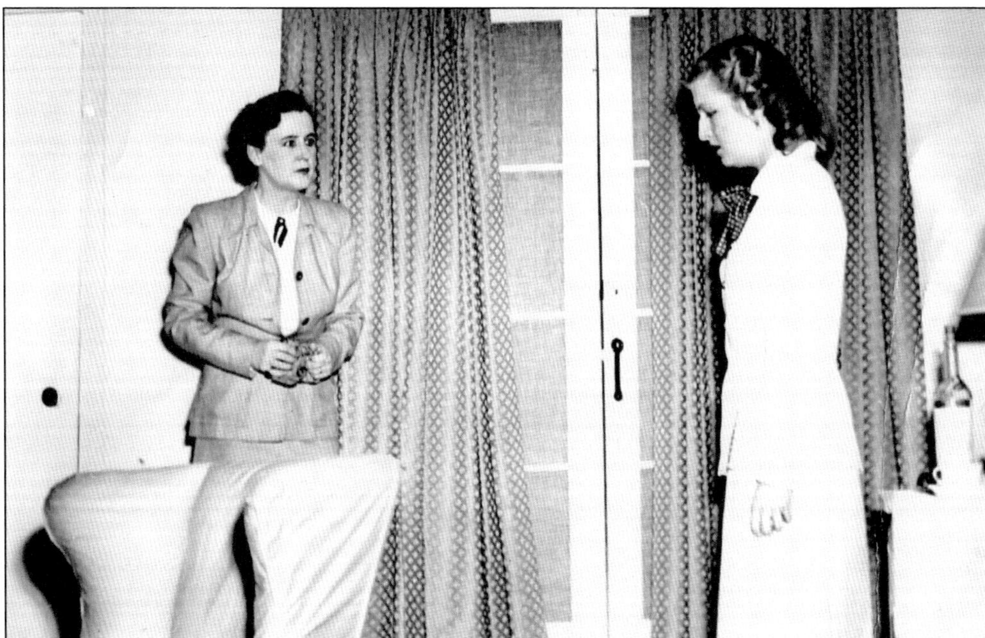

Laura is a mystery written by Vera Caspary and George Sklar. It opened at the Cort Theater on Broadway on June 26, 1947. The North River Theater production debuted on March 6, 1952. *Laura* was also a film classic from 1944, starring Gene Tierney. Shown here in a scene are Barbara Sweetser and Ruth Chipman.

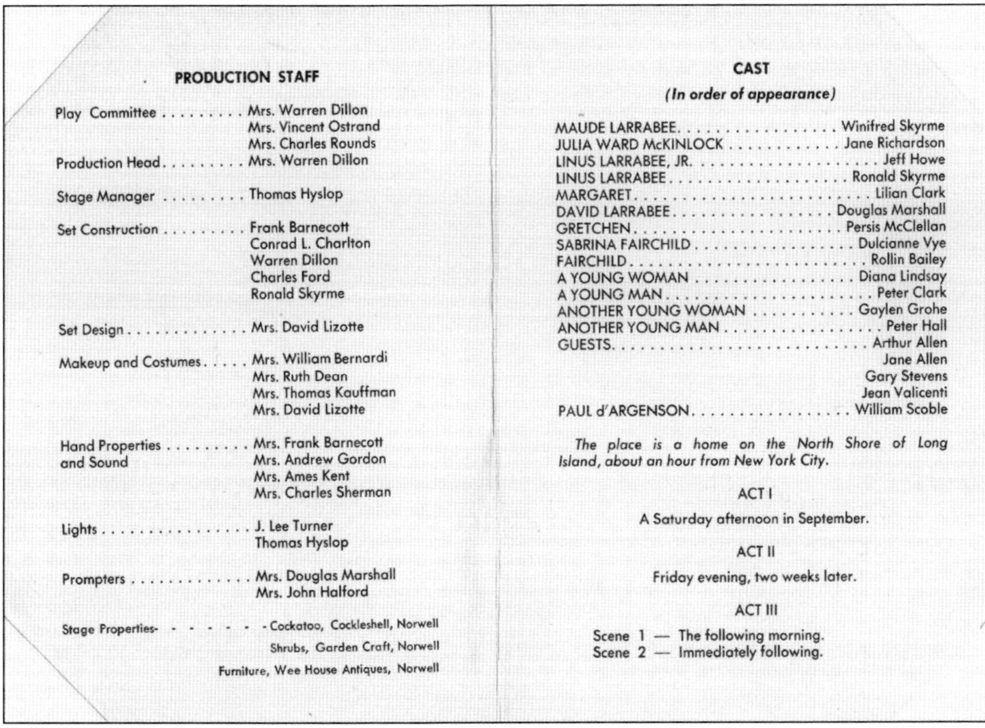

PRODUCTION STAFF

Play Committee . . . . Mrs. Warren Dillon
Mrs. Vincent Ostrand
Mrs. Charles Rounds

Production Head. . . . . Mrs. Warren Dillon

Stage Manager . . . . Thomas Hyslop

Set Construction . . . . Frank Barnecott
Conrad L. Charlton
Warren Dillon
Charles Ford
Ronald Skyrme

Set Design. . . . . Mrs. David Lizotte

Makeup and Costumes. . . . . Mrs. William Bernardi
Mrs. Ruth Dean
Mrs. Thomas Kauffman
Mrs. David Lizotte

Hand Properties . . . . Mrs. Frank Barnecott
and Sound Mrs. Andrew Gordon
Mrs. Ames Kent
Mrs. Charles Sherman

Lights . . . . J. Lee Turner
Thomas Hyslop

Prompters . . . . Mrs. Douglas Marshall
Mrs. John Halford

Stage Properties- - - - - - Cockatoo, Cockleshell, Norwell
Shrubs, Garden Craft, Norwell
Furniture, Wee House Antiques, Norwell

CAST

(In order of appearance)

MAUDE LARRABEE. . . . . Winifred Skyrme
JULIA WARD McKINLOCK . . . . Jane Richardson
LINUS LARRABEE, JR. . . . . Jeff Howe
LINUS LARRABEE. . . . . Ronald Skyrme
MARGARET. . . . . Lilian Clark
DAVID LARRABEE. . . . . Douglas Marshall
GRETCHEN. . . . . Persis McClellan
SABRINA FAIRCHILD . . . . Dulcianne Vye
FAIRCHILD. . . . . Rollin Bailey
A YOUNG WOMAN . . . . Diana Lindsay
A YOUNG MAN. . . . . Peter Clark
ANOTHER YOUNG WOMAN . . . . Gaylen Grohe
ANOTHER YOUNG MAN. . . . . Peter Hall
GUESTS. . . . . Arthur Allen
Jane Allen
Gary Stevens
Jean Valicenti
PAUL d'ARGENSON. . . . . William Scoble

The place is a home on the North Shore of Long Island, about an hour from New York City.

ACT I

A Saturday afternoon in September.

ACT II

Friday evening, two weeks later.

ACT III

Scene 1 — The following morning.
Scene 2 — Immediately following.

Here is a playbill for the North River Community Club production of *Sabrina Fair* from October 25, 1962. The romantic comedy was written by Samuel Taylor and premiered at the National Theatre in November 1953. The Broadway stage play was the basis for the 1954 film *Sabrina* starring Humphrey Bogart, William Holden, and Audrey Hepburn. It was later remade starring Harrison Ford.

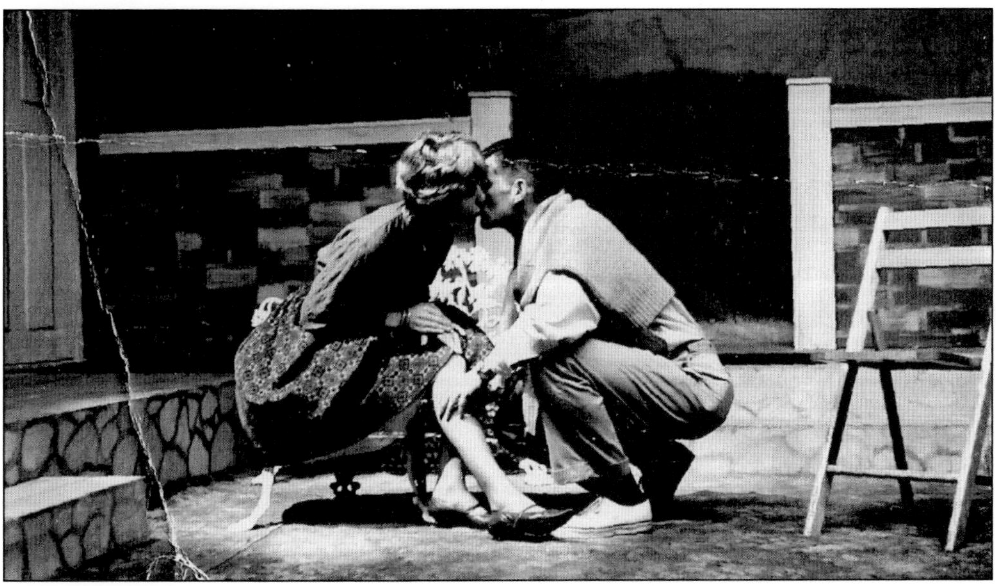

The story for the North River production is about a young lady named Sabrina Fairchild, played by Dulcianne Vye, who falls in love with her family's chauffer named David Larrabee, played by David Marshall. Shown here in an embrace are the principal players Vye and Marshall.

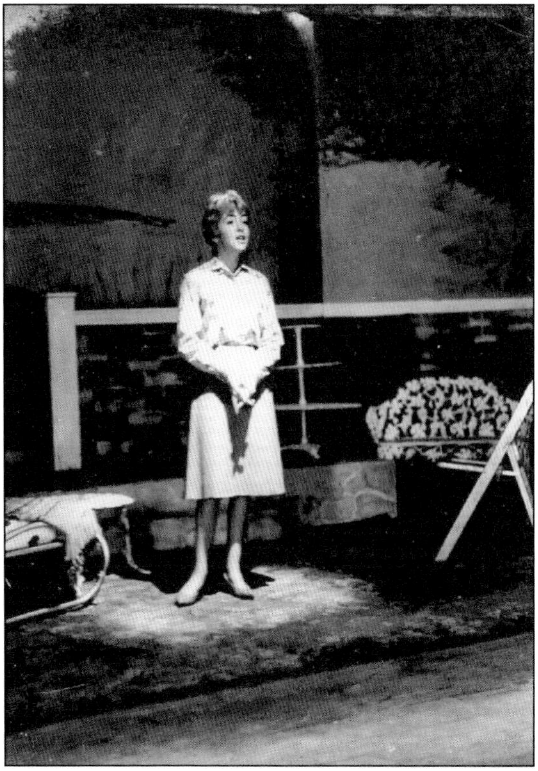

In a solo scene, Dulcianne Vye is shown stating her case for the womanizing David Larrabee. The managers of the North River Community Club who worked on this play included Mr. and Mrs. Harold Ross, Mrs. Charles Ford, Mrs. John B. Arnold, Mrs. William T. Graham Jr., and Mrs. William T. Ritchie.

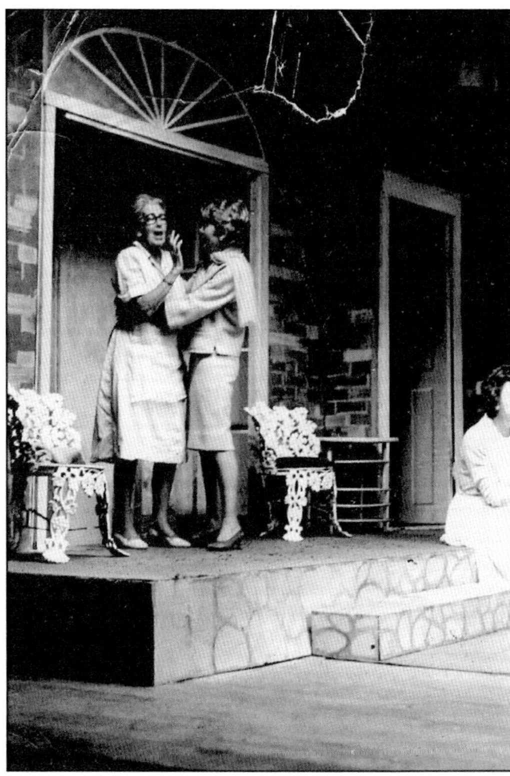

Lillian Clark, playing the part of Margaret, is shown here acting out a scene with Dulcianne Vye. Clark was a longtime member of the North River Community Club for over five decades. Rollin Bailey, a 95-year-old Norwell resident, also acted in several plays through the years including *Sabrina Fair*. Ushers for the show were Kirsten Ostrand, Patricia Ritchie, Linda Burbank, Lynn Ritchie, Mary Jane Stella, and Deborah Strohn.

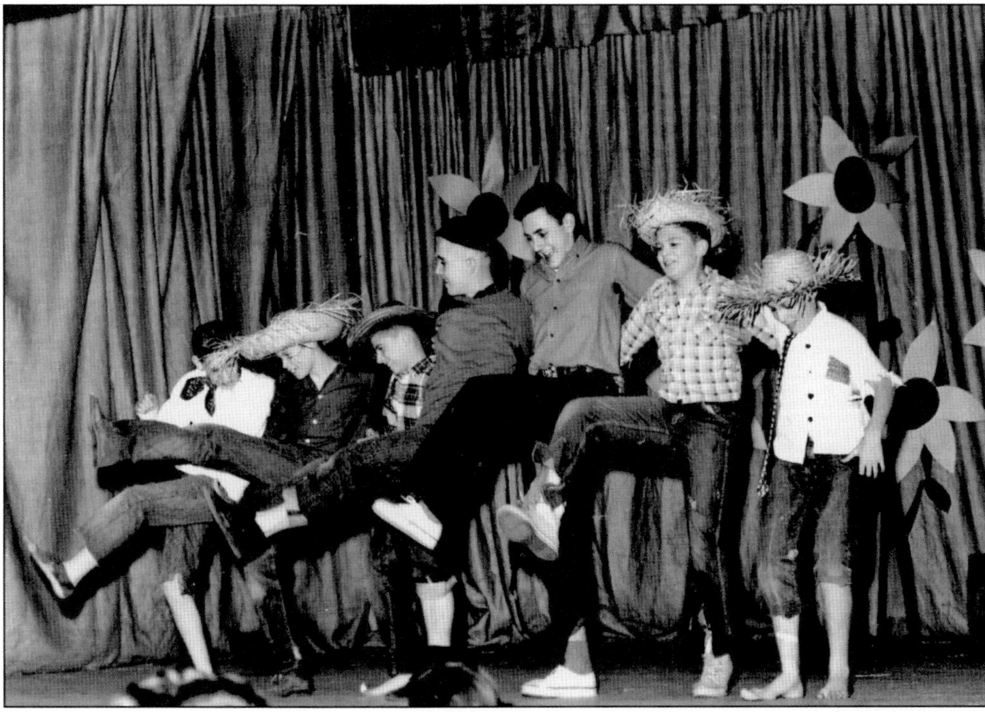

This early 1950s production was a musical variety show called *Skits and Variety*. Among performers seen here doing a musical number are brothers Peter MacKay and Benny MacKay from Scituate. The North River Community Club Incorporated was an active club with well over 100 families from towns comprised of Norwell, Hanover, Scituate, and Marshfield.

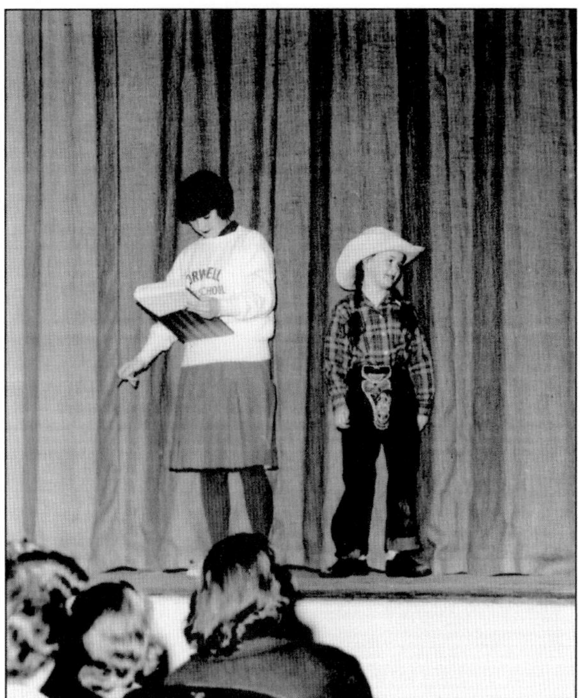

Betsy Reardon, wearing her Norwell High School sweatshirt, is shown here in a musical number with Bess Gordon during the *Skits and Variety* show.

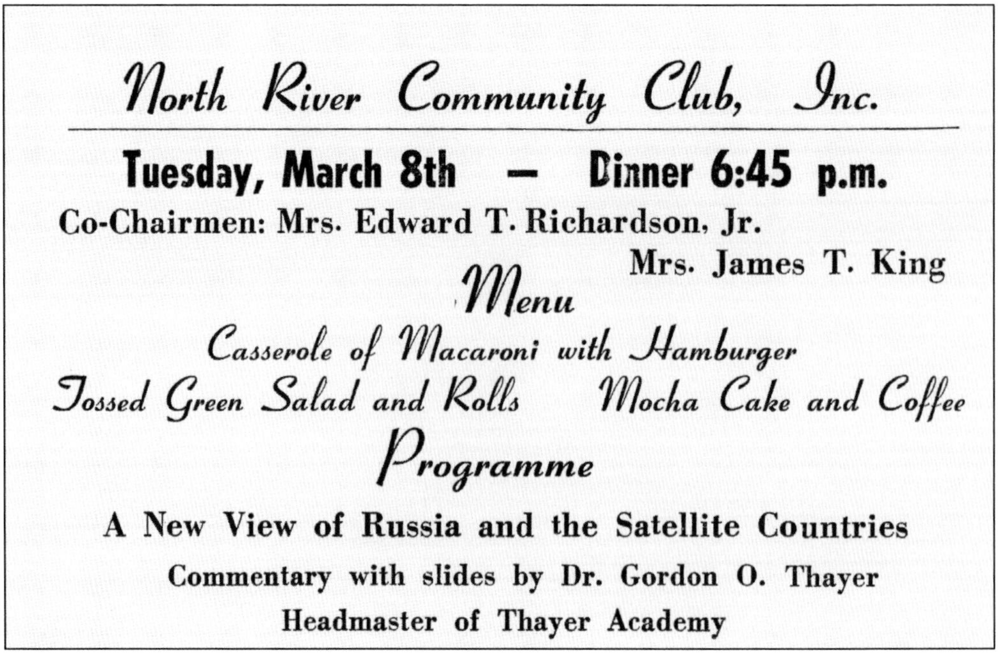
North River Community Club, Inc.

Tuesday, March 8th — Dinner 6:45 p.m.

Co-Chairmen: Mrs. Edward T. Richardson, Jr.
Mrs. James T. King

Menu

Casserole of Macaroni with Hamburger
Tossed Green Salad and Rolls *Mocha Cake and Coffee*

Programme

A New View of Russia and the Satellite Countries
Commentary with slides by Dr. Gordon O. Thayer
Headmaster of Thayer Academy

In addition to putting on dramatic arts at its River Street Theater, the North River Community Club also conducted many activities for its members. Shown here is an invitation card for a 1966 dinner program. Notice the menu was quite simple but the speaker Dr. Thayer from Thayer Academy must have been impressive indeed. At the time, the Cold War was still raging on and the topic seemed very pertinent.

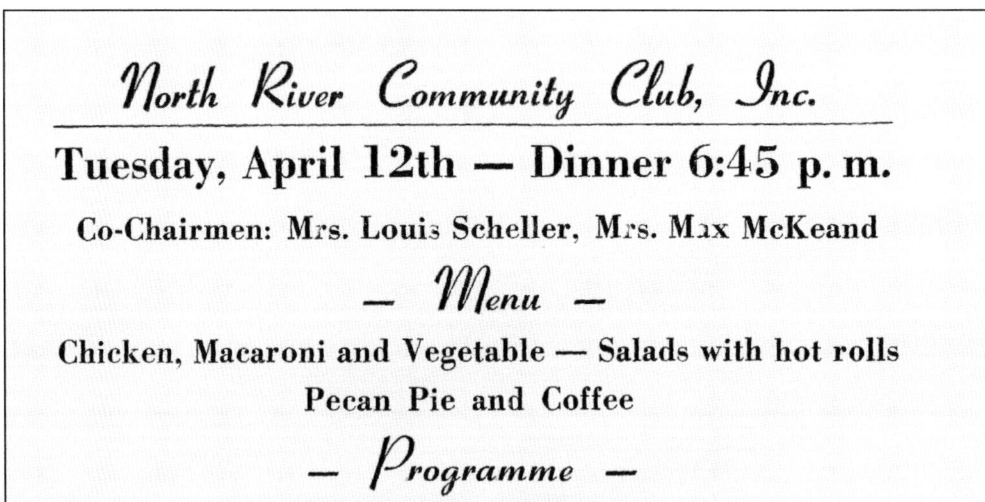
North River Community Club, Inc.

Tuesday, April 12th — Dinner 6:45 p. m.

Co-Chairmen: Mrs. Louis Scheller, Mrs. Max McKeand

— *Menu* —

Chicken, Macaroni and Vegetable — Salads with hot rolls
Pecan Pie and Coffee

— *Programme* —

"MONEY IS THE ROOT OF ALL"
Speaker - Donald Greenlaw, Vice President of Rockland Trust Co.

The monthly dinner program meetings were well-attended events if not for the spectacular menu perhaps for the speakers. In this 1966 invitation, the topic "Money is The Root of All" must have been an interesting speech. Maybe it could have been coined "money is the root of all evil?"

North River Community Club, Inc.

TRYOUTS "The Unwicked Witch" by Madge Miller

SUNDAY, SEPTEMBER 18, 1966 2:00 — 5:00 p. m.

WANTED

3 Wicked Witches

1 Unwicked Witch

2 Males

WE NEED PRODUCTION PEOPLE TOO.

– PLEASE COME AND TELL YOUR FRIENDS –

To bring a production to fruition, a director must audition a group of performers and cast the right mix to ensure the best possible end product. In this instance, the North River Community Club sent out audition cards for the *Unwicked Witch*. Madge Miller wrote plays for *Alice in Wonderland, Robinson Caruso, Pinocchio,* and *Hansel and Gretel*.

North River Community Club

announces

Paul Revere Brawl

Saturday, April 16, 1966

A "Tea" Party 8:00 to 9:00 p. m.

at 9 p.m., British Beef vs. Boston Beans

for dancing - Community Club Band

Entrance Requirement —

. mottoed flag - minimum size 2' x 3'

To be hung, admired and judged for valuable prizes.

Reservations Close April 14th

$10.00 per member couple, $12.50 per guest couple

— Please mail check to —

Douglas A. Donahue, Main St., Norwell

"British Beef versus Boston Beans?" The North River Community Club certainly had fun through the years with its many gatherings such as this one. The two invitation cards on this page, from 1966, shows just how imaginative the club got with its activities. They held their events in the small antiquated theater, and discussion at monthly meetings ensued for years on how to raise funds to improve the building's seating capacity, plumbing, and storage space.

The North River Community Club

announces **A POP OP PARTY**

Saturday, June 18, 1966

Camp Meeting 8:00 p. m. to 9:00 p. m.

Bopuffet Dopinner 9:00 p. m.

Music for Dancing, Community Club Band

Appropriate dress please

Reservations close Thursday, June 16

$10.00 per member couple — $12.50 per guest couple

•

Please mail check to:

Douglas A. Donahue, Main St., Norwell

And finally the members of the North River Theater should be commended for carrying on a historic legacy in the town. Without the hard work and dedication of just a few individuals, Norwell and the surrounding communities would lose a local treasure. They need support so please consider going to a performance and contributing a little extra so that it may long endure for future generations.

Ten

PEOPLE AND PLACES

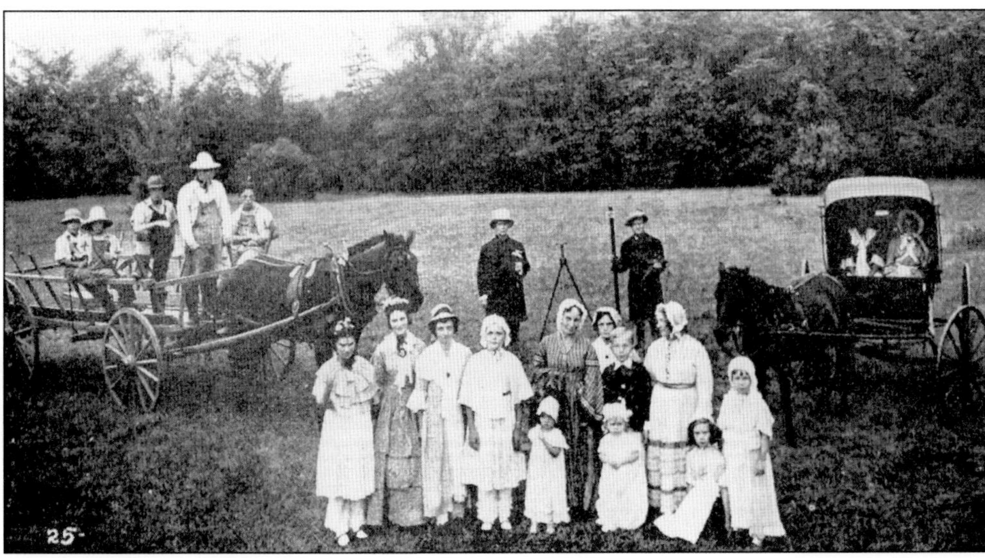

On September 2, 1936, this group of Norwell reenactors gathered for a photograph at the Scituate-Norwell town line located at Sherman's Corner. The residents were reenacting the incorporation of South Scituate as a new town in 1849. The westerly section of Scituate had much more tax revenue from its farms, heavy pine forests, and shipbuilding by the North River. Consequently, "West Enders" held most of the town offices. The ultimate reason for South Scituate splitting from Scituate was control over their finances.

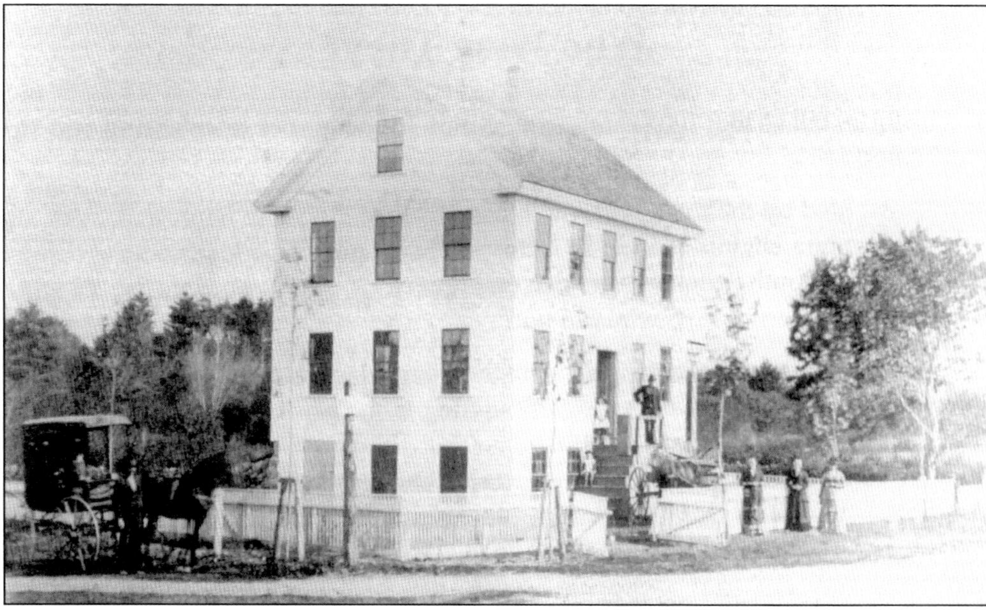

In 1877, Alonzo Tilden built this shoe factory at the corner of Winter and Cross Streets. About 15 people worked at this manufacturing firm, which was of medium size for this particular era. Alonzo operated the business with his brother Amos and a partner named Wilbur Nichols. In time, Alonzo moved to Philadelphia, and the business eventually folded. The building was destroyed by fire on July 4, 1938.

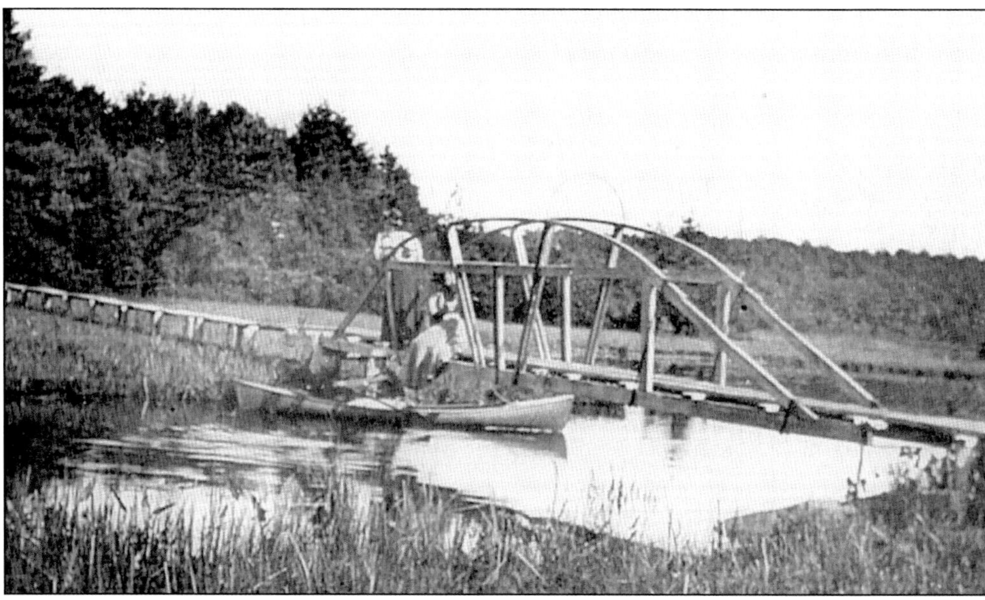

Taken around the end of the 19th century is a tranquil photograph of the Third Herring Brook. This is the Rainbow Bridge which was a vital footbridge used by shipbuilders from Hanover Four Corners to cross into Norwell. The workers would travel across the Third Herring Brook to get to Barque Hill to work each day. Over 80 vessels were built along the banks of the North River at Barque Hill. This bridge was destroyed by the Portland Gale of 1898, which relocated the mouth of the North River.

On December 13, 1954, at 8:00 p.m., an F-94C United States Air Force jet interceptor took off from Otis Air Force Base on a routine training mission. Flying the jet was Lt. Alfred Yahanda of the 58th Fighter Interceptor Squadron. His observer on the jet was Lt. Herbert Forman. About 10 miles south of Norwell, Yahanda noticed that there was a fire in the engine and he ordered Foreman to eject at 15,000 feet.

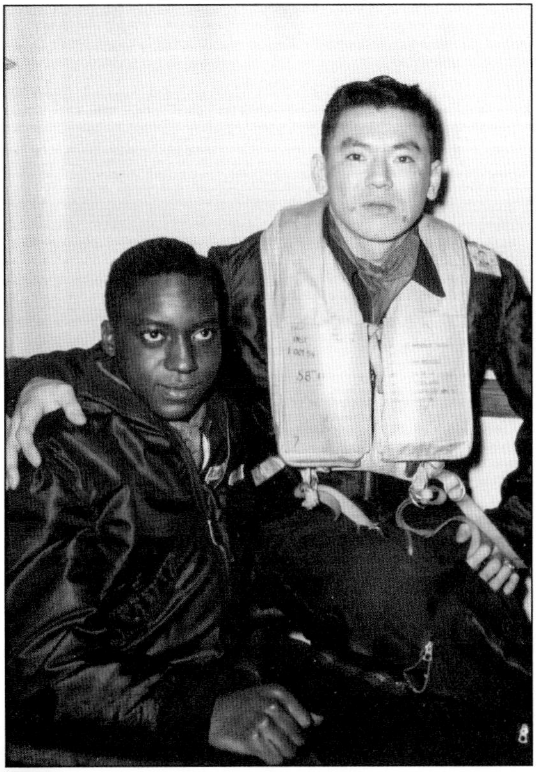

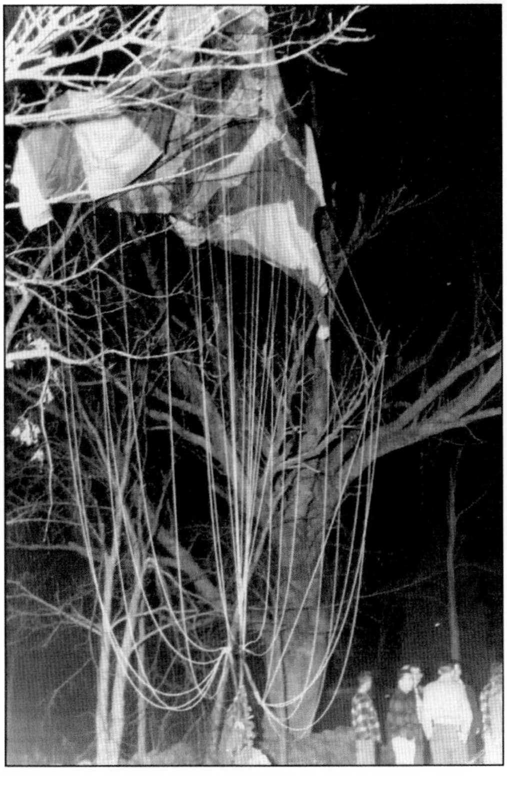

Yahanda stayed with his jet longer while lowering it to an altitude of 2,000 feet. He then looked for an uninhabited area where he could safely abandon his jet and parachute to safety. The plane crashed into a densely wooded area on Forest Street not far from the home of Norwell fire chief Richard Gaudette. Yahanda parachuted to safety into a tree on Circuit Street.

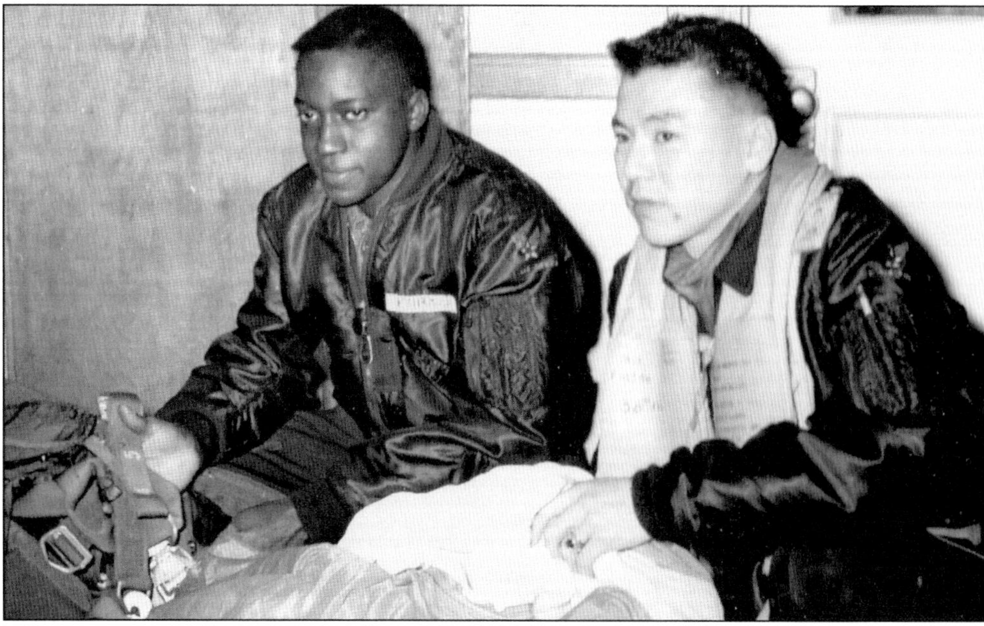

Yahanda waved down a motorist who gave him a lift to the Massachusetts State Police barracks. Meanwhile, Foreman crashed a baby shower quite literally. Foreman landed in a backyard of a home in Hanover that was throwing a baby shower at the time. His calls for help went unheeded for a time because of the loud cries of laughter inside the home. Eventually, a party goer heard Foreman and he was also driven to the state police barracks.

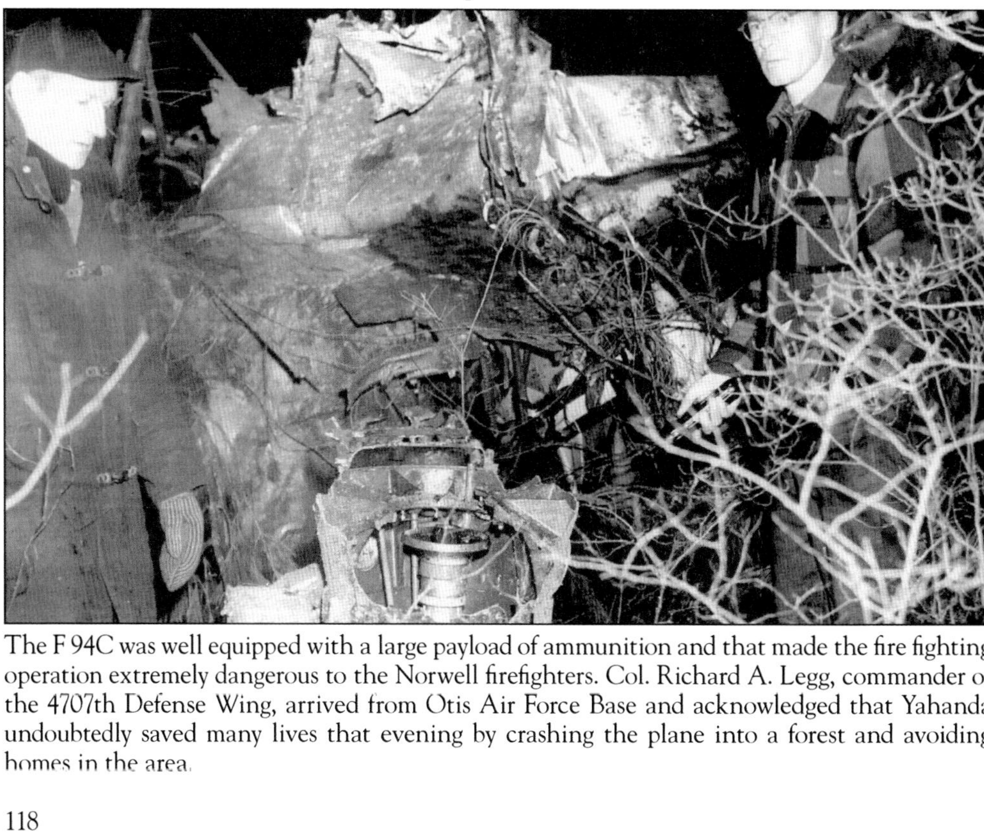

The F 94C was well equipped with a large payload of ammunition and that made the fire fighting operation extremely dangerous to the Norwell firefighters. Col. Richard A. Legg, commander of the 4707th Defense Wing, arrived from Otis Air Force Base and acknowledged that Yahanda undoubtedly saved many lives that evening by crashing the plane into a forest and avoiding homes in the area.

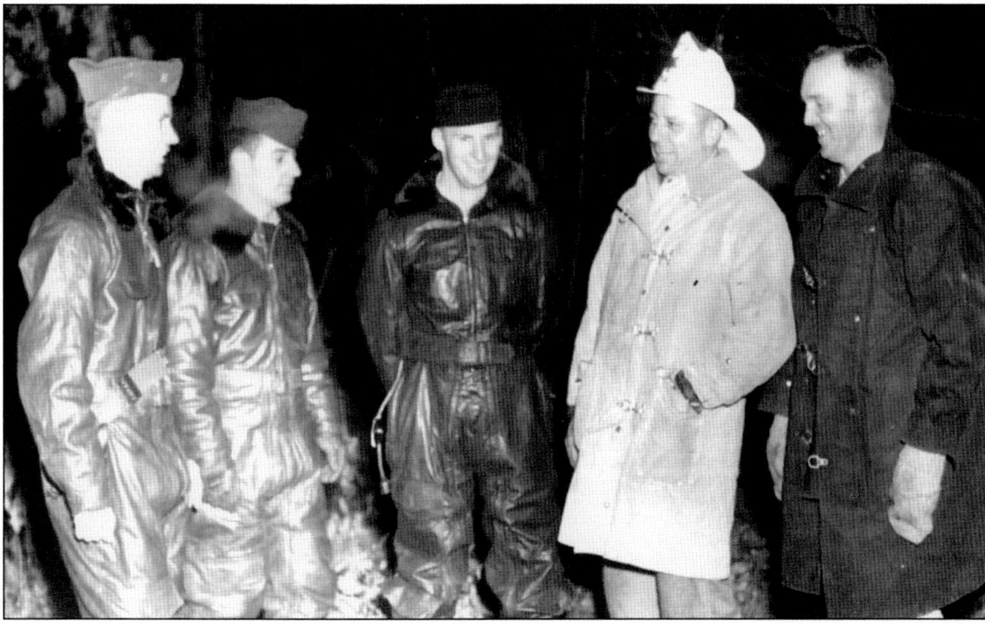

Engine One was the first fire truck to arrive on the scene, but it was unable to battle the blaze because of all of the explosions. To assure the safety of the firefighters, the military quickly ordered an evacuation of the crash site. Conversing after the crash site was secure and contained are Norwell Fire Chief Gaudette, Colonel Legg, and Col. Luther Richmond, commander of Otis Air Force Base.

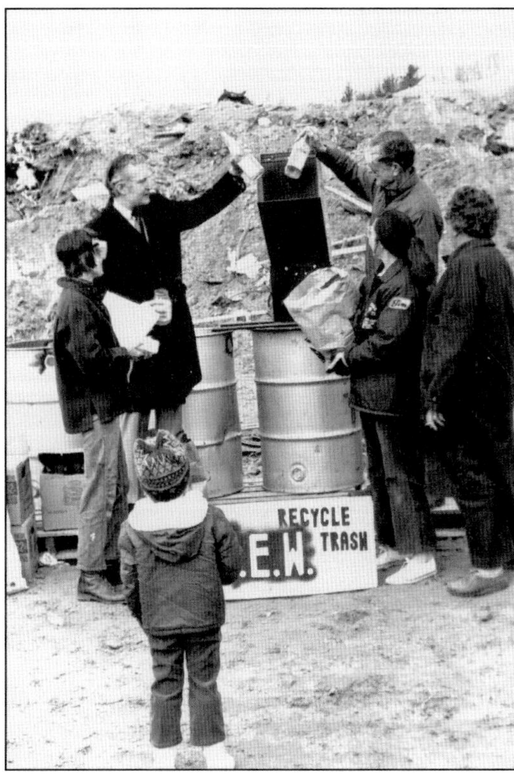

In 1972, a group of concerned Norwell residents formed an organization to begin a recycling program in town. It was named the Norwell Environmental Workers (NEW). The object of the NEW was to initiate a change in the refuse habits of the community. Pictured here from left to right are Phyllis Lindsay, membership chairman for NEW; State Representative Robert Baab; Jim Hall, chairman of the Norwell Board of Selectman; Persis McClellan, chairman of NEW; and Kay Fuller, Chairman of the Norwell Board of Health. In the foreground is Angela McClellan.

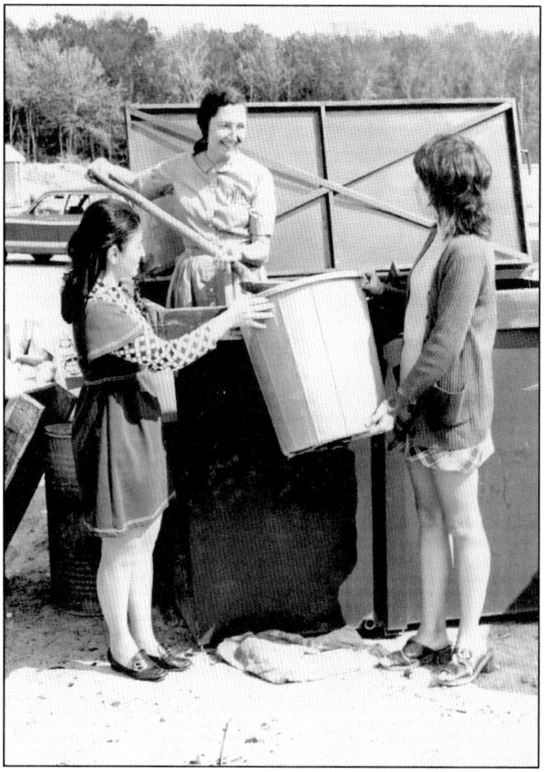

Now that is what one would call really into the job at hand! Shown here is the chairman of the NEW, Persis McClellan, shoveling glass inside the dumpster. Aiding her in this endeavor is Mrs. Ronald Licata, chairman of Community Services for the Norwell Woman's Club, and on the left Mrs. Frank Chicko, Norwell Woman's Club president. The Woman's Club was very helpful in the NEW efforts because they provided the funding for the three dumpsters.

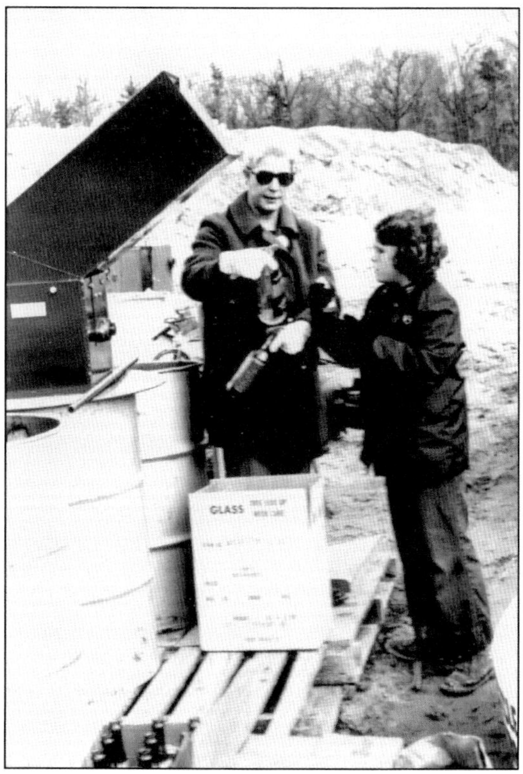

The sanitary landfill on Pine Street opened with much fanfare and success as townsfolk came and dumped over a ton of glass the first weekend it was open. Pictured here are Ann Henry and her daughter Kristen. They are inspecting each glass bottle to make sure it is clean and free of any glass rings before tossing it into the glass crusher.

The NEW recruited hordes of volunteers to help run this important initiative. One of the jobs was to work at the landfill as a recycling monitor. Among the monitors were Jon Bond, Tom Noble, Buz Vinal, Bill Zildjian, and Ann Henry. Shown here is Don Rust tossing glass into the crusher he designed and built.

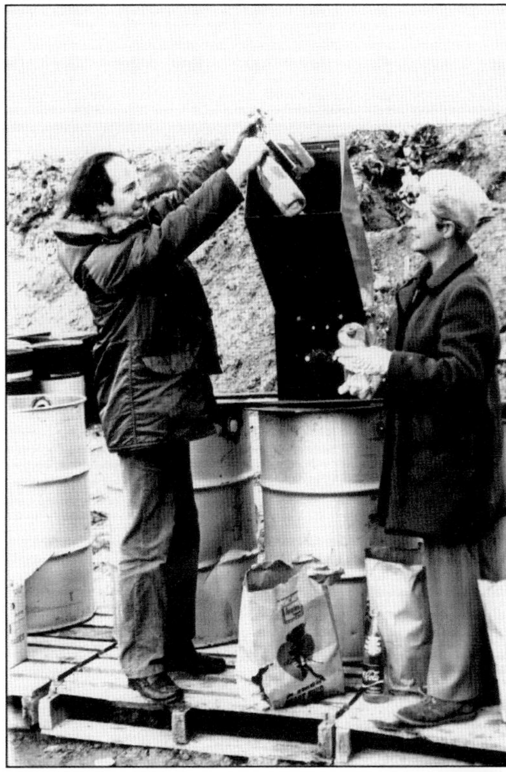

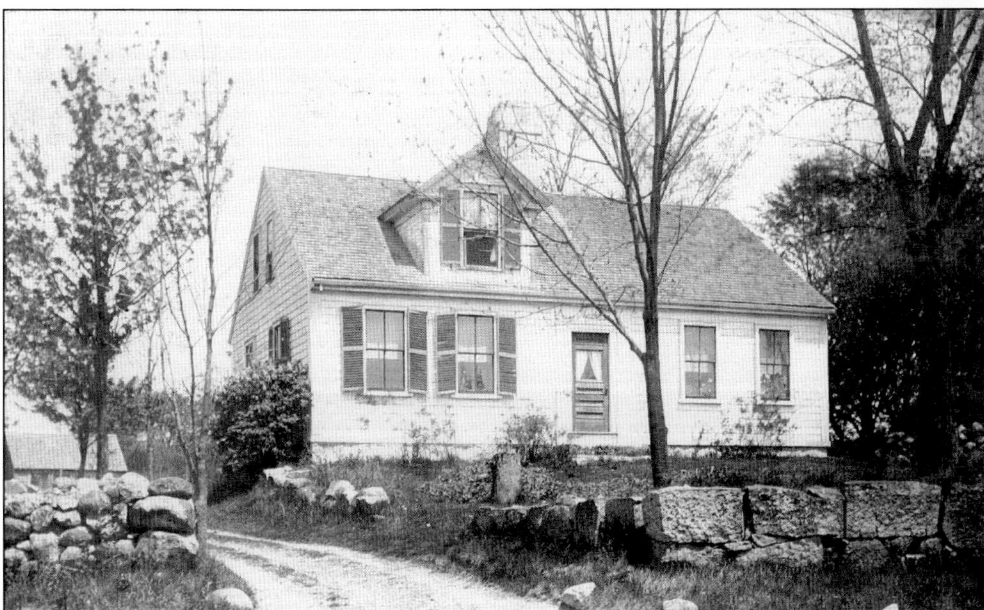

In the early 1900s, it was quite fashionable to have your home photographed and made into a postcard. Homeowners would then mail the postcards to friends and family with news, although most often it was about one aliment or another. This card was postmarked from Assinippi on May 17, 1905, addressed to Martha Marks of Clintonville, Connecticut. "Dear Martha, Just had a picture of the house taken. Does it look natural to you? Sue."

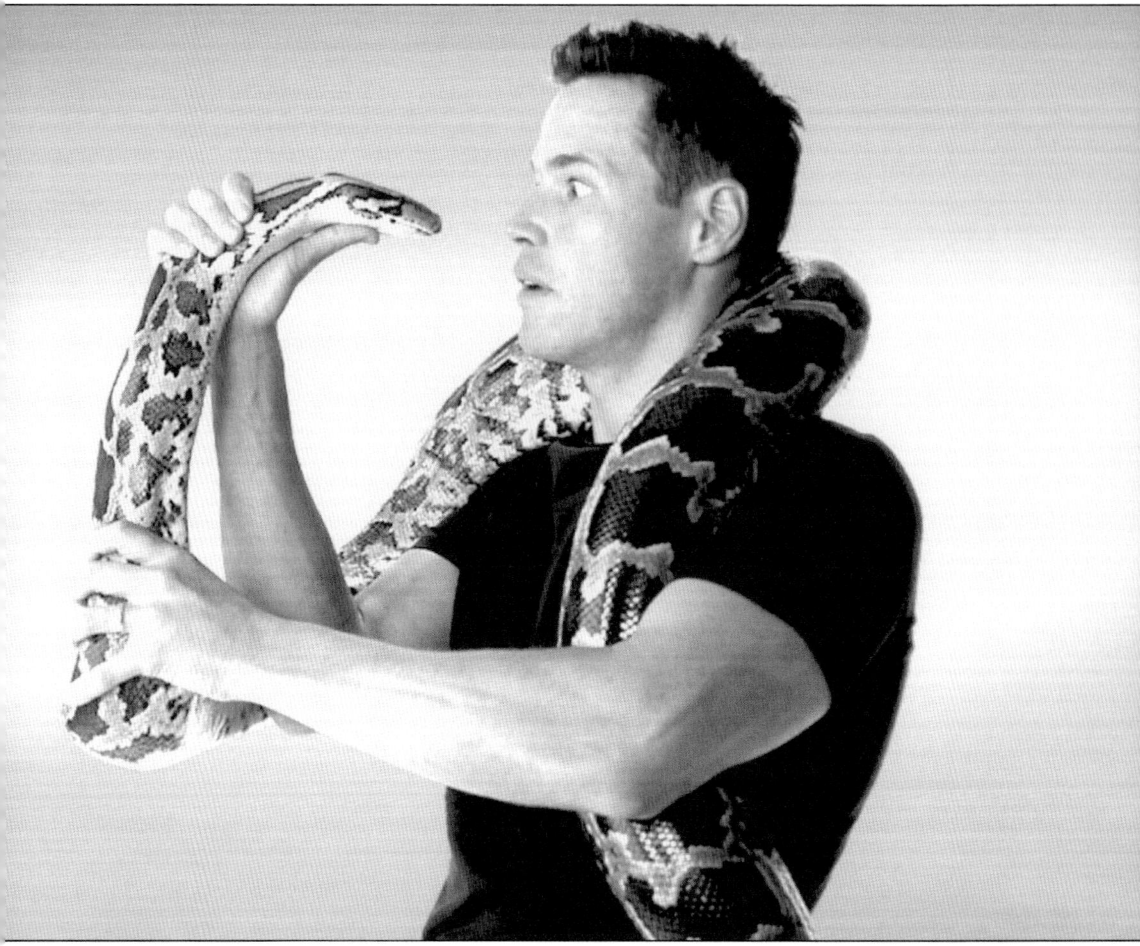

Jeff Corwin is the Emmy award winning host of the *Jeff Corwin Experience* on Discovery Channel's Animal Planet. He is currently starring in a new adventure themed series called *Corwin's Quest*. The episodes show Corwin swimming with saltwater crocodiles and traveling across the desert on an ornery camel. But where did this world famous TV star cut his teeth as an animal explorer? Corwin is a graduate of Norwell High School and is fondly remembered by longtime Norwell resident and Buttonwoods Book owner Betsy Detwiler as an integral part of the American Field Service group. As Corwin's rise to fame continues, he has appeared on *Oprah*, *CSI Miami*, and the *Tonight Show*. He also was named one of *People Magazine*'s most beautiful people. More importantly, Corwin is an expert in rain forest animal habitats, and in 1993 he addressed the United Nations General Assembly. Corwin also cares about his hometown and Norwell's South Shore Natural Science Center. He has helped to create a local exhibition called the EcoZone, which features the wildlife and ecology of southeastern Massachusetts.

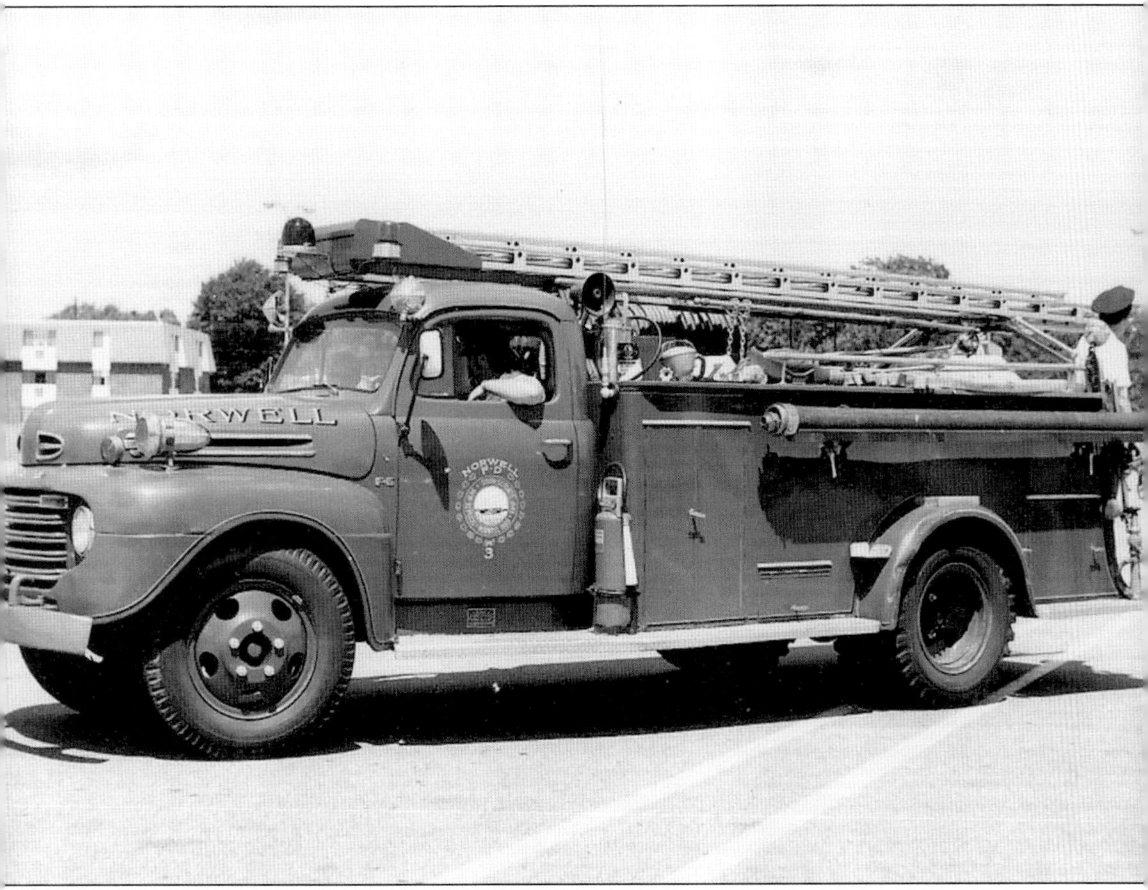

Pictured here is a 1951 Norwell Fire Department Ford fire engine. This was Norwell Fire Department Engine Number Three. This ladder truck was a longtime fire fighting apparatus used in Norwell Center. Engine Number Three played an important role in the fire in Norwell Center and the Air Force crash in 1954.

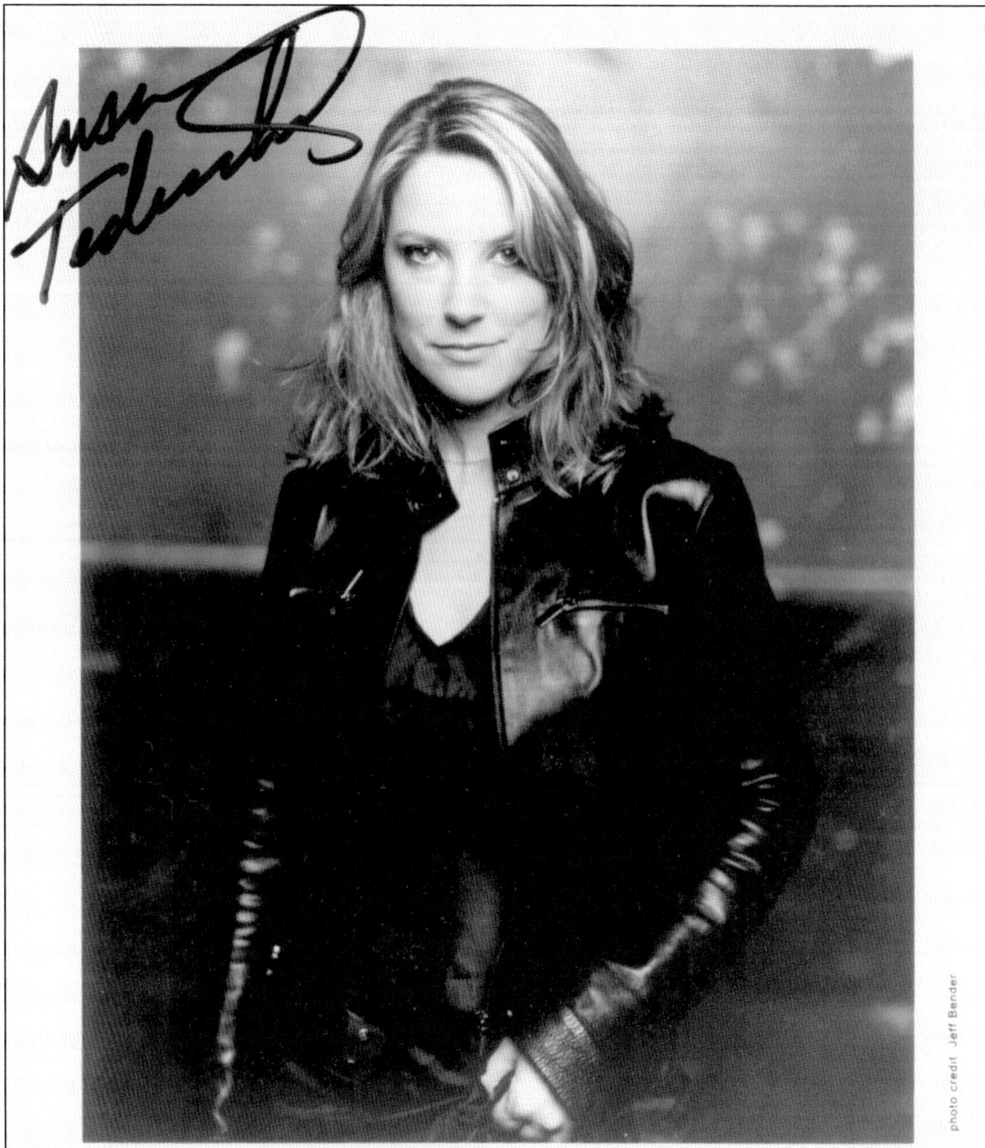

This is a recent publicity photograph of the thrice Grammy-nominated rock artist and Norwell High School graduate Susan Tedeschi. Tedeschi, a Berklee College alumna, is a national recording artist who regularly tours throughout the United States and is a headlining star in Farm Aid with Willie Nelson, Neil Young, and John Mellencamp. Tedeschi is the daughter of proud parents Dick and Pat Tedeschi.

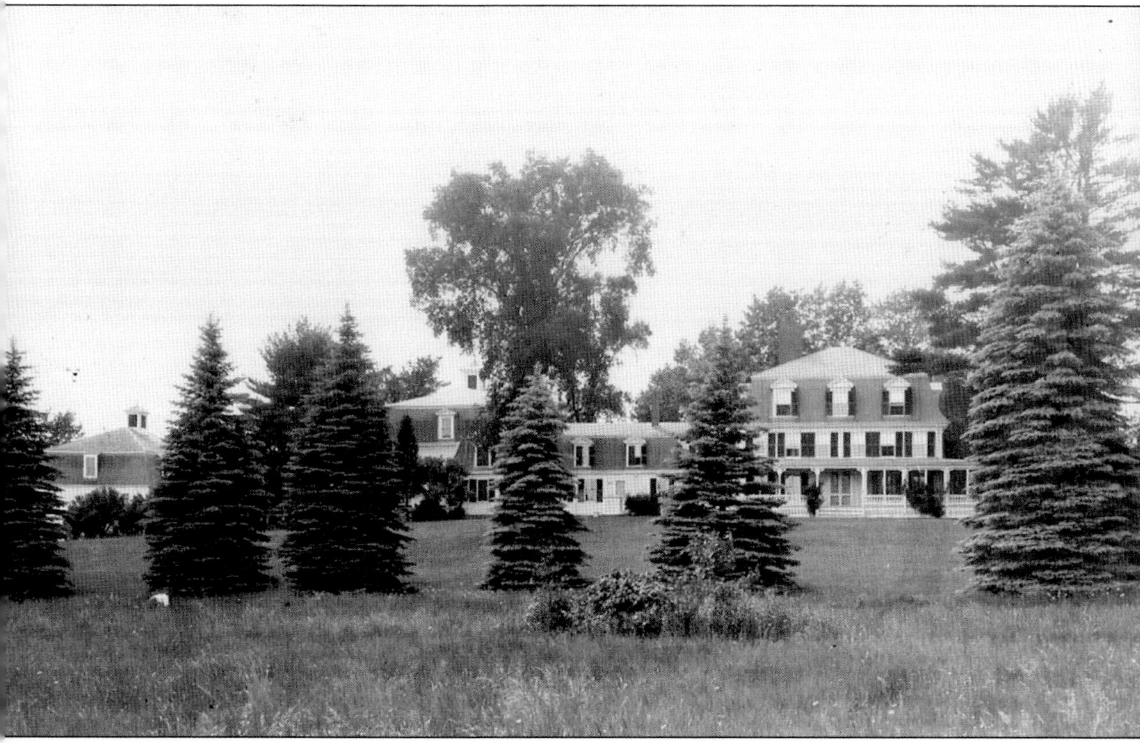

Pictured here is a nice landscape view of Henry Norwell's summer retreat, which in later years was owned by E. R. Bacon. Today the home is owned by Mark and Karen Norwell. What is interesting about this is not Henry's home but the correspondence on the back of the postcard. People would often write to update their friends or family about the latest illnesses or aches and pains. Addressed on July 3, 1906, to Mira Keene, "Called to see Aunt A. last night, was eating her supper, think she didn't come out of the bedroom during the day. He came for the bed pan this a.m. said she wasn't going to get up this a.m. Dr. could hardly find any pulse but seems rather better today-With Love H. R. C."

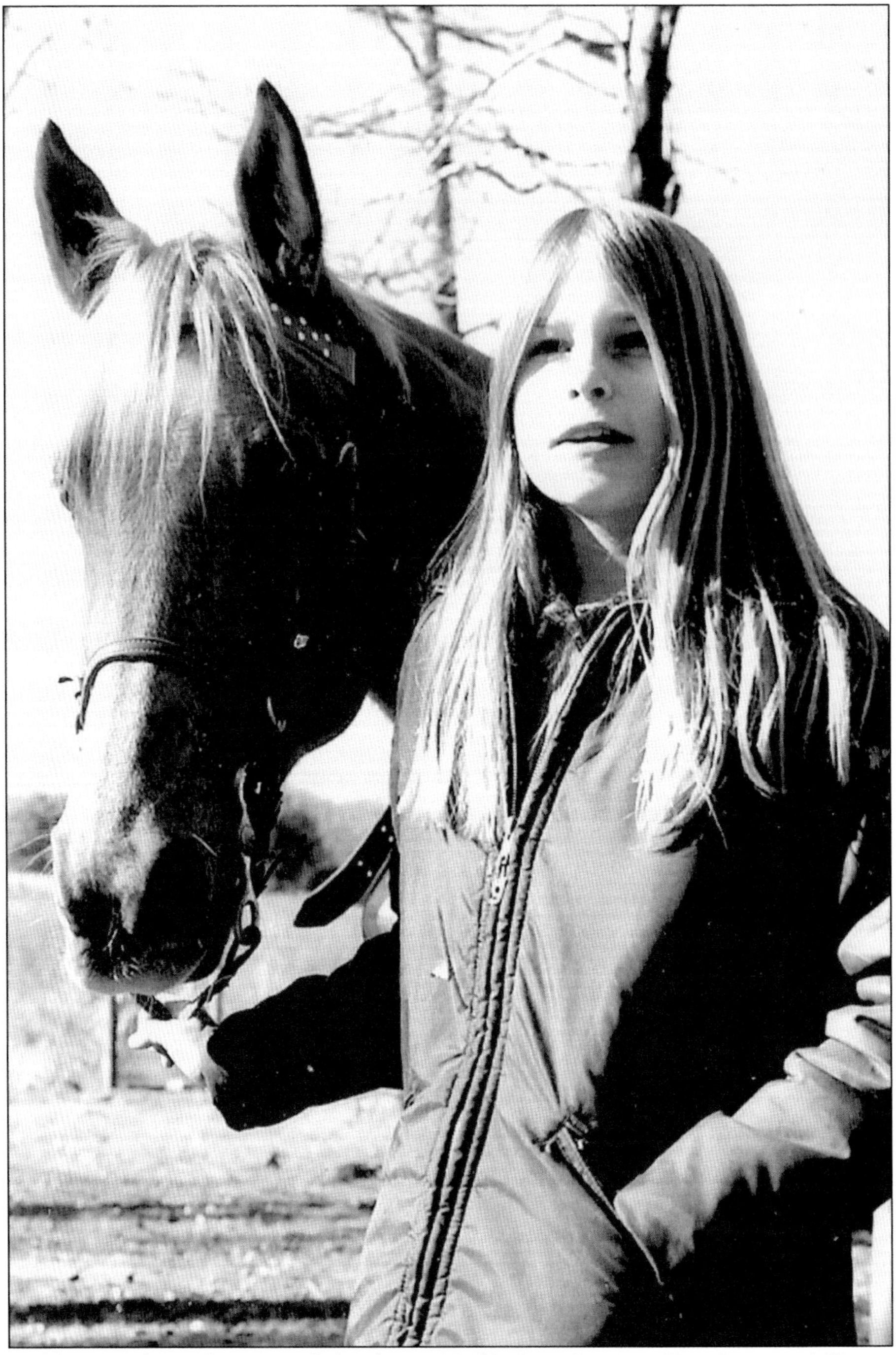

Pictured here in the mid-1970s with her horse "Goldie" is television, Broadway, and film actress Jennifer Coolidge. Coolidge grew up in Norwell and is a graduate of Norwell High School, and her family still lives in Norwell near the Third Herring Brook. Coolidge is an Emerson College alumna who has enjoyed great success in Hollywood. She has starred in *Best in Show*, *American Pie*, *Legally Blonde*, *Cinderella Story*, *Robots*, and *Date Movie*. Coolidge is currently starring on the NBC sitcom *Joey* as a Hollywood agent.

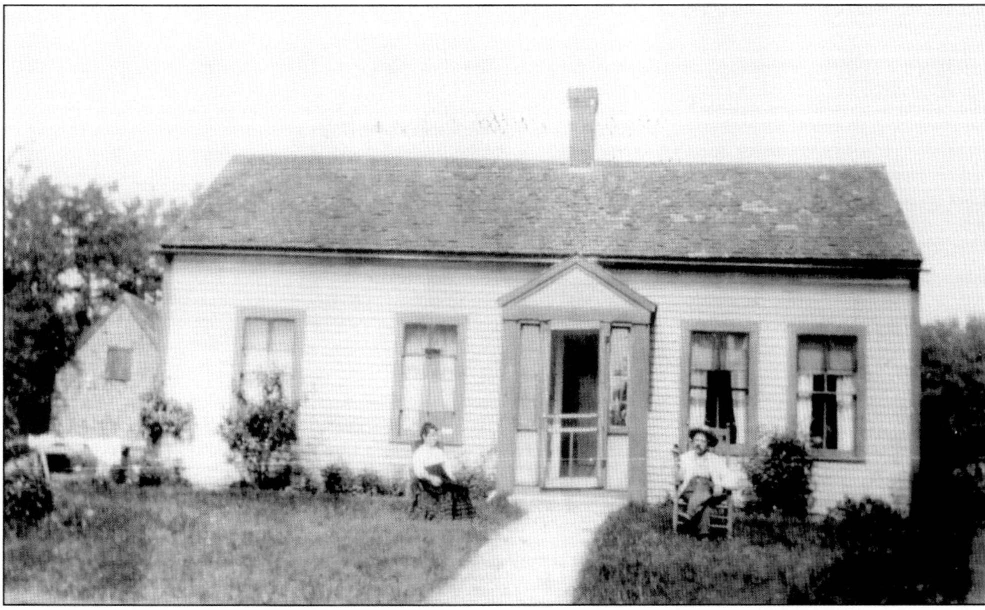

This is a photograph submitted by the Norwell Historical Society. The first president of the Norwell Historical Society was Joseph Foster Merritt. Merritt made a considerable contribution to the historic legacy of Norwell by writing the definitive history of South Scituate-Norwell, Massachusetts, in 1938. The current president is Robert Norris. This scene shows an unidentified couple rocking in their chairs on a lazy summer day.

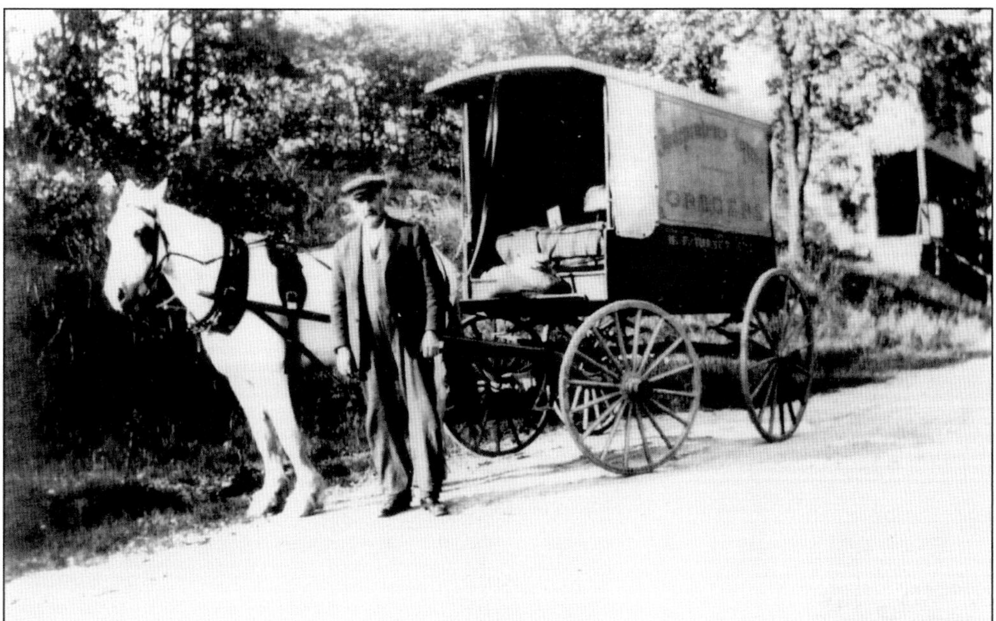

Before the proliferation of Walmarts across the globe, there were small "mom and pop" sundries shops. Some of these markets in Norwell delivered their wares to customers' homes. Pictured here is the W. F. Turner and Company Grocer wagon on a delivery run.

ACKNOWLEDGMENTS

After having completed the Postcard History Series: *Hingham* last winter, I felt the itch to write about another town on the South Shore and saw many similarities in Norwell that I had researched on Hingham. Being the self-professed carpetbagger that I truly am, and thus having no roots in Norwell, I realized that I needed help in writing this book. One person came forward whose aid was invaluable and deserves recognition. His name is Jon Bond, and I have dedicated the book *Norwell* to him. I did not dedicate the book to Bond just because he helped me with this book project, but rather after talking with him for many hours, I learned a great deal about this Norwell "townie." Jon has served the community in several capacities over the years and has been recognized for his efforts too, but I wanted to call attention to him again. Thank you, Jon. Norwell is indebted to you. As the writing progressed, I sought out others who helped me as well. Thank you to Joe McAlarney from the North River Theater, Paul Coolidge and his daughter Jennifer, Jeff Keller, Mr. and Mrs. Nick Tedeschi, Mr. and Mrs. Dick Tedeschi, Susan Tedeschi, Terry Tedeschi, the Joseph family, Geoff Gordon, Don Spradlin, Bob Norris, Mr. and Mrs. Tom Hyslop, Mrs. Jonathan Bond for her wonderful proofreading, and Jeff Corwin. Thank you to my mentors Christopher Bean and Peter Holden for their support. And thanks to Kim and Matt Zayotti for encouraging me to go forward with the book when things appeared a bit off kilter. And lastly to my wife, Brenda Pierotti, for letting me ignore her late at night while I typed away. The author royalty proceeds will benefit the South Shore Natural Science Center off Jacobs Lane, in particular, the EcoZone project that has been Jeff Corwin's passion. I wrote this book with the hope that the many families who have moved to Norwell for the great schools and neighborhoods would learn a little something about their adopted hometown. And what a great hometown it is!